north island

TROUT FISHING GUIDE

north island

TROUT FISHING GUIDE

JOHN KENT

REED

For revisions and updates to this edition of the
North Island Trout Fishing Guide, visit the following
location on the Reed Publishing website:

http://www.reed.co.nz/products.cfm?View=338&CatID=4

Reed Publishing
Te Karuhi tā tāpui o Reed (Aotearoa) (NZ) Ltd

Established in 1907, Reed is New Zealand's largest
book publisher, with over 300 titles in print.

For details on all these books visit our website:
www.reed.co.nz

Published by Reed Books, a division of Reed Publishing (NZ) Ltd, 39 Rawene
Rd, Birkenhead, Auckland. Associated companies, branches and representatives
throughout the world.

ISBN 0 7900 0737 1

© 2000 John Kent text and photographs

The author asserts his moral rights in the work.

Cover designed by Sharon Whitaker
Cover photographs by David Hallett
Maps by Jonette Surridge

First published 1989, reprinted 1991
New edition 1995
New edition 2000
Reprinted 2004

Printed in New Zealand

contents

acknowledgements

I would like to thank my mother, Lucy, for encouraging my angling interests and accompanying me on a number of field trips, and the late Robert Bragg of Christchurch, who really inspired me to fish as a teenager.

Many people throughout the North Island, including Fish and Game officers, supplied valuable information for this book. My regular fishing companions helped me check out many rivers and lakes, and I am very grateful for their continuing friendship.

Finally, I would like to thank many North Island farmers for their unfailing hospitality, and Patti Madsen for her companionship and help with the photography and text.

foreword

Imagine a tall, well-built New Zealander suspended beneath a heavy overhanging branch by two long legs crossed at the ankles. His left hand holds onto a branch a little further out, while his right arm horizontally casts a treasured nymph slightly upstream of an unsuspecting rainbow trout. His dark eyes gaze unflinchingly at his tail-quivering quarry.

This is how you might meet John Kent, the author of this book. Of course, to do this you would first have had to drive or tramp for several hours into New Zealand's remote back country.

Alternatively, you might imagine a tall figure running backwards in lakeside sand, bending low to avoid detection by a cruising rainbow trout. If you bide your time you will see a superb cast unroll from the rod to fall silently into the water. Wait awhile and you will see the strike of the rod, hear the triumphant 'Yahoo' and be able to watch the patient but intensely concentrated playing of the fish until it is deftly beached without the use of the landing net.

Now is your chance to go over and talk to the fisherman, for this one is keen to share all he knows, and that's heaps! Just wander over, say hello, and ask John Kent about fishing. He has been teaching me for over twenty years now.

Read this book and share in his vast experience and knowledge. Whether you are a newly interested learner or an addict of the tantalising sport of fly fishing, John's book has something to offer you.

Pick it up and start reading. See if you can get the big brownie out of the deep, slow-flowing hole in the bend, or maybe you'll pick that dashing rainbow from the tail of the run while sipping your after-dinner coffee. Good luck, I wish I could join you!

Peter Bygate
A friend
(Past Deputy Director, Department of Conservation)

introduction

It has been a privilege to write this book. Many New Zealand anglers with great skill and knowledge have readily imparted their secrets, and I am greatly indebted to them all.

I was brought up on the banks of the River Avon in Christchurch and began fishing for trout with bread, worms and luncheon sausage at the age of ten. At secondary school, along with four other boys, I was caned by the headmaster for 'bunking' a music lesson in order to catch trout in the school grounds. Being an English scholar, the headmaster at least had the decency to ask whether I had read *The Compleat Angler* by Izaak Walton before he administered his punishment.

As a shy thirteen-year-old, I joined the Canterbury Anglers' Club and well remember watching a rotund George Ferris demonstrating the art of casting a fly while lying flat on his back. His skills were beyond my comprehension. At fourteen, I had the great good fortune to be introduced to the late Robert Bragg, a quiet, unassuming Scotsman who earned his living as a professional fly tier and rod maker. Robert's patience and his fund of anecdotes were an inspiration for a gauche teenager. No doubt many of his stories were stretched by his 'angler's licence', but listening to his yarns while watching him tie up a gross of flies was an experience I will never forget.

My first attempts at fly fishing upset my mother. To supplement my earnings from tomato and raspberry picking, I had pestered her for money in order to purchase my first fly rod. I could not convince her that I needed improved gear. 'You catch plenty of trout in the Avon with the rod you have,' she said. My rod, freshly cut each year from 'Bamboo Island', had hand-twisted rings of copper wire bound on at intervals by black insulation tape. The old wooden Nottingham reel had been given to me by a neighbour. It had a nasty habit of jamming each time I left it out in the rain, and that was quite often. At the end of each season, my rod would end up in my father's garden firmly staked to a tomato plant.

The design had come from Tisdall's sports store. 'Want to buy a rod?' the salesman would ask. 'No thanks, I'm just looking,' would be my embarrassed reply.

At a family picnic on the shores of Lake Lyndon, I attempted fly fishing. Casting in the approved manner of a fly fisher was out of the question with this rigid bamboo pole and light cutty-hunk line. I propelled the fly like an arrow from a bow to land eight metres from the rod tip on a good cast. An angler with sophisticated gear arrived. 'Had any luck, lad?' he enquired, as if he didn't know. He began casting some distance away down the beach. To my utter astonishment, after ten minutes of bow and arrow fishing, I hooked a takeable rainbow on my Bloody Butcher fly and dragged the flapping fish up the beach. My angling companion had no such luck. 'There you are,' said my mother, in a voice loud enough for my companion to hear, 'you don't need a new rod after all. That one's perfectly alright.'

When I was fifteen my tramping companion, Skip, introduced me to the bait caster, a much cheaper method of angling than fly fishing and a wonderful transition between worms and artificial flies. At least I caught fish! We happily tramped the back country of Canterbury and Otago and became very skilful at using such gear. On more than one occasion, we landed fish weighing over 4.5 kg from isolated high country streams seldom visited by anglers. We used Devon minnows and other more intricate patterns festooned with treble hooks and made by McCarthy's Tackle Shop in Dunedin. Unfortunately, bird's nests were common as the revolving minnows twisted the nylon line into all manner of knots. At eighteen I purchased my first fly rod and, as I gained confidence, the bait caster was gradually phased out.

My special love is to combine tramping with fly fishing and to visit new water with a good friend. I have been most fortunate in having been able to fish from Fiordland to the Motu. It is difficult to convey to non-angling friends the companionship, excitement, joy, tranquillity and challenge that back country fishing offers, especially if one arrives home empty-handed. It is impossible to convey the satisfaction gained from stalking a good fish in gin-clear water, deceiving it with a home-tied artificial, landing it and then gently releasing it.

There are hundreds of streams, rivers and lakes in the North Island that hold trout. At least 30 streams draining off Mt Taranaki alone contain fish. I make no apology for omitting many of these, as I have tried to select those that are worth visiting. To describe each run, pool and bend would likewise be impossible, and intricate details about access would fill an encyclopaedia. I hope, however, that there will be sufficient information to allow you to explore new territory and fish with a degree of confidence. There is no substitute for knowledge gained by visiting 'virgin water'. Do not be afraid to ask others for advice; most Kiwi anglers will be only too willing to help. I suggest you purchase detailed maps from the Automobile Association, specialist map stores, or the Department of Survey and Land Information.

It is also very important to check local fishing regulations. I have given many of these throughout the book, but changes occur from year to year. Ignorance is no defence if you contravene regulations. Enquire at local sports stores or fish and game councils.

Over 400 rivers and streams, and 60 lakes and dams, are described in this book. I have visited almost all the water described and fished much of it, but not always with success. It is also important to remember that rivers flood and change from year to year, the Tongariro River being an obvious example. What happens next year may well alter a description in this book. Good luck and tight lines.

John Kent and Patti Magnano Madsen with a small spring creek brown trout

safety and equipment

New Zealand is a long, narrow, mountainous, windy country with unpredictable weather patterns. Weather forecasting is not easy. It is frustrating to the fly fisher to carefully plan a day's fishing, then arrive to find a howling downstream wind preventing any chance of casting. I have described the general direction each stream follows and strongly recommend studying the weather map and obtaining a forecast before leaving for your day's fishing.

In the mountains, special care must be taken with planning routes, carrying survival equipment and informing others of your intentions. Do not attempt a river crossing when the river is high. Camp out for the night, miss a day at work, but come home alive. Even in high summer, mountain storms are not uncommon. I have spent four days in February camped under a tent fly sheltering from teeming rain and marking the rising river level with sticks. However, we had waterproof matches, fire lighters and a piece of car tyre.

Clothing and equipment will vary according to conditions. Stalking smelting fish along a Taupo beach in summer is very pleasant in sandshoes and shorts. Fishing the same area in June may only be tolerable in chest-waders, survival-type clothing, balaclava and parka.

Books are available on mountain safety and these contain valuable information for the exploring angler. The lists given in this chapter are my personal lists that I have used for many years and are directed specifically towards the angler.

Equipment for fishing and camping in the mountains

General gear
Fire lighters or piece of rubber
Lightweight torch

Small lightweight tent
Frame pack

Pot scrubber
Compass
Camera and film
Towel, toothbrush, soap, etc.
Fishing licence
Waterproof matches
Lightweight axe in some
  circumstances

Sleeping bag
Sleeping pad
Cooker and fuel
Billies (2) and fry-pan
Knife
Sunscreen and insect repellent

Clothing

Boots (rubber or leather but
  with a good grippy sole)
Woollen jersey, Swanndri,
  Synchilla or polar fleece jacket
Socks (4 pairs)
Nylon over-trousers (for wading,
  windchill and sandflies)
Watch (can be used as a compass)

Parka
Sandshoes or Teva sandals
Polypropylene T-shirt
Flannelette shirt
Hat with brim
Underwear
Longs (lightweight and warm)

Fishing gear

Fly rod (preferably 4-piece)
Reels and lines
Flies and tippet material
Eel line (simple line and hook,
  great for survival)

Polaroid glasses
Large plastic bags
Spring balance for optimists
Fishing licence

Food

There is great scope for individual tastes but I choose varying quantities from the following list. Although I release most trout caught in the back country I still enjoy one cooked over an open fire or smoked in the chimney of a hut. An eel, or venison if a rifle is taken, makes a welcome addition.

Wholegrain bread
Butter or margarine
Brown sugar
Oatmeal
Tea and coffee
Pasta, macaroni cheese, etc.

Salami
White and brown rice
Packet soups
Honey
Dried vegetables
Cheese

Salt	Bacon
Dried milk	Muesli
Trail mix or scroggin	Dried fruit

Smoking trout in the chimney of a back country hut

Equipment for a day's fishing

Clothing can be selected according to the season and area being visited, bearing in mind that all four seasons can sometimes occur on one day in the mountains.

I wear neutral colours when fishing, to blend in with the background. Green, brown and blue are satisfactory, red and yellow spook fish. When fishing in boots and shorts, I often wear nylon over-trousers in cold or windy conditions. On a warm day, anklets can be worn to keep stones out of your boots. Instead of a fishing vest, a 'bum' bag or a jacket with large secure pockets can be substituted to keep the weight down. A hat with a brim and Polaroid glasses are essential for spotting fish.

I have a small day pack for carrying a Thermos, fishing extras, knife, camera, plastic bag, spare clothing and a good lunch.

I only use waders for lake, stream-mouth and night fishing and during the colder months of the year. Neoprene waders are a vast improvement on rubber but I find the lightweight Goretex-type waders do not last long in back country scrub. Don't forget your rod, flies, tippet material, artery forceps, clippers, sunscreen and insect repellent. Last but not least, your fishing licence!

Fly fishing gear

Personal preferences and the type of fishing govern the choice of rods, reels and flies. High-tech carbon fibre rods have superseded greenheart, split cane and fibreglass rods. While there are still a number of anglers who prefer their exquisitely crafted bamboo rods, for all-round use carbon fibre is the answer. Although one rod can cover small-stream, lake and large-river fishing, my preference is for two rods.

Small streams and back country rivers

I use a four-piece 6 weight rod holding a 6–7 weight, weight forward floating line. I find this useful early and late in the season when fishing heavily weighted nymphs or casting into a strong wind. My reel has an interchangeable spool holding a medium sinking line. For spring creeks I prefer a 6 weight double tapered floating line.

For nymphing the Tongariro River and for competing with other anglers

At stream mouths I use an 8 or 9 weight rod and a weight forward floating line to match the rod. The same set-up can be used for lure fishing at shallow stream mouths but a slow sinking line should also be carried. For downstream lure fishing, I use a shooting head line with a number 3 floating line as backing. When fishing Taupo or Rotorua I recommend not less than 100 m of backing for your reel.

Some anglers find a 7 weight rod with appropriate lines will cover all circumstances.

Traces and tippets

There is a large selection available but I use Maxima brand nylon and make up my own leaders. Maxima seems relatively resistant to chafing and is probably conservatively labelled as far as strength is concerned.

For nymph and dry fly fishing my leader consists of 60 cm (2 feet) of 12 kg (25–30 lb) for the butt section, 150 cm (5 feet) of 7 kg (15 lb), 60 cm (2 feet) of 4 kg (8 lb), 150 cm (5 feet) of 1–2 kg (3–5 lb) for the tippet. The length of the tippet can be varied to suit the conditions.

The only problem with a knotted leader is that it picks up weed at the knots. For this reason, I often use an unbroken length of 3 kg nylon when night fishing at a stream mouth. I also use a short leader/tippet of 150 cm of 3–4 kg nylon when fishing a shooting head line.

Flies

When I first began fly tying at fifteen, I tied every pattern in C.H. Kendrick's *Modern Fly Dressings* (1949) and most of those listed in Eric Taverner's *Fly Tying for Trout*. Now I fish with confidence using a few well-tried and trusted varieties, many being modifications of original patterns. My favourites have changed over the years, and with increased angling pressure trout have become more discerning. Fly tying materials have also improved and the range enlarged. However, many patterns will catch fish and it is clear there are other factors to consider, the most important being whether or not the trout are feeding. When a school of Taupo trout madly chase smelt into the shallows, a piece of string tied to a hook will be as deadly as the most sophisticated smelt fly, provided it is handled correctly. There are many flies tied that have no parallel in nature, yet they take fish regularly.

Accurate presentation, the size of the fly, the depth and way it is fished and whether the fish are feeding are factors that have greater significance than exact attempts to match the hatch. Sometimes there are 'no fish' days, when trout are either lying under banks or simply not feeding. It is worth looking for fresh footprints! However, entomology as it applies to trout fishing broadens one's appreciation of the finer arts of angling, and Norman Marsh's excellent book *Trout Stream Insects of New Zealand* should have pride of place in every serious angler's library.

With few exceptions, New Zealand trout are relatively unsophisticated as to the choice of fly. We do not have well-defined hatches that occur at certain times of the day in favourable weather conditions, nor do we have the 2000 species of mayfly that exist in North America. However, on spring creeks it is very important to establish whether the fish are feeding above or below the surface or in the surface film. Close observation is generally sufficient but to determine the hatching insect I also carry a small piece of nylon stocking in my vest for use as a seine. By stretching it over the palm of your hand and immersing it in the current you can then trap any insect that is floating down the stream either on or beneath the surface. Whether or not you can match that insect in your fly box is another matter. Because a fish is not rising, do not believe it can't be induced to do so with a well-presented dry fly. Remember, however, that over 80 per cent of trout food is taken sub-surface. A refusal suggests you should change to another pattern or a smaller version of the same fly, as repeat presentation will eventually spook the fish. Here is a list of patterns I have found useful.

Lures
Night fishing Hairy Dog, Fuzzy Wuzzy, Black Prince, Craig's Nighttime and Black Marabou.

I have tied my own night lures for many years from black cat's fur and a short dark squirrel tail. The soft fur sends out the right underwater vibrations and the fly swims well. Undetected feather wrap-round is a disaster when night fishing and I don't want to check every second cast. The luminous body material, Aurora Skirt, is favoured by some anglers, especially those fishing two flies. It seems effective in the Rotorua lakes.

I use night lures in sizes 2 to 8. When all else fails try a daytime smelt pattern.

Day fishing These three well-tried patterns are good all-purpose lures. I have used them for smelt fishing and for run fish, river-mouth fishing and back country river fishing.

Rabbit flies in sizes 4 to 10. Body colour can vary from red or orange to yellow, white or silver depending on conditions. A Black Rabbit can even be used for night fishing, although the fur is never very black, while a Silver Rabbit imitates an inanga or smelt.

Red Setter in sizes 4 to 8. This Sanderson-designed lure is excellent for run fish, back country lure fishing, stream mouths and even night fishing. The originator of this fly nearly evicted me from his fly shop many years ago when I had the temerity to ask whether he stocked nymphs. He was an 'old school' downstream lure fisherman and despised nymph anglers.

Parsons' Glory in sizes 4 to 8. Although this is an excellent and well-tested pattern it does suffer from feather wrap-round. An angling friend overcomes this problem by tying it in the same fashion as a Red Setter or Fuzzy Wuzzy and not as a tail fly. A long shank hook and a shortened wing will also help.

Smelt fishing Many patterns will work well when the fish are smelting but I like a small fly around size 10. Grey Ghost and Taupo Tigers are excellent lures but suffer from feather wrap-round unless tied short on a long shank hook. A small Yellow or Silver Rabbit can also be very effective. There are many types of flash or glitter material now available to incorporate into a pattern, including Flashabou and Crystal flash, and I am sure this adds to the attractiveness. Pearl Mylar tubing over an underbody of white wool makes a very attractive smelt pattern but breaks down rapidly after a couple of fish are landed, unless reinforced by silver wire or nylon leader material ribbing.

Mayflies

Mayfly dry flies When fishing dry flies, I like a pattern that I can clearly see in riffly water. For this reason, many of my dry flies are tied parachute style with a white calf tail or polypropylene post.

I use Dad's Favourite, Kakahi Queen and Parachute Adams. I also tie my own parachute pattern with a dubbed or peacock body, brown tail and hackle and a calf hair post in sizes 12 to 16. It is an excellent searching pattern and is often taken as a mayfly.

Mayfly nymphs It is hard to go past Hare and Copper (Hare's Ear) and Pheasant Tail patterns tied in sizes 12 to 18. Early in the season, I incorporate a bead, sometimes tungsten, if I want to fish a deep run. In fact, if the water is high or swift, I will use two well-weighted nymphs. This technique is essential when fishing for run fish on the Tongariro River or early in the season with increased water flow.

When using an indicator, I like natural unwashed merino sheep wool collected off a farmer's fence. A tuft of bright green or orange polypropylene material soaked in floatant can be tied in as well, especially when there is glare on the water. However, trout will often rise to a red or orange indicator and this is disconcerting.

Caddis

Caddis dry flies Deer Hair Sedge, Goddard's Caddis and Elk Hair Caddis. A soft hackle wet fly fished either upstream or across and down works very well at dusk.

Caddis nymphs I am sure the old faithful Hare and Copper and Pheasant Tail nymphs are taken for caddis pupae and larvae. Half Back nymphs tied on a curved caddis hook are a more true representation. Most of my nymphs are well weighted and many are tied with a bead head. Gary La Fontaine's Deep Sparkle and Emerging Pupa in varying colours can be useful.

Midges

Midge dry flies Griffith Gnat. I have been surprised to find trout in high country lakes specifically taking midges so it is worth carrying a few patterns. A size 18 Parachute Adams can be a substitute.

Midge nymphs Midge Pupa or Serendipity.

Emergers

Mayflies spend some time in the surface film as emergers or cripples, whereas caddis flutter off the water in a great hurry; hence the splashy caddis rise in late evening. A midge pupa will also hang in the surface film before flying off as an adult. An unweighted nymph is a fair representation but in order for the thorax of the fly to float and the body to hang beneath the surface film, I often incorporate a small piece of closed-cell foam encased in nylon stocking or use Cul de Canard feathers as an emerging wing. A small soft hackle wet fly is often a good emerger pattern, as is a Half Humpy. These small flies are hard to see, especially towards dusk, so I often fish them in tandem with an easily seen dry fly acting as an indicator.

Terrestrials

Manuka beetle (green and brown) Coch-y-bondhu, Half Humpy or a specific representation. I tie my Coch-y-bondhu flies parachute style to increase visibility and allow the peacock body to float low in the surface film. Both beetles can be imitated specifically with closed-cell foam or deer hair patterns. A Royal Wulff is probably taken for a manuka beetle at times.

Cicada Parachute Hopper, again with a white post, or Stimulators work well.

Willow grub Must be tied on an 18 or smaller hook.

Blowflies Black Gnat or an iridescent Blue Humpy.

Dragonflies Only the nymph is worth representing. A brown Woolly Bugger is a fair imitation.

Damselflies Damselfly nymph, Olive Woolly Bugger or Hamill's Killer.

Snail Black and Peacock.

Corixa or water-boatman Specific imitation.

Attractor patterns

These flies do not specifically represent any insect but trout obviously view them as food. Who worries when they work well! It is very important to me that they are highly visible. They are good searching flies, especially in rough water.

I use Royal Wulff, Royal Humpy, Irresistible and Trudes.

Visiting anglers would be well advised to visit local fly shops or sports stores in each location to obtain up-to-date information on 'hot' localities and the preferred fly patterns.

Spin-fishing gear

Spin fishing is a great way to start fishing. It is easy to learn and the gear is less expensive than the fly fisher's. There are many waters more suitable for spin fishing than fly fishing, and the catch rate will be correspondingly greater. This is especially true on the lower reaches of most rivers, where the water is large and heavy.

Rods
There are various lengths and weights of rods available in most sports shops. A fibreglass rod 1.7–2 m long is recommended. It is an advantage to be able to collapse the rod down so it can fit into a pack. Some telescopic varieties fold to less than 50 cm.

Reels
The old bait-casting reels controlled by the thumb have been replaced by the fixed-spool reel. These can be either open or closed face. The closed face reel is ideal for beginners but the casting distance is less than with the open faced variety. The open faced reel has a far greater line capacity and snarl-ups are easier to deal with. To achieve maximum casting and retrieving capability, the drum should be filled to capacity with line.

Line
Monofilament line weights can vary, depending on conditions, from 1.5 kg to 4.5 kg. An average line weight is 4 kg.

Spinners
There are many varieties on the market and these change from time to time. A selection from Toby, Cobra, Hexagon Wobblers, Panther, Tasmanian Devil, Flatfish, Billy Hill, Rapala and Zed in different colours and weights is desirable. The smaller Veltic and Mepps spinners are useful in low water summer conditions. The

Tokoroa Chicken has a place in heavy water and lakes, especially the Upper Waikato River system, where it is probably taken for a small carp or goldfish. Some anglers use a bubble or lead weight to enable them to fly fish with spinning gear. This technique is very useful for parts of the Waikato River where the water is deep and fast and fish hug the bottom.

It is important to vary the speed of the retrieve as some fish will follow right into shore and actually pick up the spinner at the angler's feet when all motion has ceased. Anglers using spinning gear should be aware of the regulations pertaining to stream mouths and other fly-only waters.

Boat-fishing gear

Full safety equipment is essential when boat fishing. The larger lakes can become very rough and treacherous even for sizeable craft. In half an hour, Lake Taupo can change from a millpond to a raging sea. I have been embarrassed by these conditions on more than one occasion, even in a 5.5 m cabin boat. The same safety equipment for offshore saltwater fishing should be taken on Taupo. This should include an auxiliary outboard, oars, flares, life-jackets, tool-kit, anchor and warp, and a bailer. A radio or cellphone can be very useful.

Fishing equipment can include boat rods, fly rods, reels and lines, flies and spinners, landing net, down-rigger, fish box and knife. Don't forget sunscreen as the burn time is less over water.

If an auxiliary outboard is not used for trolling, boat speed can be reduced by towing a bucket or sack.

Trout tend to inhabit areas close to the thermocline, or the junction between cold and warm water. By mid and late summer, most trout lie very deep in the lake during the day and can only be reached by deep trolling. Acoustic echograms have shown fish in Lake Taupo at depths of 100 m and more, especially in late summer. Obviously, these depths cannot be reached by the angler. Generally, the most productive trolling can be obtained by following the blue-line or drop-off, or trolling over reefs and the edges of weed beds. An echo sounder or fish finder offers a distinct advantage, especially to those boats equipped with a down-rigger. The regulations state that down-riggers are legal in Lake Taupo only but the cable length is restricted to 40 m. No added weight can be attached to the line using a down-rigger. At present, few private boats are equipped with a down-rigger and those using such a device account for less than 10 per cent of the fish caught from a boat. A wire line will go to greater depths than a down-rigger but when a trout is hooked on the end of 200 m of wire line the angler can be totally unaware of the strike.

When using a lead line, remember every 10 m (one colour) will sink 1–2 m. If fishing in 3–5 m of water, use only 20–30 m of lead line. At the end of the lead line, attach 6–7 m of 6.5 kg nylon and then a 4–5 kg trace 3 m long. This will enable fish to fight better and if the line should snag the lead line will not be lost. If using monofilament line, a colour or two of lead line can be used to help it sink.

When harling, use a fast sinking fly line and let it all out including 20 m of backing. Jigging will account for fish in some areas and can be fun.

A selection of flies recommended for harling or trolling includes Rabbit patterns, Green Orbit, Parsons' Glory, Red Setter, Taupo Tiger, Grey Ghost and Ginger Mick.

Useful spinners include varieties of Cobra, Tasmanian Devil, Panther Martin, Toby, Flatfish and Zed. The selection may change from time to time so I recommend visiting the local sports store to find out the hot lure.

It is wise to check your licence for regulation details as these vary for each lake fished. Remember to keep 300 m from any stream mouth.

conservation and etiquette

While collecting information for this book, I have been saddened by my own observations and by anglers reporting stream deterioration and the reduction in the fish population in many parts of the North Island. Without doubt, streams that have native bush-clad banks in their headwaters are of superior water quality and generally offer the best fishing. While I am sympathetic towards sensible land development there can be no excuse for clear-felling the banks of streams and allowing stock to graze the stream margins, break down the banks and pollute the waterway. A buffer zone of scrub and trees along the banks helps absorb fertiliser run-off and stabilises the bank during a fresh. Electric fencing is a simple way to protect stream margins but despite education by Federated Farmers, some farmers remain ignorant of the problems or simply don't care. New Zealand has a priceless resource and is recognised as the best trout fishing destination in the world. The cost of repairing damaged waterways is exorbitant so it is tragic that some streams have already deteriorated to the point of no return. Some farmers still use the river as a rubbish dump, and I have no desire to snare a trout from the back seat of a rusting car. Water extraction for irrigation is another threat and should be carefully monitored by local councils. Anglers should report evidence of stream or river degradation to local fish and game councils.

The unstable nature of the East Coast, Gisborne and Hawke's Bay high country is well known and contributes to the serious run-off, flooding and silting that so disturbs trout habitat in those regions. The Taranaki streams once offered superb trout fishing before clear-felling of the banks and pollution by dairy cows occurred. Climatic changes and clearing bush cover from stream banks lead to water warming to the point where trout no longer survive.

There are exceptions to this general degradation of the waterways where farmers, local authorities, Fish and Game councils and conservation organisations have cooperated to improve water standards. Lake Tutira in Hawke's Bay is a fine example.

Discarded cans and bottles hardly improve the environment. Although many Taupo rivers are subjected to heavy angling pressure, I am delighted to find very little rubbish along the banks. Some boat owners using the lake need reminding, however.

Unlike large productive lakes like Lake Taupo, very few streams can cope with being heavily fished. Back country streams and rivers are especially vulnerable to overfishing. There is still room for local Fish and Game councils to reduce the bag limit and create more 'catch and release' sections. Who in their right mind would want to take five trout from the Waione Stream or the Kaniwhaniwha Stream? I am not opposed to killing the odd fish but to take home more than two fish from most streams is an unnecessary waste in my opinion. Waters that are regularly stocked with hatchery trout ('put and take') like the Waikato and Rotorua lakes are a different story. Les Hill and Graeme Marshall, in their excellent book *Stalking Trout*, outline principles for successful catch and release.

These are:
- The use of the strongest practical tippets to facilitate the quick landing of fish. Long playing leads to metabolites such as lactic acid building up in the muscles and this kills fish.
- The use of a wide mouthed net to minimise handling.
- The use of barbless hooks. A pair of pliers is all that is needed to crimp the barb.
- The use of artery forceps or slim-jawed pliers for removing hooks.
- Care in handling fish: wet the hands first, avoid the gill area, do not squeeze the stomach, and take care not to rub off scales. Holding the fish belly-up often quietens it. Take care not to drop the fish from a height when taking a photograph.
- Once the hook has been removed, hold the fish back in the water, head facing upstream if fishing a river, and do not release it until it begins to gently struggle.

If the fish is bleeding, especially from the gills, then its chance of surviving is considerably reduced. Anglers can help local fish and game councils and the Department of Conservation by weighing and measuring all trout caught, and supplying details from their diaries at the end of each season. This is especially important for fish that have been marked or tagged. Tags should be returned, along with the measurements, to local Fish and Game councils or the Department of Conservation. Metal or plastic tags are usually attached to the dorsal fin. Fish can also be marked by fin clipping or even fin removal. To determine right or left, look down on the fish's back with the head facing away from you. Always measure from the fork of the tail to the tip of the snout. Send details of species, weight, length, and time and area of capture. Anglers' co-operation can be vital in managing a fishery.

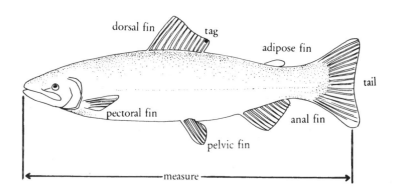

I think more back country areas should be set aside as true wilderness zones, where helicopters are prohibited. A challenge would then still be left for those anglers keen and fit enough to seek out trophy fish. Helicopters have their place and I have used them to my advantage in the past, but it can be depressing to have a machine land upstream from where you are fishing after you have spent three days tramping into a so-called remote spot.

Anglers must extend courtesy to landowners. Few farmers will deny access to fishing water provided permission is sought first. Please shut gates or leave them as found, avoid disturbing stock, be aware of fire risk and offer thanks on the way out. Remember, the cost of fishing in most countries is well out of the reach of most anglers. Fortunately, we have not yet reached that stage, but treat landowners with respect so access for others will not be denied.

Finally, a comment about fishing etiquette. One winter morning my friend Dick and I were determined to be first to reach a certain pool on the Tongariro River. Unfortunately, although we arrived at dawn, another angler was first in the pool. This fisherman began upstream fishing right at the tail of the pool, so Dick and I sat shivering patiently on the frosty bank waiting to start behind him. After ten minutes, he had not moved one step upstream so I walked into the rapids below him and waited another ten minutes. Finally, I asked whether he would mind moving upstream a little so my friend and I could start fishing.

'Look,' he said, 'I got here first and you were second. I'm going to fish every inch of water in this pool even if it takes me all day.'

Finally, after some none too gentle persuasion, he decided to move up a little. A confrontation on the river is entirely unnecessary and always detracts from the pleasures of angling. Usually, if another angler offends against our ideals of fishing courtesy it is through inexperience or excitement. A gentle word may be all that is required. If anglers are already fishing a pool, you may join in but not in the water someone is just about to fish. If the pool is being fished downstream, start upstream of those already fishing. If they are fishing upstream, start downstream. Never start fishing a pool downstream when someone is already fishing upstream or vice versa. If in doubt, ask the angler fishing where you might start so as not to disturb the water. It is only common courtesy. When fishing for run fish on a Taupo river, fish disturbance is not crucial for success. In fact sometimes, when the fishing has been quiet, an angler hooking a fish and disturbing the pool can be a positive action. Not so on a back country river! Fish may not return to feed for a couple of days after being spooked. For this reason, an angler fishing such a stream, and especially a small one, should be given 3 km of undisturbed river. If you find another angler has arrived first it is often better to find another stream close by.

If your neighbour hooks a fish, leave plenty of room for him to play it and reel in if necessary. Never fill a gap left by an angler landing a fish. This also applies to stream mouths. Join a line of anglers on the end unless there is a large gap. Even then, check with the anglers first. Try not to disturb other anglers' water by excessive wading or walking close to the river bank. Finally, watch your back-cast and do not impede others by straying within casting range.

Two trout fishing licences are required to fish the North Island: a New Zealand licence and a Taupo licence. The New Zealand licence covers the whole of New Zealand except Taupo. Day, month and junior licences are available. Although I have included most of the regulations, these change from year to year. I suggest anglers obtain a copy of the *Sports Fishing Guide* published annually by Fish and Game councils. There is no excuse for regulation ignorance, and anglers should be aware that rules change from season to season.

The terms true right and true left are used frequently in this book when describing rivers. Both are determined by looking downstream.

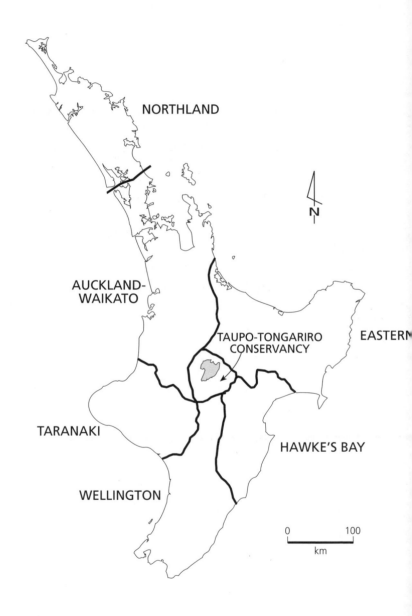

NORTHLAND

AUCKLAND-
WAIKATO

TAUPO-TONGARIRO
CONSERVANCY

EASTERN

TARANAKI

HAWKE'S BAY

WELLINGTON

0   100
km

North Island Fish and Game council regions

Northland Fish and Game Council region

Generally, Northland waters become too warm in summer to sustain trout. Those rivers and streams that do hold fish usually arise from bush-clad catchments that shade the stream's headwaters. In other less fortunate unprotected streams, the water warms in summer, weed and algal growth become a problem and the water quality deteriorates. Then the oxygen concentration falls to a level where both invertebrate life and trout have difficulty surviving.

There is very little sight fishing in Northland, in part due to the poor water quality but also because fish seek shelter under shady banks and in the colder depths of pools when the water temperature rises beyond 18°C. The best time to fish Northland is in the cooler months of the year. Most streams can be fished in boots and shorts but anglers fishing the Kaiiwi Lakes are advised to wear waders. Around twenty rivers or streams and five lakes or reservoirs hold trout. Only some of these can be recommended, however.

The season for all rivers and streams is 1 October–31 April. All lakes and reservoirs are open all year round. There are no restrictions as far as fly fishing only or bait fishing is concerned. The daily bag limit in streams and rivers is two fish; in lakes and reservoirs, three sports fish. (A sports fish is any fish the law requires the angler to hold a licence for). Minimum length is 30 cm.

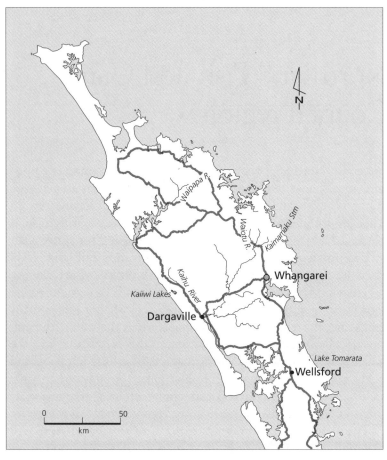

Northland

Kaiiwi Lakes

Location These three sand dune lakes lie 35 km north-west of Dargaville off SH 12.

Access Turn off SH 12 on to Omamari Road and travel 11 km to the Kaiiwi Lakes Road, which in turn leads to the Taharoa Domain and Pine Beach camping ground. The Promenade Point camping ground lies beyond the Kaiiwi Road turn-off.

Restrictions No mechanical powered boats are permitted on Lake Kaiiwi. Boat anglers must stay 50 m away from shoreline anglers.

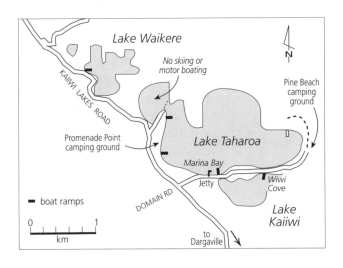

Kaiiwi Lakes

These lakes were first stocked from the Ngongotaha Hatchery in 1968 and have been regularly stocked since that time, the last with late maturing 'r' type rainbows. Lake Taharoa, covering 237 ha and 37 m deep, is the most productive lake, especially for the shoreline angler. Lake Kaiiwi, covering 33 ha, is surrounded by bullrushes and is best fished from a boat either by trolling a spinner, harling or casting a fly. Lake Waikere is 35 ha in area and is mainly used for water-skiing.

The best time to fish these lakes is from May to October, with lure and nymph being most successful. Use a medium density line and fish over the drop-off. Water quality is good, wading is safe and the odd fish can be spotted cruising the drop-off. Trout food consists of a small smelt, *gracilis*, koura or freshwater crayfish, snails, bloodworms and fresh-water mussels and crabs. Rainbows up to 3 kg and rudd occupy these lakes.

Recommended flies during the day include Parsons' Glory, Muddler Minnow, Woolly Bugger, Rabbit patterns, Hamill's Killer and Red Setter. Any small weighted nymph, Black and Peacock or even a small San Juan Worm will catch fish. At night, use Fuzzy Wuzzy, Black Marabou, Hairy Dog or any black fly that swims well.

Fish can also be caught by trolling, jigging, harling and bait fishing.

Kaihu River and its tributaries, the Waima and Mangatu

Location and access The Kaihu River rises in the Tutamoe Range, flows close to the Trounson Kauri Park and meets SH 12 at Kaihu. It then flows south parallel to and east of SH 12 to join the Wairoa River at Dargaville. The Kaihu is best fished upstream from the township of Kaihu.

The Waima River can be reached 45 km north of Dargaville from Donnelly's Road to Donnelly's Crossing.

The Mangatu River joins the Kaihu 5 km north of the Whatoro Motor Camp along Oputeke Road.

All three rivers hold a small population of self-sustaining rainbow and brown trout in the 0.5–1 kg range. Use small nymphs and fish upstream. Although the water quality is reasonable, fish are not easy to spot. Don't neglect the ripples and white water as fish often enjoy well oxygenated water when the temperature rises.

Waipapa River and its tributary, the Waihoanga Stream

Location Rises in the Puketi Forest inland from Kerikeri and joins the Waihou River, which empties into Hokianga Harbour.
Access Turn right 9 km north of Okaihau off SH 1 onto the Puketi Forest Pools Reserve Road. The Waihoanga Stream can be accessed from the Waihou Valley Road to Puketi.

Because this medium-sized stream flows beneath a canopy of native bush it remains cool in summer and is one of the more desirable Northland streams to fish. Holds small rainbows in the 0.5–1 kg range which can be spotted in the brownish water in bright conditions. These respond to small nymphs, terrestrials and smelt flies. There are good, deep holding pools and the river is easy to wade and fish for 10 km upstream.

Punakitere River

Location and access Drains the Punakitere Valley, flows east just south of Kaikohe to enter the Waima River and Hokianga

Harbour. Both the Mangakahia and Mataraua roads running south from Kaikohe cross the river.

Water quality is far from virginal in this often silt-laden river but it does hold small rainbows which are best fished to with a spinner. The banks are overgrown with scrub and fly fishing is difficult.

Lake Manuwai

Location and access This large irrigation reservoir lies west of SH 10 some 15 km north of Kerikeri.

Fly fishing is difficult from the shore as the banks are generally steep but a boat that is not mechanically powered is permitted on the lake. Holds rainbows up to 2 kg.
    The lake is stocked annually. Try spinners or a well-weighted Woolly Bugger.

Waipapa Stream

Location and access Drains Lake Manuwai, flows east and enters Kerikeri Inlet. There is access to the stream from SH 10, which crosses just north of Waipapa village. Elsewhere, permission should be sought to cross private land.

This is a small stream, holding small rainbows. It is best fished downstream from the main road bridge and, like all the Northland streams, during the cooler months of the year.

Kerikeri River

Location and access Rises in the Puketi Forest, flows east just south of the village of Waipapa on SH 10 and enters Kerikeri Inlet. There is access from SH 10 but as with the Waipapa Stream, permission must be sought from landowners north of Kerikeri township.

Holds rainbows averaging 0.5–1 kg. The Kerikeri River gets very warm in summer so fish it either early or late in the season. Best downstream from SH 10.

Waitangi River

Location and access Flows east from Waimate North to Haruru Falls just north of Paihia. Best access is from the Bay of Islands Holiday Park, Puketona Road or SH 10 at Puketona.

Holds small rainbows, but fish it early in the season before campers and swimmers arrive.

Tiriohanga Stream

Location and access Drains Russell Forest and flows east to Kawakawa. This stream is not easy to access as it crosses private farmland southeast of Kawakawa.

Holds small rainbow trout.

Wairua River and tributaries

Waiotu River

Location and access Drains Russell Forest and flows south beneath SH 1 near Waiotu 28 km north of Whangarei. Joins the Whakapara River 6 km downstream from the main road bridge to form the Wairua River. There is good access from a road and rail bridge at Waiotu both up and downstream, and from a turn-off to the right off SH 1, 50 m north of the Hukerenui Hotel.

Holds small rainbows and best fished early in the season before algal slime and weed choke the river.

Kaimamaku Stream

Location and access Flows south alongside Old Russell Road. This road runs north from the village of Whakapara, 22 km north of Whangarei, to Helena Bay. Peach Orchard Road, a branch road from Old Russell Road, also furnishes access.

There is good water quality in this stream once the winter rains have ceased but fish often lie deep in pools when the water warms. Early in the season, there is pleasant upstream nymph fishing for small rainbow trout.

Whakapara River

Location and access From SH 1, 22 km north of Whangarei at Whakapara village.

There is reasonable fishing upstream to the confluence of the Kaimamaku and Kaikanui streams and downstream for 5 km to the confluence of the Waiotu River.

A close approach with a short cast is required here to prevent drag

Kirikiritoki Stream

Location and access Turn off SH 1, 20 km north of Whangarei, onto Whananaki Road. The Kirikiritoki Stream is reached 6 km along this road. Marua Road on your right provides good access.

Because of vegetation along the banks, fly fishing can be difficult in some sections. Short casting with a small nymph into the shady areas under overhanging scrub is often fruitful.

Mangahahuru Stream

Location and access Travel 10 km north of Whangarei on SH 1 then turn right across Main Road Bridge. From the railway line 150 m along this road, there is upstream and downstream access.

Like all these tributaries, this stream offers small rainbow fishing early in the season.

Wairua River

Location and access Starts where the Waiotu and Whakapara rivers meet, 6 km south of Waiotu village, then flows south-west to enter Kaipara Harbour at Dargaville. Access is available from many roads:

- Turn left off SH 1, 250 m past the turn-off to Hikurangi, onto Jordan Valley Road. Once past Apotu and Rushbrook roads, this eventually crosses the Wairua River.
- Travel down Rushbrook Road and turn right at the intersection to a bridge over the river.
- Turn left 0.5 km past the Kamo shopping centre onto Ruatangata Road. This crosses the river after 20 km.
- The Maungatapere–Kaikohe road leaves SH 14 12 km south-west of Whangarei. About 12 km along, it crosses the Wairua River.

A medium-sized river offering some fly fishing early in the season but generally it is best fished with a spinner.

Location and access Turn left at the Whau Valley Dam shopping centre on SH 1, 3 km from the Whangarei Central Post Office. The Whangarei water supply reservoir is at the end of this road.
Restrictions No boating permitted.

The Whau Reservoir is stocked annually and holds browns and rainbows up to 2.5 kg. Shoreline angling is available, especially when the dam level is low. All methods of fishing are productive. For the fly angler, try a small nymph on a long tippet, or a size 8–10 Hamill's Killer, Green Woolly Bugger or Marabou Damsel.

The North River near the Waipu Caves holds small rainbows.

Fly selection

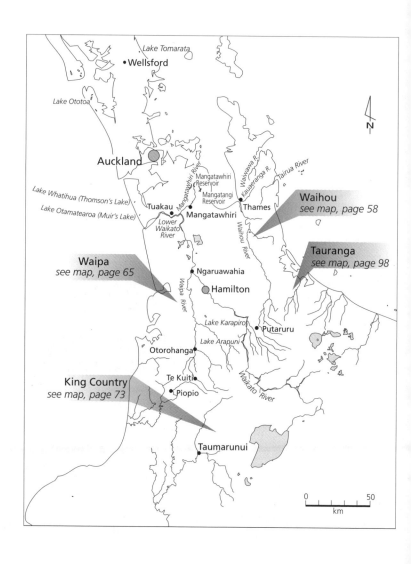

Auckland–Waikato region and Tauranga District

Auckland–Waikato Fish and Game Council region

This region covers a large area from Wellsford in the north to Taumarunui and Awakino in the south. Also included are the Coromandel Peninsula and the fertile farmland around Matamata and Putaruru. For ease of description, the region is discussed under Auckland lakes and rivers, Coromandel rivers, the lower Waikato River and hydro lakes, the Waihou River system, the Waipa River system and the King Country.

Unless otherwise specified the daily bag limit in this region is five sports fish. Minimum length is 30 cm.

Auckland lakes and rivers

All lakes are open for fishing year-round. Unless otherwise specified, the season for streams and rivers is 1 October–30 June.

There are numerous small lakes in the Auckland area, many of which contain coarse fish such as rudd, tench and carp. Only those holding trout and worthy of fishing will be described in any detail. Virtually all of these lakes have no natural spawning habitat so they are stocked annually with hatchery fish.

Lake Tomarata

Location This lake, 20 ha in size, lies between Wellsford and Mangawhai. The lake is north-east of Tomarata, almost on the coast.
Access Turn off SH 1 at Wellsford on the Te Hana–Tomarata road.

Travel 13 km on Ocean View and Tomarata Lake Road to the lake.

Contains small rainbow trout which can be fished to from a boat or by casting from the eastern shore. Best fished in winter when the water temperature has dropped, weed growth has diminished and the water-skiers have gone home. Try a small weighted olive or brown Woolly Bugger on a floating line.

Lake Ototoa

Location Lies 30 km north-west of Helensville near the Woodhill Forest.
Access Take South Head Road and Donohue Road to the lake. There is public access.

Ototoa is a sand dune lake regularly stocked with 'r' type late maturing rainbows from the Ngongotaha Hatchery. Trout average around 1 kg with some larger fish over 2 kg not uncommon. The water is clear and at times trout can be spotted cruising the shallows or drop-off. It is best fished in the cooler months of the year as during summer trout avoid the warm shallows and retreat to the cooler depths of the lake. Trout food includes inanga, koura, bullies, snails and terrestrial insects and their larvae. From April to October fish can be taken fly casting from the shore or from a float tube paddled around the weed beds and rushes. Try various shades of Woolly Bugger, Lord's and Hamill's Killer, smelt patterns, Red Setter and Rabbit flies on a medium or slow sinking line. Small nymphs and a snail imitation such as Black and Peacock are also worth trying. Rudd, tench, carp and trout are all present in this lake.

The remaining lakes in the Woodhill region — Kuwakatai, Kerata, Karaka, Piripoua, Pautoa and Ngaharu — all hold coarse fish. Other Auckland lakes holding coarse fish are Okaihou at Muriwai Beach, Wainamu at Bethell's Beach and Puketi at Waiuku.

Lake Pupuke

Location This popular water-sports lake occupies an old volcanic crater in the middle of North Shore City.
Access From the end of Northcote Road and from Sylvan, Henderson and Killarney parks.

This lake is also regularly stocked with trout but tends to be under-fished. Holds a variety of fish including rainbow and brown trout, tench, rudd, catfish, goldfish and perch. All types of lure and bait can be used, but trout are generally caught in winter on spinners. Night fly fishing with a large black streamer fly is worth trying when the television programmes are dull and other recreational users have gone home.

Lake Whatihua (Thomson's Lake)

Location and access Reached from Waiuku on Karioitahi Road. Access is down a drive and over a stile, but permission must be sought from the landowner.

This 5 ha lake is shallow, weedy and exposed. It is surrounded by farmland and holds rainbows up to 2.5 kg and koi carp. Wading is safe but should be avoided if possible so as not to disturb shoreline cruisers. Trout cannot be spotted but on calm, warm evenings there can be a rise. Try bully-type lures, damsel- and dragonfly nymphs and midge pupae. Best in the cooler months of the year.

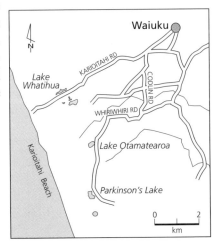

Waiuku Lakes

Lake Otamatearoa (Muir's Lake)

Location and access Lies 6 km south-west of Waiuku off Whiri-whiri Road via the Waiuku–Otaua road. The Waiuku race track encircles the lake. Permission must be obtained from the farm.

This 7 ha lake can only be fished from a boat or float tube but dinghy launching is easy. The lake is surrounded by reeds and holds browns and rainbows up to 2.5 kg. Tench are also present. Use similar flies to those described for Lake Whatihua.

Parkinson's Lake

Location and access Lies south of Lake Otamatearoa near the end of Whiriwhiri Road.

A small lake covering 1.5 ha, with good shoreline access. Holds rainbows up to 3 kg which can be caught by shoreline wading. Best fished in the cooler months when weed growth is not a problem. Similar methods to those described for Lake Otamatearoa.

Mangatangi Reservoir

Location and access Lies in the Hunua Ranges south of Auckland. Take SH 2 to Thames but turn off past Mangatawhiri on Mangatangi, Kaiaua and Workman roads.

This Auckland city reservoir has recently been opened for fishing but angling is restricted to the dam wall. Limited boat access is available to members of the Auckland Freshwater Anglers' Club. Holds both stocked and wild rainbows that can be caught on lures and spinners.

Wairoa River

Location Rises near Paparimu and drains the Hunua Ranges south-east of Papakura. Flows north to enter the sea near Clevedon.

Access For the lower gorge, take the Clevedon main highway and McNichol Road. For the upper gorge, take Hunua Falls Road.
Season Open all year.
Restrictions Fly fishing only above Hunua Falls.

The Wairoa is a small, fragile stream offering nymph and dry fly fishing for wild rainbows and the occasional brown trout up to 1.2 kg. Fish are difficult to spot and weed becomes a problem in summer. Catch and release recommended.

Mangatawhiri River

Location Rises in the Hunua Ranges, flows south-west to Mangatawhiri on SH 2 and enters the Waikato River south of Pokeno.
Access From Lyons Road in the vicinity of Hotel du Vin.

Despite reduced water flows for the Mangatawhiri Reservoir, this river provides small stream fishing in the upper reaches for rainbow trout averaging 0.75 kg. Could be an interesting diversion when staying at the hotel.

Coromandel rivers

Although it rises in the Coromandel Range, the Kauaeranga River is a tributary of the Waihou River and is discussed under the Waihou River system. All these rivers are best fished in the cooler months of the year.
Season 1 October–30 June.

Mahakirau River

Location Drains the Coromandel Range west of Whitianga, flows east to empty into Whitianga Harbour.
Access From the Whitianga–Coromandel road (309) in the vicinity of Mahakirau.

This small, stable stream, popular with local anglers, has well developed pools holding a good stock of small rainbow trout. The overhanging native bush along some stretches makes it attractive to fish. Wading and crossing are still easily accomplished.

The Kaimarama Stream, which joins the Mahakirau at Kaimarama, also holds trout.

Waiwawa River

Location This river also empties into Whitianga Harbour but from a southerly direction.
Access From the Coroglen–Tapu road.

The Waiwawa is a medium-sized river stocked with a population of rainbow trout bred from Ruakituri stock. It has been postulated that as fish living above the Waitangi Falls on the Ruakituri River cannot migrate downstream to the sea, their progeny will hopefully do likewise and remain in the river. There is 10 km of fishable water, and rainbows up to 2 kg have been taken. There are some deep holes, but despite this the river warms in summer and fishing is best in the cooler months of the year.

Waiwawa tributaries holding trout include the Kapowai River east of Coroglen, and the Taranoho and Rangihau streams.

Tairua River

Location This river flows north from the bush-clad hills to discharge into Tairua Harbour.
Access Take Hikuai Valley Road from SH 25A at Hikuai.

There are some deep pools and attractive runs in this river but fishing is best in the cooler months and especially when rafting has ceased.

Lower Waikato rivers and hydro lakes

Season The Waikato River and associated hydro lakes are open all year. However, the season for the Waikato River tributaries described is 1 October–30 June. Bag limit is five sports fish.

Lower Waikato River

Location The lower reaches of this very large river flow north-west through Cambridge, Hamilton and Ngaruawahia. It then turns north to Mercer and finally west to the sea at Port Waikato.
Access SH 1 parallels the river from Lake Karapiro to Mercer. Small boats are very useful for access and can be launched at numerous spots. There is a popular access track below the Karapiro Dam on the true left bank and riverside tracks in Hamilton and Cambridge.

This large, deep, slow-flowing river holds many trout but, because of its size, is difficult to fish with a fly. Most trout are taken on spinning gear although night lure fishing is popular. There are rainbows upstream from Hamilton but the lower river contains more brown trout as well as carp, catfish, goldfish, perch and mullet. While the water quality has improved somewhat over recent years more progress is still required.

Popular fishing spots include below the Karapiro Dam on the true left bank, the mouth of Karapiro Stream near Cambridge, at the Narrows between Hamilton and Cambridge, Cobham Bridge and Ferry Bank in Hamilton, Horotiu Bridge and the wall at Huntly Power Station. This river is not for the purist, but it flows through a number of population centres and yields good trout to local anglers.

Lake Karapiro

Location and access Lies on the Waikato River south-east of Cambridge. SH 1 follows the lake and there are boat ramps off this road and at the mouth of the Little Waipa Stream. There are good access roads on both sides of the lake, with Horahora Road crossing the mouth of the Little Waipa and Pokaiwhenua Streams.

Restrictions If a boat is used for fishing the tailrace below the Arapuni Dam it must be securely anchored.

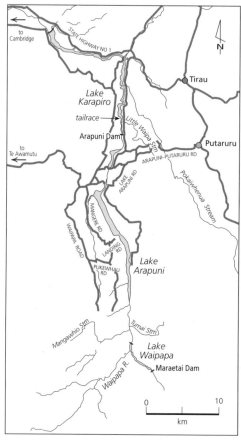

Lower Waikato hydro lakes

This hydro lake is used for a variety of water sports and is famous as a rowing venue. The best fishing is from an anchored boat in the upper reaches or tailrace below the Arapuni Dam. The current is fast and deep, and anchoring can be difficult. Your lure should be fished close to the bottom, and while some anglers use shooting head and high density fly lines others have more success fishing a well-weighted fly and a lead weight on spinning gear. You are fishing deep enough when you lose tackle on snags. However, there are trophy browns and large rainbows present and a good-condition fish of this size in swift water can be very difficult to manage. At night use at least a 4 kg tippet. During the day try Rabbit and smelt patterns, while at night use Black Marabou, Fuzzy Wuzzy and Black Prince.

Trout intent on spawning congregate at the mouths of the Little Waipa and Pokaiwhenua streams from April until July. There is good fly casting from an anchored boat at both mouths providing weed is not too troublesome. Trolling in the lake can also be an effective way to catch fish in weed-free areas, especially in the cooler months.

For shoreline anglers there is good night fishing between Arapuni Power Station and the mouth of the Little Waipa Stream. On warm summer evenings, there can be a prolific caddis hatch so a Deer Hair Sedge or an Elk Hair Caddis should be tried in among the willows. As the night darkens, large fish move in close to the bank to feed. Even a Deer Hair Mouse at night should be tried for big browns.

The Arapuni Dam itself is popular for worm fishing but anglers hooking fish from the dam need a wire basket on a long rope or pole to land their fish.

This lake is regularly stocked with late maturing Tarawera progeny from the Ngongotaha Hatchery. Anglers should be aware of fluctuating lake levels.

Landing a brown trout

Location Rises near Tokoroa from springs, flows north 10 km west of Putaruru and enters Lake Karapiro on the opposite side of the lake to Horahora.

Access As the river generally runs through private farmland away from roads, access is difficult. However, most farmers in the area are very obliging when approached. The river is divided into two sections by falls at Buxfields Reserve on the Putaruru–Arapuni road. Above the falls, good water can be reached from Old Waiotu Road, which branches south off the Putaruru–Arapuni Road. There is also access from Hildreth Road, and Horahora Road crosses well below the falls near the mouth, south of SH 1.

Above the falls, there is spring creek fly fishing for small resident rainbows. Below the falls, the main attraction is the spawning run of large browns and rainbows from Lake Karapiro during April, May and June. Fish can be spotted and stalked with small nymphs and egg patterns, but take a long-handled net as the banks are high and difficult in places.

Pokaiwhenua Stream

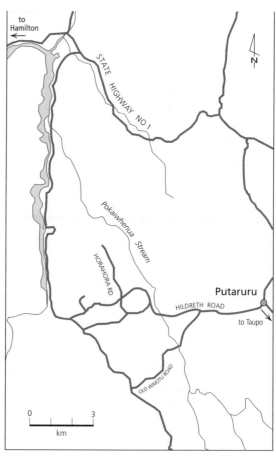

Little Waipa Stream

Location Like the Pokaiwhenua Stream, this medium-sized spring creek also rises in the forestry near Tokoroa. It flows north, parallel to and west of the Pokaiwhenua, and enters Lake Karapiro 5 km south of the Pokaiwhenua mouth.
Access From the Putaruru–Arapuni, Pearsons, Waiotu, Hodderville and Huihuitaha roads and often across private farmland.
Restrictions Fly fishing only above Horahora Bridge at the mouth.

Trout can be readily spotted and stalked in this weedy, clear, spring creek but fishing is a real challenge. Accurate presentation of small nymphs and dry flies on a fine tippet is necessary for success. A landing net is useful.

Lake Arapuni

Location and access Another hydro lake on the Waikato River, lying 16 km south-west of Putaruru. There are five boat ramps, including the popular Jones and Arapuni at the northern end. On the western side there is access from Bulmers, Landing and Barnetts roads and from a boat ramp just below the Waipapa Dam at the southern end.

This is the most popular of the Waikato lakes and is stocked mainly with late maturing 'r' type and Ruakituri rainbows averaging around 1.5 kg. Browns up to 3 kg are not uncommon. A boat is a great advantage both for access and for fishing as shoreline angling is limited to beaches on the western side off Landing Road and at the mouth of Tumai Stream (reached via a track from the eastern side of Waipapa Dam). The mouth of Mangawhio Stream is also worth visiting but casting from a boat is much easier than attempting to walk through bush and swamp. Popular lures seem to be green bodied and include Green and Yellow Rabbit, Green Orbit, Green Marabou and Green Smelt. However, the majority of trout are caught by trolling a spinner such as a Black Toby or a green and gold Cobra.

Location Rises in Pureora Forest Park south of Ngaroma and enters the tailrace beneath the Waipapa Dam on the western side.

Access The lower stretches can be reached in 20 minutes from a bush track below the Waipapa Dam. The mouth is more easily reached by boat as the banks can be swampy.

Season Above the falls, 1 October–30 June. Below the falls, open all year.

Above the falls, the upper reaches lie in an inaccessible gorge and only mountain goats keen on scrub-bashing should attempt to fish this section.

Below the falls, the river is overhung by trees and scrub but is more accessible. There is only 1 km of river to fish between the falls and the mouth. The river can be crossed immediately below the falls but it then becomes deep and slow flowing. From April to the end of June, trout congregate in the lower section to spawn and these fish can offer good sport. Red Setter, Green Rabbit and Red Fuzzy Wuzzy are favourite lures to use on a slow or medium sinking line.

Lake Waipapa

Location and access Mangakino lies on the shores of Lake Maraetai. Lake Waipapa is the next hydro lake downstream. The Te Awamutu–Mangakino road follows the western shore. There is one boat ramp just south of the bridge over the Waipapa River.

Shoreline fishing is very limited on this lake and most fish are caught trolling or fly casting over weed beds from a boat. Weed growth in summer becomes frustrating for anglers. Holds both rainbow and brown trout but the fish are smaller in size than those in Karapiro and Arapuni. The flooded lower reaches of the Waipapa River below the falls is a hot spot in winter for boaties when fish congregate to spawn. Try casting a luminous green-bodied lure on a high density fly line across the current. The Tokoroa Chicken lure is a favourite with local anglers. Trout probably take this to be a small perch.

Location Rises in Pureora Forest Park, flows north-east and empties into Lake Waipapa above the power station. The section below the falls is open all year (see Lake Waipapa).

Access

• Turn right off the Te Awamutu–Mangakino road about 8 km beyond Waipapa Bridge onto Ranginui Road. An unmarked, private, dry weather road closed to vehicles runs off to the right. Drum Bridge over the Waipapa River is reached after a 40-minute walk down this road. From this bridge, overgrown tracks lead downstream on the true right bank and upstream on the true left bank.

• Through private farmland near Ngaroma after a steep climb downhill through scrub.

• Access to the upper reaches can be obtained across private pastoral land off Ranginui Road.

Season Above the falls, 1 October–30 June. Below the falls, open all year.

Restrictions Fly fishing only above the falls.

Although access is difficult, the Waipapa is an excellent medium-sized rock and stone river offering plenty of fishing for agile anglers prepared to walk, wade and bush-bash. It holds a good stock of rainbows up to 2.5 kg but wading can be tricky in places owing to deep slots in the slippery papa rock. The river is best fished in boots and longs for leg protection as the banks are very overgrown in parts by blackberry and gorse. The native bush in the upper reaches is very scenic but an overnight camp is recommended when fishing this section of river. Because of the bush cover in the headwaters the water quality is excellent in this river and sight fishing is possible in some pools. However, due to the bedrock configuration many fish can be missed so all likely looking water should be covered. The stretch of river upstream from Drum Bridge offers superb nymphing water. Be careful downstream from the bridge as the river is swift and dangerous right to the top of the falls.

The Waihou River drains the Mamaku Plateau and the rugged, bush-clad Kaimai Range. It flows generally north and discharges into the Firth of Thames north of Ngatea. It is supplied by numerous feeder streams, most of which hold trout especially in the cooler months of the year. During hot summers when water flows are reduced and the water temperature rises, fish drop back to the main river. This river system runs for 150 km and, along with the Waikato River and its tributaries, is a very important fishery in the Auckland–Waikato region.

The main river holds a large stock of fish and even when the tributaries are scoured by floods and the fish swept downstream, stocks are rapidly replenished from the main river when the floods moderate.

Waihou River

Season The Waihou River and its tributary the Waimakariri are open all year.

Restrictions Artificial fly and lure only above Okoroire. Bait fishing is legal below the Okoroire Falls. Both browns and rainbows are present below these falls with rainbows only above the falls.

Lower reaches

Location and access The river flows north from Matamata to the Firth of Thames and is readily accessible west of Te Aroha and east of Waharoa and Matamata from the Okauia road (Old Te Aroha Road) and Manawaru Road. There is good access from Armadale Road at Gordon, although landowner permission should be obtained.

The lower reaches are unattractive, being sluggish, deep, willow-lined and often muddy. Trout are very difficult to spot in this quiet section of brownish river meandering through dairy farms. Brown and rainbow trout can be caught but mainly on spinning gear. However, there are some large fish in this section of river, with one of 9 kg accidentally snared in a net near Paeroa.

Middle and upper reaches

Location Rises from springs on the Mamaku Plateau east of Putaruru and flows north through Okoroire to Matamata.

Access *Headwaters* Through private farmland from Whites and Leslies roads.

Middle reaches From SH 5, which crosses the river east of Tirau, from Okoroire behind the hotel, from SH 29 west of Te Poi and from the Tauranga–Matamata road.

The headwaters are gin-clear and do not discolour. There are some good-sized rainbows present but they are wary and need to be approached with fine, long tippets and small flies. Many of these larger fish lie under the banks during the day. The smaller fish can also be testing, and when spooked they race upriver and frighten other fish. Early morning and evening are the best times to try for the larger fish. The stream has true spring creek characteristics with a pumice and weed bed.

Below Whites Road but upstream from Okoroire, there is excellent water with drift dives revealing 55 medium-sized rainbows per kilometre of river. In this section, the river flows sedately through farmland. There are grassy banks, some swampy sections and patches of scrub but access to the river is generally good. All methods of fly fishing including dry fly, nymph and soft hackle wets can be productive. The local lads use spinners and worms below SH 5. In April, May and June, there is an excellent spawning run from the lower reaches.

Kauaeranga River

Location Rises in the heavily bush-clad Coromandel Range, flows south-west and enters the tidal estuary of the Waihou River just south of Thames.

Access Kauaeranga Valley Road leaves SH 26 on the outskirts of Thames and follows up the true right bank.

Season 1 October–30 June.

This is a small to medium-sized stream flowing through native bush in its upper reaches, and farmland in its middle and lower reaches.

Water quality is generally good although the river is tidal in the lower reaches up as far as Smiths Corner. From the Christian Heritage camp upstream to the Wainora camping ground, there is pleasant water to fish with good access in most stretches. The stream can be waded and crossed but the rocks are extremely slippery. There are some deep holding pools and attractive rocky runs. Fish can be spotted on bright sunny days. Above Wainora, the river becomes rather thin and divided.

Holds a reasonable stock of small to medium-sized rainbow trout averaging 0.5–1 kg. Fishes best early and late in the season when the trampers and swimmers have gone home. Try Coch-y-bondhu, Black Gnat and Royal Wulff dry flies and small Pheasant Tail nymphs.

Tramping is very popular in this valley and there are many attractive campsites.

Puriri River

Location and access From the Thames–Paeroa highway (SH 26) 12 km south of Thames.
Season 1 October–30 June.

The Puriri is a small, shingly, willow-lined spawning stream crossing farmland. Holds limited stocks in summer and is best fished early in the season before trout return to the main river. Sight fishing is possible.

Hikutaia River and the Maratoto tributary

Location and access From SH 26 at Hikutaia, then from the Hikutaia–Maratoto road. There is a good camp site in this valley with access to Coromandel Forest Park.
Season Open all year except the Maratoto tributary. On this tributary and above the ford on Whangamata Track the season opens on 1 October and closes on 30 June.
Restrictions Fly fishing only in the Maratoto tributary. The Maratoto is another spawning stream for the Waihou River, hence the restrictions.

Best fished early or late in the season when a few good-sized rainbows enter the river. Resident fish tend to be small — drift dive surveys have found 18 fish in the 20–30 cm range. The Hikutaia is a small, shingly, willow-lined stream flowing across pastoral land with stretches of clear nymph water and stable pools. Not heavily fished.

Komata Stream

Location and access 6 km north of Paeroa, take Komata Valley Road from SH 26.
Restrictions Fly fishing only.
Season 1 October–30 June.

The Komata is a small, gravelly stream lined by willows and flowing across pasture. Holds small rainbow trout and fishes best either early or late in the season.

Ohinemuri River

Location Drains the southern Coromandel Range and the northern Kaimai Range. Flows west from Waihi to Karangahake then north through Karangahake Gorge to Paeroa, where it joins the Waihou River.
Access SH 2 follows the river from Paeroa to Waihi. There is an access road to an excellent picnic spot at Taylor's Reserve opposite Rahu Road at Mackaytown.
Season Above Victoria Street Bridge in Waihi, 1 October–30 June; elsewhere, open all year.

During the Waihi gold rush over a hundred years ago, this medium-sized river was polluted with cyanide used in gold recovery. Despite regular monitoring of water quality, the river was again polluted quite recently from gold mining but complete recovery seems to have taken place. The river has been prone to severe flooding in the past but fish stocks are rapidly replenished from the parent river, the Waihou.

Above Karangahake Gorge there are pools, runs and backwaters but trout are difficult to spot in the brownish water. The best fly

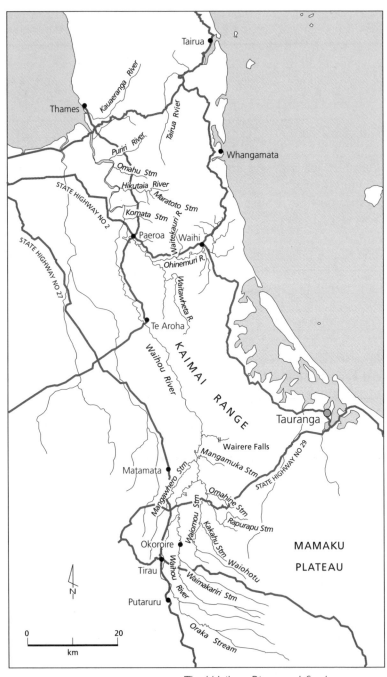

The Waihou River and feeder streams

fishing is upstream from Waihi, where dry flies can be used in summer. Through the gorge there is a wide variety of water, with the rougher water more suitable for nymphing and spinning. Holds a good stock of browns and rainbows in the 0.5–1 kg range but fish seem to move about in this river, leaving some pools barren while others hold plenty. Late in the season, a spawning run of larger trout enters the river from the Waihou.

Below Karangahake Gorge, the river is best fished with a downstream lure, smelt fly or spinner. Mullet are present in this stretch and are easily mistaken for trout.

Waitekauri River

Location and access Flows south from the Coromandel Range to join the Ohinemuri River at Waikino on SH 2. Waitekauri Valley Road follows upstream and eventually crosses the river. Private farmland may need to be crossed to reach the stream.

This is a pleasant small stream holding a small stock of brown and rainbow trout in the 0.5–1 kg range. Fish can be spotted under optimum conditions and will respond to small dries and nymphs. Dairy farm pollution has been a problem at times and the stream is overgrown in places. Best early in the season.

Waitawheta River

Location Rises on the eastern slopes of Mt Te Aroha in the Kaimai Range west of Katikati. Flows north through bush, across farmland, then through a gorge to enter the Ohinemuri River downstream from Waikino.

Access *Lower reaches* From SH 2 at Karangahake. Cross the Ohinemuri River Bridge to a car park and walk up the rocky gorge on a well-defined track.

Middle reaches From SH 2 at Waikino, take the road to Waitawheta and turn off on Dickies Flat, Deans or Franklin roads to the river.

Upper reaches A DoC track follows upstream from the end of Franklin Road. There are huts and camp sites off this track in the Kaimai Range.

Season Upstream from Franklin Road, 1 October–30 June. Below Franklin Road the river is open all year.

This heavily fished, medium-sized stream offers plenty of good water, especially in the middle and upper reaches. Fish stocks are not high (10 trout per km in the 30–40 cm range) with fewer fish in the upper reaches. Despite good-looking water in the gorge, I have found this section disappointing, although a late spawning run in May and June boosts fish numbers.

Trout can be taken on dries, nymphs and well-sunk lures fished across and down.

Mangamuka Stream

Location and access Crosses the Okauia road (Old Te Aroha Road) 1 km north of the Crystal Hot Springs at Okauia.
Season 1 October–30 June.

This small, spring-fed stream rising in the Kaimai Range holds limited numbers of small rainbow trout.

The Wairere Falls Stream also holds a few small fish in the lower reaches before it enters the Waihou.

Omahine Stream

Location and access Crossed by SH 29 (the Tauranga–Matamata road) just before joining the Waiomou River. Access also from Omahine Road.
Season 1 October–30 June.

A small rock and stone stream that often remains clear when the Waiomou floods. A good spawning run of brown trout arrives from the Waihou River late in the season. These can be sight fished and taken on small nymphs. The stream is overgrown in its upper reaches.

Location Rises in the Kaimai and Mamaku Ranges, flows north-west at first through native bush, then through pastureland to join the Waihou River north of Te Poi.

Access

- The Tauranga–Matamata road crosses the stream near Stopfords Road, 11 km from Matamata.
- The Tauranga–Hamilton highway (SH 29) crosses the stream at Swaps Bridge east of Te Poi.
- The Te Poi–Tapapa road runs parallel to but west of the stream with access available from Rapurapu, Smith's and Waiomou side roads.

Season 1 October–30 June.

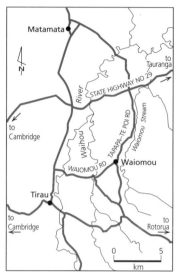

Waiomou Stream

There is 30 km of fishable, wadeable water in this medium-sized river, flowing over a shingle and mud bed. There is an hour's fishing upstream from where the river emerges from the bush, although a lot of scrambling is required. At Okoroire School the stream is narrow and deep in parts and not easy to fish. There is good water where the Tauranga–Matamata road crosses, the river being wider and intermittently willow-lined. However, the river enters a difficult gorge an hour downstream from this bridge.

In April, May and June, a spawning run of brown trout enters the river from the Waihou but these fish are not easy to catch. Resident fish are mainly rainbows in the 0.5–1.5 kg range but an occasional fish of 3 kg is landed.

Try well-weighted nymphs, caddis and mayfly dry flies on summer evenings, and lures such as Red Setter, Woolly Bugger and Red Hairy Dog fished across and down for spawning browns late in the season.

Rapurapu Stream

Location and access From Rapurapu Road, which branches off the Tauranga–Matamata road at the foot of the Kaimai Range. The upper reaches flow through private farmland.

Another small feeder stream that is best fished early or late in the season when water flows are adequate. Trout are generally small and can be stalked with a dry fly or nymph.

Kakahu Stream

Location and access Rises in Kaimai–Mamaku Forest Park, flows north-west and joins the Waiomou Stream near the old Selwyn School. Access from Kakahu Road linking Rapurapu Road with Waiomou Road.
Restrictions Fly fishing only.

A small, clear-water nursery tributary of the Waiomou that is easy to cross and fish. Holds a reasonable stock of small rainbows. Tree planting by Okoroire School and conservation-minded locals have helped stabilise the banks and conserve this stream.

Oraka Stream

Location and access Rises near Tokoroa, flows north, east of Putaruru and Tirau, to join the Waihou just south of SH 29, west of Te Poi. Access from Lake, Langlands and Taumangi roads off SH 27 (the Tirau–Matamata road).
Season 1 October–30 June.

This small stream is best fished between Tirau and Putaruru. It is overgrown in places and stocks of small browns and rainbows are not high. As the banks can be high along some stretches, a landing net should be carried.

Location Rises from springs on the Mamaku Plateau east of Putaruru, flows north-west across farmland and joins the Waihou 3 km above Okoroire Falls.

Access Crossed by SH 5 (the Tirau–Rotorua highway) just west of Tapapa. Waimakariri Road follows upstream on the true left bank.

Season Open all year. There is no bag or size limit under 30 cm but only two fish over 30 cm can be taken.

This busy, medium-sized stream holds a large population of small rainbows and is a great learner stream (79 trout in the 20–30 cm range per kilometre). There is 12 km of fishable water suitable for both fly and spin fishing. It is willow-lined in parts, easy to wade and cross, and has a stone and mud bed. Trout are not easy to spot so the stream is generally fished blind. The Auckland Acclimatisation Society had a hatchery on this stream some years ago.

Waipa River and tributaries

This river system is another important Auckland–Waikato fishery offering many small-stream angling opportunities close to population centres.

Season 1 October–30 June, except for the Puniu River below Seafund Road bridge, where it is open all year.

Waipa River

Location Rises south-east of Te Kuiti in Pureora Forest Park in the Rangitoto Range. Flows generally north across pastoral land close to Otorohanga and Pirongia to enter the lower Waikato River at Ngaruawahia.

Access *Lower reaches* Off the back roads from Ngaruawahia to Otorohanga. Also from the Pirongia–Kawhia road and the Otorohanga–Kawhia road (SH 31).

Middle reaches Otewa Road follows the river for 16 km from SH 3 to Toa Bridge.

Upper reaches Walking is required above Toa Bridge although there is access from Owawenga Road on the eastern side of the river across private farmland.

Season Below Toa Bridge this river is open all year. Above the bridge, 1 October–30 June.

Restrictions Daily bag limit above SH 3 bridge is two fish. Below this bridge, five fish.

This long, medium-sized river is a highly recommended trout fishery, especially above Otorohanga, where the water quality is reasonable.

In the lower reaches, where the river is deep and slow-flowing, the water quality deteriorates and runs silt-laden for much of the year. However, this unattractive section still yields an occasional good-sized trout, usually taken on spinning gear.

Above Otorohanga there are 30 km of pools and runs. The river has a rock, gravel and mud bed and there are patches of native bush along the banks. There are reasonable numbers of browns and rainbows up to 2 kg. However, the best water lies an hour's walk upstream from Toa Bridge and there are at least two days of fishing in this section up as far as Owen Falls. The last 7 km below the falls become rough, bouldery and turbulent.

From February to May is the most popular time to fish this rather inaccessible upper section, as a spawning run of brown trout arrives from the Waikato River. These fish can be taken on dry flies such as Coch-y-bondhu, Lace Moth, Twilight Beauty and Humpy, nymphs such as Half Back, Hare's Ear and Pheasant Tail, and red-bodied lures fished deeply through the pools and runs. In bright conditions, fish can be spotted.

Kaniwhaniwha Stream

Location Flows off the northern, bush-clad slopes of Mt Pirongia and enters the Waipa north of Karamu.

Access Turn off at Te Pahu onto the Karamu Limeworks loop road.

Restrictions Fly fishing only.

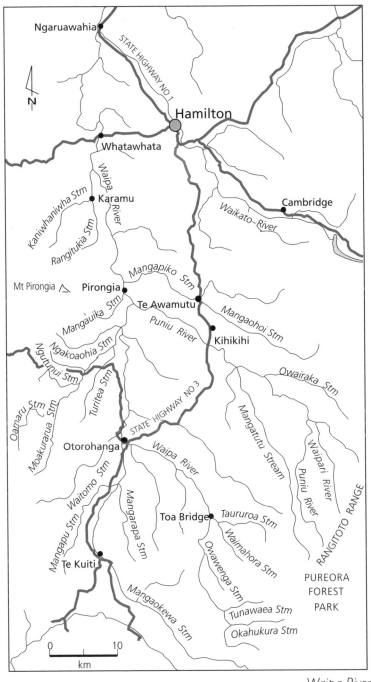

Waipa River

Kaniwhaniwha and Ngakoaohia Streams

This popular, clear-water stream emerging from native bush is heavily fished. With its rock and stone bed and well-defined pools, some trout can be spotted on bright days although they are very shy. Holds rainbows and browns in the 0.5–1.5 kg range, and drift dives have counted 25 fish in the 20–30 cm range per kilometre of river in the upper reaches. As a number of fish lie concealed beneath the banks and overhanging vegetation, fishing the likely looking water is well worthwhile.

Early in the season there is good fly fishing above the Limeworks loop road bridge. Beware of a low telephone wire on the backcast! It is festooned with flies, including one of mine. Early in the season there are fish upstream beyond the fork in both bush-lined tributaries (Kaniwhaniwha and Blue Bull streams). There are also some productive stretches downstream of the loop road. This area is popular for tramping and picnicking.

Mangauika Stream

Location and access Enters the Waipa at Pirongia. Access from Mangauika and Hannings roads.

A small stream flowing across farmland holding a few small rainbow trout. It is very pleasant to fish but water flow in summer can be reduced by the Te Awamutu water supply draw-off.

Ngakoaohia Stream

Location Flows east from the southern slopes of Mt Pirongia.
Access From the Pirongia–Kawhia road (SH 31) and Pekanui Road at Ngutunui.
Restrictions Fly fishing only upstream from the Pirongia–Kawhia bridge.
Season 1 October–30 June.

This small to medium-sized stream holds small brown and rainbow trout in clear pools and runs over a rock and gravel bed. It flows through native bush in the upper reaches, then across pastoral land. Below the Pirongia–Kawhia road, willows and high banks make fishing difficult in places. Upstream from this road there is 10 km of fly fishing water.

Moakurarua Stream

Location and access Rises from bush-clad hills west of the Waitomo Valley, flows north just west of Honikiwi and joins the Waipa near Te Awamutu. There is access to the upper reaches from the Otorohanga–Honikiwi road, Carlin Road and Tapuae Road across private farmland. The Otorohanga–Kawhia road (SH 31) crosses the middle reaches.

This is an excellent small stream flowing across pastoral land. The quality water and a gravel and sandy bed allow trout to be sight fished. There is a good day's fly fishing upstream from Honikiwi Road right up into native bush. This section of river is easily waded and crossed.

The middle and lower reaches cross farmland but

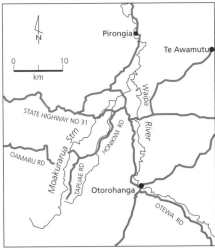

Moakurarua Stream

there are well-developed, stable pools holding browns and rainbows up to 2 kg. This section is best fished with spinning gear as the water quality deteriorates and willows choke some stretches.

Oamaru Stream

Location and access Joins the Moakurarua Stream just downstream of the Honikiwi Road bridge. Access is from Oamaru Road, which parallels the stream.

This delightful small stream has unfortunately deteriorated as a result of farming operations and becomes very weedy in summer. Only worth a look early in the season.

Ngutunui Stream

Location and access Flows off the southern slopes of Mt Pirongia and joins the Moakurarua Stream near the Otorohanga– Kawhia road (SH 31). Flows parallel to this road.

The upper reaches of this small stream are difficult to fish in places because of overhanging bush and high banks. Best where it flows across farmland. Holds small browns and rainbows.

The Turitea Stream is another small tributary of the Moakurarua Stream. It is crossed by SH 31 just east of the Moakurarua.

Waitomo Stream

Location Rises near Waitomo Caves and flows north to enter the Waipa River just west of Otorohanga.
Access Across private farmland from Waitomo Valley Road.

A small stream that quickly becomes silt-laden after rain. The overgrown banks and poor quality water make fishing difficult. Not recommended.

Mangaokewa Stream

Location Drains the Ruapehu Range north of Benneydale, flows north-west, parallel to and east of the railway line from Kopaki to the eastern suburbs of Te Kuiti. Then follows SH 3 and joins the Mangapu Stream near Hangatiki.
Access From Mangaokewa Reserve off SH 30 just south of Te Kuiti, and from Mangaokewa Road also off SH 30.

Holds a reasonable stock of browns and rainbows averaging 0.75 kg. Fish are hard to spot in the brownish water but the stream is pleasant to fish above Mangaokewa Reserve. Popular with the locals.

Mangarapa Stream

Location and access Flows north-west to join the Mangapu near Hangatiki. Access off SH 3 from Mangamutu Road near Hangatiki.

Best in the upper reaches as this small stream is often silt-laden further downstream.

Waimahora Stream

Location and access Enters the Waipa River at Toa Bridge on Otewa Road.

A small, willow-lined, shingly stream flowing over farmland and holding small numbers of trout. Best fished early in the season before water flows are reduced and fish drop back to the main river. It is a spawning stream for the Waipa River.

Mangatutu Stream

Location Rises in the Rangitoto Range in Pureora Forest Park and flows generally north to join the Puniu River near Waikeria.
Access From Wharepuhunga Road, which runs parallel to the stream for 5 km. There is another 10 km of stream that can be

accessed on foot upstream from the Wharepuhunga Road bridge.
Restrictions Fly fishing only upstream from the Lethbridge Road
bridge near Korakonui.

This highly regarded, medium-sized, rock and stone stream is one
of the larger tributaries of the Puniu River. In the fly-only section,
there are well-developed stable pools and runs, the water is clear
and trout can be sight fished. Holds some good-sized fish up to 2.5
kg but tends to be overfished by the locals. Drift dives found 12–15
takeable fish per kilometre of river. I would suggest trying mid-
week and early in the season.

The headwaters flow through bush and scrub, whereas below
the quarry near the Mangatutu Road junction the stream crosses
farmland. There are very few fish in the headwaters above a sink
hole, and fly casting becomes difficult in the scrub. The best fishing is above Lethbridge Road, where the stream is easily waded and
crossed. Below this point spinning is the best option as the water
quality deteriorates.

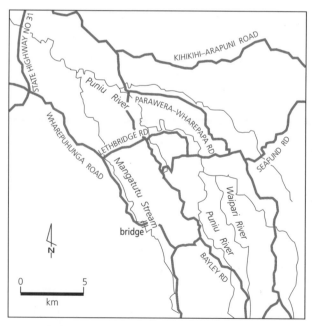

Waipari and Puniu rivers and Mangatutu Stream

Location Like the Mangatutu, the Puniu also rises from the Rangitoto Range in Pureora Forest Park. The river flows north-west from Wharepuhunga to join the Waipa near Pirongia.

Access *Upper and middle reaches* From the Kihikihi–Arapuni road, turn right at Bayley Road 5 km beyond the Orakau Battle site. Then take Newman, Bayley, Wharepapa or Duncan roads.

Lower reaches From SH 3, which crosses south of Kihikihi, and from Tiki Road.

Season Below the Seafund Road bridge this river is open all year. Above the bridge, 1 October–30 June.

Restrictions Fly fishing only upstream from Bayley Road bridge.

This popular, medium-sized river offers good fishing in the upper and middle reaches but the lower reaches are polluted by farming operations and bank clearance. Emerging from native bush, the upper reaches have good water quality and trout can be sight fished. The slower flowing middle reaches are generally blind fished but rainbows and browns in the 0.75–1 kg range can be expected. The upper reaches can be waded and crossed but the middle reaches have long deep pools and crossings can be difficult, especially when you cannot see the stream bed because of the brownish water.

Try small Parachute Adams, Coch-y-bondhu and Dad's Favourite dry flies, Pheasant Tail and Hare and Copper nymphs, CDC emergers or a small soft hackle wet fly.

Owairaka Stream

Location and access Runs parallel to the Kihikihi–Mangakino road beyond the Bayley Road junction.

This narrow, deep, spring-fed stream winds its way across farmland. It has a shingle, mud and weed bed and holds small rainbows. Because of high banks in some sections, anglers are advised to carry a landing net. The stream suffers from farm run-off, with weed and algal growth a real problem in summer.

Waipari River

Location Flows parallel to, but east of, the Mangatutu Stream to join the Puniu east of Waikeria.
Access Near Wharepapa south of Whatauri Settlement Road via Seafund Road. Permission is required to cross private farmland.

This stream is similar in size and character to the Mangatutu but holds fewer fish. A delightful stream to fish either early or late in the season. Sight fishing can be difficult except on a bright, sunny day.

Mangaohoi Stream

Location and access Flows from Pukeatua through Te Awamutu. Access is from Parawera and Monkton roads, off the Kihikihi–Mangakino road.

Runs silt-laden for much of the year but holds small rainbows.

Although not tributaries of the Waipa River, two other worthwhile streams in this vicinity are the Oparau and Awaroa rivers. Both drain into Kawhia Harbour on the west coast and look to be interesting streams to fish. Surprisingly, the stocks are low.

Oparau River

Location and access Drains Mt Pirongia and flows west to Kawhia Harbour. Access is from a loop road off SH 31 linking Ngutunui with Oparau.

This small stream, bush-clad in its upper reaches, holds a limited stock of small rainbows and sea-run browns that enter the lower reaches toward the end of the season. A walking track up Mt Pirongia follows upstream where the loop road leaves the river.

Location Rises from the hills south-east of Kawhia Harbour and north-west of Te Anga. Flows north from Te Koraha to enter Kawhia Harbour north of Hauturu.
Access From the Hauturu–Te Koraha road.

The middle and upper reaches of this stream are bush-clad and very scenic. Holds a small population of brown trout. The best stretch of river to fish is where the road leaves the stream for a short section and enters a scenic reserve. There are some very deep holes and trout are not easy to spot.

King Country

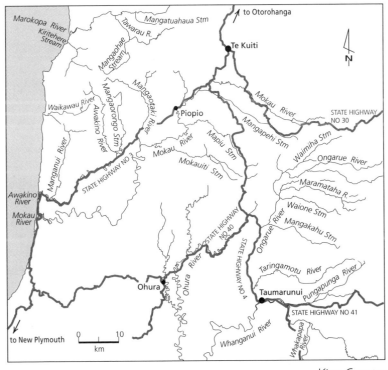

King Country

The area described in this section includes all the country lying between Te Kuiti in the north and Taumarunui in the south, the Hauhungaroa Range in the east and the Tasman Sea in the west. Originally, dense native forest clothed these hills, but now much of the bush has been burned and clear-felled to make way for pasture. This has caused deterioration of the water quality in many of the rivers. The main river systems include the Marokopa, Awakino and Mokau rivers draining to the Tasman Sea and some Whanganui headwater tributaries north of Taumarunui.

 Marokopa River and tributaries

Marokopa River

Location Rises in the bush-clad hills west of Waitomo Caves, flows on a westerly course through rugged limestone country and farmland to enter the Tasman Sea at the small seaside settlement of Marokopa.
Access From the Waitomo Caves–Te Anga road, which leaves SH 3 8 km south of Otorohanga.
Season Above the confluence of the Mangatuahaua Stream, 1 October–30 June. Below this confluence the river is open for fishing all year round.

The lower 4 km are tidal and, along with whitebait, mullet, herring and kahawai, an occasional large sea-run brown is caught, not always by legal methods. Below Te Anga, the river is best suited to spinning, being deep, wide and slow flowing.

Between Te Anga and the Marokopa Falls, there is good water for all types of fishing. Fly fishing is best above the falls, where the river flows sedately for 12 km across farmland. There are patches of scrub, grassy banks and long, slow pools and runs. Because the banks have been cleared for pastoral farming, and with a stream bed of papa and mud, the river discolours rapidly in a fresh and takes 3–4 days to clear. Even in low-water summer conditions, the water is never crystal clear and trout are not easy to spot in the deeper stretches. For this reason fly fishing is best after Christmas, when the river is low.

The headwaters are a challenge for the bow and arrow anglers as the river is overgrown by native bush and full of snags. Trout are present upstream beyond the naturally formed Marokopa Tunnel.

There are reasonable numbers of rainbows and browns averaging 1.2 kg in this river and they respond to all fishing methods. In favourable conditions, trout can be spotted and often reveal themselves by their rise forms. The browns have very attractive markings with bright red spots along their flank.

Mangatuahaua Stream

Location and access This small stream joins the true left bank of the Marokopa River at Piripiri. Access is from the Waitomo Caves–Te Anga road at Piripiri.

Only energetic and fit anglers wearing boots and shorts should explore this stream, but it does hold trout and is seldom fished.

Mangapohue Stream

Location and access Follows the Waitomo Caves–Te Anga road close by the natural bridge and joins the true right bank of the Marokopa River upstream from Piripiri.

This small tributary holds good trout but they are very difficult to catch and land as the stream is overgrown by scrub and bush. There is a small stretch where the bush has been partially cleared but generally the stream requires bow and arrow techniques and lateral thinking. The water is clear and it is frustrating to spot good-sized trout lying in impossible places. Take a landing net and use it quickly after a fish is hooked!

Mangaohae Stream and Tawarau River

Location Rises near Waitanguru north-west of Piopio, flows north and enters the Marokopa at Te Anga. The upper reaches are known as the Mangaohae, while the same river downstream of the Orekopa Stream becomes the Tawarau River.

Access *Mangaohae Stream* Take Oparure Road from SH 3, 3 km north of Te Kuiti to Oparure, Pakeho and Ngapaenga. Then Weres Road to Mangaohae. A DoC track follows downstream from the end of Weres Road.

Tawarau River From Te Anga take Speedies Road, a short no exit road following the true left bank. A DoC track follows upstream and connects to Weres Road 16 km upstream.

This medium-sized tributary of the Marokopa offers good quality fly fishing from Te Anga all the way upstream to beyond Mangaohae. The river gorges in places and is partially lined by bush but offers deep stable pools and enticing runs. Fish can be spotted in the shallower sections on bright days but the river has a brownish tinge and any likely looking stretches should be fished blind. The river holds mainly rainbows in the 1–2 kg range, which respond to mayfly and caddis imitations. The eels are healthy and prolific in this river. Crossings can be tricky because of slippery stones.

Energetic, keen anglers should take two days and fish the 16 km of river from Te Anga to Mangaohae. There are excellent camp sites along the river bank.

The Kiritehere Stream and Waikawau River are best described in this section. Although not tributaries of the Marokopa River, they empty into the Tasman Sea south of the Marokopa settlement.

Kiritehere Stream

Location Rises in the bush-clad Herangi Range, flows north and enters the Tasman Sea just south of Marokopa at Kiritehere Beach.
Access Across private farmland from Kiritehere Road running south over the hill from Marokopa.
Season 1 October–30 June.

This small stream holds medium-sized brown trout that can be spotted and stalked in low-water summer conditions. The upper reaches, upstream from the bridge, flow over a shingle bed and hold few fish. The middle reaches, which meander slowly across farmland, offer the best fishing, while the lower reaches become sluggish and tidal and are more suited to whitebaiting. This stream is not easy to fish as the unprotected banks are high in places and the fish become very spooky. It is difficult to see fish and remain hidden. Trout are light in colour and blend in well with the sand and mud river bed. Fishing is best early in the season. There is a camp site at the second bridge.

Waikawau River

Location and access Also rises in the Herangi Range and flows west to enter the sea midway between Marokopa in the north and Awakino in the south.

A small, willow-lined stream winding across cleared farmland and entering a large estuary. It only holds a few trout but each year there is often a large sea-run brown caught on spinning gear. Not worth a special visit but the coastal scenery is recommended and the man-made tunnel to the beach is unique.

Awakino River and tributaries

Season 1 October–30 June.

Awakino River

Location Rises from the Herangi Range west of Piopio, flows south to Mahoenui, then south-west through the Awakino Gorge to reach the Tasman Sea at Awakino.
Access *Upper reaches* Follow up the winding Gribbens Road for 12 km from Mahoenui. Permission to fish should be obtained from the first farm in the valley.
Middle and lower reaches From SH 3 between Mahoenui and Awakino.
Restrictions Fly fishing only upstream from Mahoenui Bridge. Bag limit is two fish.

Below the gorge, the river is sluggish and often silt-laden. It is usually fished with spinners. Between the gorge and Mahoenui there is reasonable fly water, especially during the summer months when the river is low and clear. However, this section still discolours readily after rain, and spotting is usually difficult.

Above Mahoenui, the river is smaller, easy to wade and cross, and a delight to fish. There are clear pools and runs on a rock and stone bed and fish are easy to spot. This section above the Mangaorongo confluence is partially bush-lined and seldom becomes unfishable except after heavy rain. In the bush section upstream from the farmland, fish numbers are low. Accurate casting is required during the day but at dusk fish often rise to caddis and can be taken on a soft hackle wet fished across and down. During the day try any small lightly weighted nymph or Coch-y-bondhu, Parachute Adams, Elk Hair Caddis or Royal Wulff dry flies in sizes 14 to 16. It is my opinion that the upper section of this stream should be catch and release.

The Upper Awakino after a fresh

Manganui River

Location Flows in a southerly direction parallel to the coast to join the Awakino River just upstream of the mouth.

Access Waikawau Road follows upstream on the true right bank.

This is an important spawning stream for the Awakino. For this reason, it is best fished either early or late in the season. It only holds a small population of resident fish. The upper reaches are gorgy in parts with some bush cover, but the lower reaches are willow-lined and cross farmland.

Mangaorongo Stream

Location Flows south, parallel to and east of Gribbens Road, to join the Awakino at Mahoenui.
Access From Mangaorongo Road, which leaves SH 3 about 4 km north of Mahoenui.

This stream is gorgy, overgrown and very difficult to fish. It is full of snags and rapidly becomes silt laden in a fresh. Despite this adverse description, an angler with bow and arrow techniques and a sound knowledge of bushcraft should hook some good fish. Whether these fish are landed, however, is another question. Take a landing net.

Mokau River and tributaries

Season Except for the lower reaches of the Mangaotaki River, 1 October–30 June.

Mokau River

Location and access Flows on a south-westerly course parallel to and south of SH 3 from Te Kuiti to the sea at Mokau. Access to the upper reaches from Puketutu on SH 30 south of Te Kuiti.

Twenty years ago, anglers enjoyed good fishing on this river. Now farming operations have severely affected the water quality. In summer, sluggish flows, fertiliser run-off, bank clearance, warm water and weed and algal growth lead to eutrophication and poor trout habitat. There are a few fish early in the season in the upper reaches but generally this river is now only useful for eeling.

Unfortunately, apart from the Mangaotaki River and the Mangapehi Stream, all other tributaries have suffered the same fate.

Mangaotaki River

Location Drains the Herangi Range west of Piopio, flowing south-east to join the Mokau River east of SH 3, just north-west of Mahoenui.

Access

- From Mangaotaki Road where it crosses the river 10 km west of Piopio at Battley's Bridge. Permission required to cross farmland.
- From SH 3, which crosses the river 10 km south of Piopio.

Season Above the lower bridge on Mangaotaki Road, 1 October–30 June. Below this bridge to its confluence with the Mokau this river is open all year.

This medium-sized river is favoured by the local anglers. Below the SH 3 bridge, the river runs through a partially bush-clad gorge that can be fished down to the Mokau confluence. Spinning is favoured in this stretch of river as the water quality is often not good.

Upstream from SH 3, there is good water holding both brown and rainbow trout up to 1.5 kg. Fish are difficult to spot in the brownish water, but there are some deep holes and some interesting riffles. Patches of native bush enhance the scenic qualities of this popular river.

Mangapehi Stream

Location and access Rises near Benneydale, flows west to join the Mokau River south of Te Kuiti, near Eight Mile Junction. Crosses SH 30 at Kopaki, flows across farmland and then runs parallel to SH 4 before joining the Mokau.

This small, sluggish, brown-water stream crossing farmland readily becomes silt-laden after rain. In summer, weed growth is a problem. Holds small rainbows and an occasional brown.

A number of excellent trout fishing rivers drain the Hauhungaroa Range in Pureora Forest Park. These tributaries join to form the Ongarue River north of Taumarunui, which after flowing south enters the Whanganui River at Taumarunui. All hold brown and rainbow trout, and fish up to 2.5 kg are not unusual, especially in the headwaters of these rock and stone rivers. The season is 1 October–30 June.

Waimiha Stream

Location Rises near Barryville on SH 30, flows south-west across pastoral land to join the Ongarue at Waimiha.
Access *Upper reaches* From SH 30, 10 km east of Benneydale, across private farmland behind a pa.
Middle and lower reaches From Waimiha Valley Road, which leaves the Waimiha–Mangapehi road just north of Waimiha settlement.

Ongarue River

This medium-sized stream holds a good stock of trout and is a delight to fish. The upper reaches are deep, clear and slow flowing but hold good-sized browns that cruise rather than hold their feeding position. They are very spooky during the day but can be deceived by a small, lightly weighted Pheasant Tail nymph cast well ahead of a cruising fish.

The middle and lower reaches are more heavily fished. The water is seldom very clear but there is good access between the willows to a succession of pools and runs. There are more rainbows in these stretches. The majority of fish landed in this section are caught on spinners.

Ongarue River

Location Drains the Hauhungaroa Range and flows parallel to and south of the Waimiha Stream.

Access *Upper and middle reaches* From Ongarue Stream Road, which runs parallel to the stream for some distance and provides access to 20 km of fishing water. Please ask permission to cross private farmland.

Lower reaches From Ongarue–Waimiha Road.

The lower reaches of this medium-sized river south of Waimiha are sluggish, muddy and channelled, and not recommended.

The middle reaches upstream from Waimiha settlement flow across farmland and are better suited to spinning. There are some deep, slow-flowing holes in the willows.

The upper reaches offer 20 km of good water with well-defined pools, long glides and shingly runs. The river winds placidly over pastoral land, access is easy, wading and crossing possible at the tail of most pools and casting generally unimpeded by vegetation. Further upstream, a few kilometres above Endean's Mill, the river becomes more difficult to fish as it is overgrown by bush and scrub. Although there are a few access tracks to some of the better pools, fly casting is still testing.

The Ongarue water is slightly peat stained, making sight fishing difficult unless fish are rising or feeding in the shallower runs. Holds rainbows and browns up to 2 kg. The stretch of water in the vicinity of Endean's Mill is very popular.

Location and access This small tributary of the Ongarue can be accessed from Ongarue Stream Road, which crosses the stream just above its confluence with the Ongarue River. The stream bed should be followed upstream from this bridge as access is very difficult from Okauaka Road.

Restrictions Fly fishing only.

This clear-water, stable stream flows down a rocky gorge that becomes progressively more overgrown with scrub, blackberry, bracken and native bush as you wade upstream. There is only half a day's fishing until you reach an impressive waterfall. The stream is easily waded and crossed and trout can be spotted in most sections. Holds a limited stock of small rainbow up to 1 kg. Drift divers discovered a few fish above the falls but how they got up there is a mystery.

Maramataha River

Location and access Flows west, parallel to and south of the Ongarue River. Waione Road, a branch road running south from Ongarue Stream Road, crosses the Maramataha River.

Waione Stream

Recommended for the energetic angler who can deal with dense manuka scrub and blackberry. Holds a few large rainbows in deep pools and gorges but unless you carry a chainsaw, I suggest leaving your fly rod at home. You are unlikely to be disturbed by other anglers on this river except near the bridge. The water is slightly peat stained. Deerstalking friends have found trout in the upper reaches in Pureora Forest Park.

Waione Stream

Location Flows parallel to, but south of, the Maramataha River.
Access From Waione Road via Ongarue Stream Road. It is the next stream south of the Maramataha Bridge, at the end of the road at Waione Station.
Restrictions Fly fishing only.

The middle reaches of this small to medium-sized stream flow across farmland and offer easy access to clear pools and runs. There are few fish in the first gorge on the farm.

In the upper bush-lined reaches the stream is stable and the pools well defined and deep. Rainbows averaging 1.4 kg can be sight fished. Although the stream can be readily crossed, it is best suited to active anglers, as scrambling over large boulders and ducking through native bush is required on some sections. There is a full day's fishing from Waione Station to a deer farm in the upper reaches. An old logging road on the south side of the stream is great to walk home on at the end of the day. A highly recommended stream but it can become unfishable after rain.

Mangakahu Stream

Location and access Runs parallel to Waione Stream but further south again. Access is from Mangakahu Road, running east from Ongarue.

A small, difficult, willow-choked stream holding a few trout only. Best early in the season.

Pungapunga River

Location and access East of Taumarunui turn off SH 41 to Ngapuke.

This is a small stream with a shingly bed, flowing across farmland and holding a few small trout. Best early in the season before the water warms in summer.

Ohura River

Location Rises north-west of Ongarue, flows south to join the Whanganui River south of Ohura.
Access Turn off SH 4 onto SH 40 at Mangatupoto, about 20 km north of Taumarunui. This road to Ohura follows the river.

This slow-flowing, brownish, willow-lined river is unattractive to fish even though it does hold both brown and rainbow trout. There are a few stretches below Matiere where one can fly fish but generally the river is more suited to spinning and eeling.

This is the final Whanganui River tributary north of Taumarunui that is described.

Upper Whanganui River

Location The Upper Whanganui River rises from rugged bush-clad country west of Lake Otamangakau.
Access
- The headwaters can be reached by 4WD or trail bike on old logging roads leaving SH 47 south of Lake Otamangakau. Local knowledge and forestry maps are essential.
- From SH 41 (the Taumarunui–Turangi road) turn right 8 km east of Manunui on an unsealed road marked Hohotaka. This road crosses the river.
- From SH 4 on roads to Kakahi, Manunui, Mahoe and Piriaka.
- From the end of Te Rena Road by wading the Whakapapa River and crossing Whakapapa Island.

- Below Taumarunui, roads follow down each bank.

Season Above the Whakapapa confluence, 1 October–30 June. Open season below this confluence.

The headwaters of this large river provide rugged back country fishing for the fit, energetic angler. There is good water to explore upstream from Hohotaka Road providing the river is reasonably low. Otherwise, difficulty in wading and crossing will be experienced. Take a wading staff for this section of river. There are rocky pools and runs with bush along the banks providing stability for the river. Trout can be difficult to spot and you should search the likely looking water with an attractor pattern dry fly or well-weighted nymphs.

Between Bennets Bridge and Taumarunui, the river is more sedate, flowing through grazing land. There are well-defined, stable pools, long glides and riffles. The river bed is sandy and stony with occasional papa outcrops, making wading hazardous. Willows and native trees line the banks.

Now that water flows have been increased in the Whakapapa River, the stretch below this confluence has improved and fish stocks increased. There is pleasant water to fish with easy access between Manunui and Kakahi.

There are good stocks of brown and rainbow trout in this large river, with fish averaging 1.5 kg. When fishing the pools and runs blind, I suggest trying bead head nymphs early in the season, size 12 Humpy, Coch-y-bondhu, Stimulator and Royal Wulff dry flies when the weather warms, and downstream lures such as Rabbit varieties, Mrs Simpson and Kilwell at any time. For the spin angler, Black Toby, Red Veltic and Daffy seem to be effective.

Below Taumarunui, the river becomes very large and usually runs silt laden below the Ongarue confluence. It is described in the Waimarino section.

Whakapapa River

Location Rises on Mt Ruapehu and joins the Whanganui River near Kakahi.

Access *Headwater tributaries* Whakapapanui and Whakapapaiti join 2 km west of SH 47 (the Turangi–National Park road). Walk downstream from SH 47 where this road crosses these streams. There are a few fish upstream from SH 47.

Main river Across private farmland east of SH 4 at Oio, from an old timber company road at Owhango, and from Te Rena Road at Kakahi. Access is difficult south of Oio because of gorges, cliffs and rugged bush country.

Season 1 October–30 June. Above the Piopiotea confluence the daily bag limit is two fish but all rainbows must be released.

Now that water flows have been increased, the fishing in this once highly regarded river has improved. The headwater tributaries below Matariki Falls hold only a few large fish early in the season. Below the hydro intake for Lake Otamangakau, there is very little water until the Otamawairua Stream joins.

East of Oio, there are good, clear, stable pools, long glides and shingly runs. The river is quite large and swift in places and needs to be crossed with considerable care. Trout can be spotted and stalked, and the scenery is rugged and attractive with native bush, steep cliffs and gorges.

At Kakahi, the water has a brownish tinge, but fish can still be spotted in low-water summer conditions. However, there are sufficient stocks to fish this section blind and there is often a rise in the evenings. There are some large brown trout in the section above the Whanganui confluence. Access is easy on this section of the river and there is an attractive picnic area and basic camp site.

Use the same flies as suggested for the Whanganui River but special mention should be made of the Kakahi Queen and Twilight Beauty dry flies, which were created many years ago by Mr Basil Humphries, postmaster at Kakahi.

Piopiotea Stream

Location Rises near National Park, flows north through Raurimu, parallel to and east of SH 4, to join the Whakapapa River at Hukapapa.

Access Across private farmland from SH 4 between Raurimu and Oio. The side road through Raurimu village also leads to the river.

The upper 6 km of this small stream lacks holding water, but below the falls near Raurimu the stream follows a more gentle course across cleared pastoral land. The stream bed contains boulders, sand, silt and mudstone while the banks are willow-lined. Holds small numbers of rainbows and browns averaging 1.2 kg. These can be spotted and are best fished early in the season before water flows diminish and the fish retreat back downstream to the main river.

A tributary of the Piopiotea, Te Pure Stream, holds a few fish only and is unreliable. Access is from Manson's Siding bridge and a gravel road that follows the stream along the main trunk railway.

Other tributaries of the Whanganui River further south are described in the Waimarino section.

Eastern Fish and Game Council region

For ease of description, this diverse and exciting region is divided into the Upper Waikato River and hydro lakes, Tauranga District, Rotorua District, Rangitaiki River system, Urewera National Park, and East Coast, Gisborne and Wairoa. One could happily fish this expansive region over a lifetime without covering all the water. There is a wide variety of fishing to be experienced all year round, with trophy rainbows in some of the Rotorua lakes and Lake Aniwhenua. There is excellent summer sight fishing in the Urewera National Park, while the Ruakituri and Rangitaiki rivers are well known to local and overseas anglers alike.

Daily bag limit Ruakituri River above Waitangi Falls and the Horomanga River (including tributaries), two trout. All other waters eight trout. The daily limit for brown trout on Lake Waikaremoana and Lake Rotorua is two trout. On Lake Tarawera, catch and release only for all male trout caught within a radius of 200 m of Te Wairoa Stream.

Upper Waikato River and hydro lakes

There are five lakes in this area — Maraetai, Whakamaru, Atiamuri, Ohakuri and Aratiatia. All have been formed by damming the Waikato River for hydro-electric power. In addition, a number of streams draining into these lakes or into the Waikato River itself warrant description.

Season The lakes are open for fishing all year round, while the streams open on 1 October and close on 30 June.

Unfortunately, eutrophication is a problem in all these lakes, with weed and algal growth being most prolific in summer when the water warms. Consequently, the best time to fish is either early in the season or during the colder winter months. As access is very difficult, shoreline fishing is limited, so a boat is a decided advantage. Both browns and rainbows are present and fish over 3 kg are not uncommon, although the average weight is somewhat less than this. At Queen's Birthday weekend each year, The Big Three competition is held. Prizes are awarded to angler/hunters skilled and lucky enough to bag a deer, a wild pig and a trout over the weekend.

Lake Maraetai

Location and access At Mangakino on SH 30, where there is a boat ramp at the lake front domain on Lake Road.

Although popular with local anglers, fishing is rather inconsistent in this lake, which was formed in 1952. Trout average 1 kg but fish up to 3 kg are not uncommon. Recent releases have been Taonui browns and late maturing 'r' type rainbows. Trolling and harling accounts for most of the fish landed while some anglers have success casting over weed beds from a boat. Sandy Bay is a popular area for trolling and Mangakino Arm for casting from a boat. Favoured spinners include Toby, Cobra, Flamingo patterns and Tokoroa Chicken, the latter most probably representing a small Russian carp — a favourite trout food in this lake. Lures that catch fish include Red Setter, Red Rabbit, Hamill's Killer, Green Smelt and damsel nymph patterns.

The Mangakino Stream, entering the top end of Lake Maraetai and crossed by SH 30 south-east of Mangakino, holds trout but is overgrown and difficult to fish.

Lake Whakamaru

Location Lies upstream from Whakamaru township. SH 30 crosses the dam and follows the northern shore.
Access There is no shortage of boat ramps. They can be found on the true right of the lake (northern shore) at Snowsill's Reserve, Duddim's Creek, Whakamaru Christian Camp, Lake Whakamaru camping area and from SH 30.

On the south side of the lake, there is access at the ski club on Pokuru Road.

Formed in 1956, this shallow lake becomes very weedy in summer, which makes trolling from a boat extremely frustrating. Rainbows average 1.5 kg but browns are much larger with a few trophy fish landed each year. Casting over weed beds from an anchored boat is the most profitable method of fishing this lake. There is some shoreline fishing near the Whakamaru Christian Camp. Use the same lures as for Lake Maraetai.

Another popular spot to fish is immediately below the Whakamaru Dam.

Lake Atiamuri

Location and access SH 1 between Taupo and Tokoroa crosses the Waikato River just below Atiamuri hydro village and dam. There is boat launching at Atiamuri.

This small, deep lake was formed in 1958. Boat fishing for both browns and rainbows can be very productive, especially at small stream mouths and in the Tahunaatara Arm. Browns up to 4.5 kg have been caught. There are some shoreline areas to fish on the true right of the lake in the Waikato Arm.

Tahunaatara Stream

Location This is one of many tributaries in the region of Horohoro on SH 30 between Rotorua and Lake Atiamuri. The Tahunaatara joins the Pokaitu, Matahana and Rahopakapaka streams to become the Whangapoa Stream. This enters Lake Atiamuri at the Tahunaatara Arm just east of Upper Atiamuri.
Access From SH 30 in the vicinity of the Rotorua Gun Club near Guthrie. Forestry roads west of SH 30 give reasonable access.
Season 1 October–30 June.

Although this stream is very overgrown in places, there are a few good stretches of water offering dry fly and nymph fishing to adventurous, scrub-bashing bow and arrow casting anglers. Rainbow trout can be spotted in clear water but conventional casting is difficult.

There are reputed to be *fontinalis* in the gorge section south of SH 30.

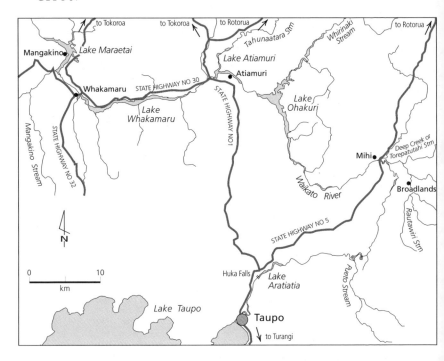

Upper Waikato hydro lakes

Lake Ohakuri

Location and access Turn off SH 1 just south of Atiamuri. The road through the pine forest is well signposted. There is a boat ramp and picnic area at the end of the road quite close to the dam. Also from Orakei Korako, where there is boat access.

This large lake, formed in 1961, is very popular for water sports in summer. Holds both browns and rainbows with recent releases of late maturing 'r' type fish. Weed is once again a problem in summer. Most fish are caught from boats as shoreline fishing is limited.

The most popular areas are the Whirinaki Arm and the Waikato River part of the lake. Use the same lures as described for Lake Maraetai.

Whirinaki Stream and tributaries

Location and access Drains farmland around Waikiti Valley and Ngakuru, flows south-west and enters Lake Ohakuri. Can be reached from SH 30 via Ngakuru on Mangatete and Whirinaki Valley roads. Generally, access is across private farmland.
Season 1 October–30 June.

There are many streams in this vicinity that hold trout but most have been affected by dairy farm operations. Early in the season, before weed growth becomes a problem, they are worth visiting. The slower flowing lower reaches above Whirinaki Arm can be fished from a boat on Lake Ohakuri.

Lake Aratiatia

Location and access Lies just downstream from Huka Falls. Access from Wairakei Village off SH 5 by turning into the Taupo Equestrian Centre, Department of Conservation reserve, from Rapids Road. This is on the true right of the lake. There are no boat ramps.

Fishing is very limited in this lake but browns and rainbows can be taken by spinning from the shore on both sides.
Note: ECNZ opens the Aratiatia Dam gates each day at 10.00 am and 2.00 pm. Anglers fishing below the dam are warned!

Upper Waikato River

Location This large river has been severely modified for hydro-electric power generation. Consequently, there are only two sections worth fishing. The most popular stretch is from below the Aratiatia Dam to the head of Lake Ohakuri. The section between Lake Taupo (SH 1 bridge) and Huka Falls 13 km downstream also

93

holds trout but fishing access is severely limited.

Access There are a number of access points. Some of the more popular to the true left bank are:

- Ohaaki Road off SH 5 north of Wairakei.
- Tutukau Road before the turn-off to Orakei Korako (there is a boat ramp).

And to the true right from:

- Rapids Road across the Aratiatia Dam.
- From Wairakei to the Aratiatia Rapids below the dam.

And off Broadlands Road to:

- St Kilda Road (permit required from Fletcher Challenge Forests at Tauhara).
- Kaiwhitiwhiti Stream access through forestry land (permit required from Fletcher Challenge Forests at Tauhara).
- River Road, where there is a boat ramp.
- Pueto Stream mouth can be reached from Broadlands Road by walking down the stream on the true left bank for 2 km through the southern side of Fletcher Challenge Forests reserve.
- Vaile Road to the Torepatutahi Stream and mouth.
- Mihi Road bridge.

Season The main river is open all year. Boat fishing is permitted.
Note The river is subject to flow variations when the flood gates at Taupo and Aratiatia are opened. The Aratiatia Dam is opened at 10.00 am and 2.00 pm each day.

This is a very productive fishery with both rainbow and brown trout present in good numbers. In summer, geothermal discharges raise the water temperature. As a result, trout congregate at the mouths of the cooler spring creeks. From October to May, the mouths of Pueto, Kaiwhitiwhiti and Torepatutahi streams offer excellent fly fishing with either a nymph or a streamer. Many fish are also caught by trolling and harling from a boat or spin fishing from the shore.

Location and access
- Pueto Stream is one of the first streams you cross on the Taupo–Broadlands road. Access from Broadlands Road is by walking down the true left bank through the southern side of Fletcher Challenge Forests reserve.
- Kaiwhitiwhiti Stream crosses Broadlands Road 3 km beyond the River Road turn-off. Permit required from Fletcher Challenge Forests.
- Torepatutahi Stream and its tributary Rautawiri Stream. Vaile Road near Broadlands gives access to the lower and middle reaches while Earles Road gives access to the upper reaches and Rautawiri Stream across private farmland.
- Otonga Stream, with access from East Road.

These are all cold, spring creeks worth exploring in the cooler months before weed growth becomes a problem. Most creeks are affected by dairy farming but the middle and upper reaches are generally clear, thereby enabling trout to be spotted and stalked. There is often a good evening caddis rise on these creeks but during the day trout are spooky and must be approached very cautiously. An accurate delicate first cast is very important. Rainbows up to 2.5 kg are present. Use small dry flies and weighted nymphs and be prepared to change the pattern after a refusal. A landing net is very useful.

Tauranga District

The most important river system in this district is the Wairoa River and its many feeder streams draining the rugged, heavily bush-clad Kaimai Range. The main river enters Tauranga Harbour near Bethlehem and is tidal in the lower reaches. Unfortunately from an angling perspective, this river system has been considerably modified for hydro-electric power generation. There are five power stations operating and thirteen tributaries have been dammed or diverted.

Other smaller streams in the Tauranga area have reduced water flows as a result of water draw-off for orchard irrigation. However, there is still some interesting water to explore.

Season Aside from Lake McLaren, Ruahihi Canal and the lower Wairoa River, which are open to fishing all year round, the season for all other waters is 1 October–30 June.

Tuapiro Creek

Location and access Enters the northern end of Tauranga Harbour at Tanner's Point. Can be reached from SH 2 north of Katikati by taking MacMillan's or Woodlands roads.

This small stream holds small rainbow trout. It is tidal in its lower reaches and used for swimming in summer. Being overgrown it is not highly rated, but local anglers using spinners, wet flies and nymphs enjoy their sport.

 Wairoa River and tributaries

Wairoa River

Location and access Drains Lake McLaren, flows north through a rugged gorge, then placidly through pastoral land parallel to SH 29. The lower tidal reaches are crossed by SH 2. Access to the gorge section is very difficult and hardly worthwhile.

Season Open all year below Lake McLaren.

There is very little water to fish in this moderate-sized river because of fluctuating water flows and difficult terrain below the McLaren Falls Power Station. This section of river is better suited to rafting than trout fishing. An occasional good fish has been taken below the Ruahihi power house on a smelt fly or silvery spinner early in the season when trout are chasing whitebait.

Ohourere (Minden) Stream

Location and access Rises in the Kaimai Range south of Te Puna and flows east before entering the Wairoa River. Access off SH 2; take Wairoa Road at the main Wairoa River bridge near Bethlehem, then Crawford's Road to a picnic area beside the stream.

This small stream flows across farmland and holds a limited stock of small rainbow trout. The stream is pleasant to fish but trout only average 0.5 kg and the catch rate is not high. Falls on the lower section prevent fish running in from the Wairoa River. The stream should be fished blind with small dry flies and nymphs.

Opuiaki River

Location and access Take Soldiers Road from SH 29 just beyond the Ngamuwahine Bridge. Soldiers Road crosses the stream on a low-level concrete bridge.

Reduced water flows from power generation have seriously affected this once excellent stream. Fish stocks are not high but rainbows can be spotted and stalked with a fly.

The Mangapapa River, entering the top of Lake McLaren, has also been affected by hydro development but, like the Ngatuhoa Stream at Ngatuhoa Lodge, holds a few rainbows. Access is difficult.

Ngamuwahine River

Location and access Drains the Kaimai Range south of Whakamarama, flows east at first through native bush, then over farmland to join other small streams that enter Lake McLaren. SH 29 crosses the river 15 km south-west of Tauranga. A single-lane, unsealed road follows upstream on the true right bank to a farm.

This small, scenic river is the pick of the Tauranga waters for fly fishing. The upper reaches in the bush hold limited stocks but in the middle reaches there are a few browns in the 1–2 kg range in the pools across the farm. Below the farm, the river is more boisterous but the odd fish can be spotted in the rocky crevices. This is a delightful place to picnic, with native bush bordering the stream.

Te Ahura Stream, easily seen from SH 29, joins the Ngamuwahine near the SH 29 bridge. Holds a few small brown trout.

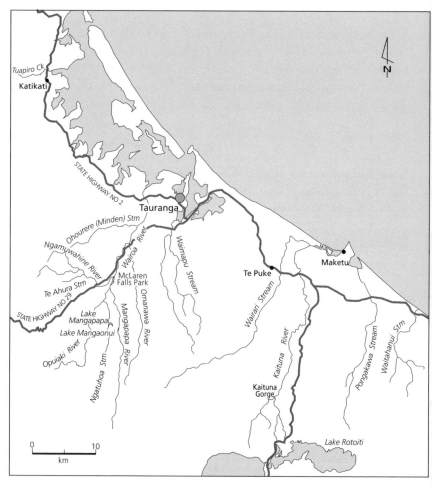

Tauranga District

Omanawa River

Location Flows north, parallel to but east of Omanawa Road from Omanawa Power Station, to enter the Wairoa River downstream from Ruahihi Power Station.

Access Across private farmland, but often very difficult because of a deep gorge.

This is not an easy river to fish; boots and shorts and a wading stick are recommended. Holds mainly rainbow up to 1.5 kg with a few browns in the lower reaches. The water is clear but the gorge section should only be attempted by active, fit anglers. Most fish are taken on spinners. Upstream from Omanawa Power Station there are a few rainbow, but this section is not highly regarded.

Lake McLaren

Location and access Take McLaren Falls Road from SH 29 to McLaren Falls Park.
Season Open all year.

A small hydro lake that is difficult to fish because of a muddy shoreline. Best suited to spinning although trout will rise on warm summer evenings. Casting from a dinghy or float tube could be worth trying. Holds both browns and rainbows.

Exotic tree planting has made McLaren Falls Park a great picnic spot.

Ruahihi Canal

Location and access Runs from the lake and is easily accessible from either end. After hours, the gates are locked but keys can be obtained from the Tauranga Angler's Club or the Ruahihi power house on SH 29.
Season Open all year.
Restrictions Closed to fishing between landmarks marking an artificial spawning bed at the southern end.

This hydro canal is stocked with medium-sized rainbow trout that can be taken on fly or spinner. The ambience leaves a little to be desired.

Waimapu Stream

Location Rises in the hills south of Oropi, flows north and enters the Waimapu estuary of Tauranga Harbour near Greerton.
Access From Oropi Road across private farmland.
Restrictions Fly fishing only above the waterfall 1 km east of the Oropi–Hereford road junction.

Although highly regarded by local anglers, this small stream has limited water available to fish. Parts of the stream are overgrown with scrub while other sections wind across pastoral land. Holds only a small stock of brown trout but the water quality is good and sight fishing is possible.

Kaituna River

Location Drains Lake Rotoiti at Okere Falls, flows north through hill country for 6 km, then enters an inaccessible bush-clad gorge. The river emerges from the gorge 20 km downstream and flows slowly and sedately across farmland to enter the Bay of Plenty near Maketu.
Access *Upper reaches* From Okere Falls turn-off on SH 33. The road follows the true left bank to the Trout Pool. There is a bridge and walking tracks downstream and stands have been constructed for anglers.
Middle reaches The gorge section can be reached by tramping through cut-over bush from SH 33. In the farmland section, access can be obtained off SH 33 from Mangarangi Road and bridge, where there is a boat ramp.
Lower reaches From Rangiuru Road, SH 2 east of Te Puke and Kaituna River Road.
Season Open all year downstream from the Lake Rotoiti flow control structure.

The most popular section of this medium-sized river is the 6 km stretch of water downstream from the outlet. The water is deep, weedy and reasonably clear in the upper reaches but most anglers fish it blind. Holds reasonable numbers of rainbow trout averaging

0.75–1.5 kg and these can be taken on dry flies, lures, wet flies, nymphs and spinners. There is often a good caddis rise in summer. Favoured flies include Twilight Beauty, March Brown, Elk Hair Caddis and soft hackle wets.

The gorge is rough and difficult to fish as there are cliffs and very deep sections where it is impossible to ford. Fish are certainly present, but be prepared to lose most of those hooked as they run off downstream, unless of course you decide to swim after them.

Across the farmland, the character of the river changes. It becomes deep and slow-flowing and the water quality deteriorates. Most fish are taken on spinners. Further downstream, kahawai enter the mouth chasing whitebait, and the occasional sea-run rainbow has been caught.

The Mangorewa River, flowing parallel to, but west of, the Kaituna River, also holds a few trout but access is difficult as the river runs through a deep gorge for most of its course. The Oropi–Rotorua road crosses the upper reaches.

Wairari Stream

Location and access Flows in a northerly direction to enter the Kaituna River north of Te Puke. Access from No 1 Road or Te Matai Road through private land, and from SH 2, which crosses east of Te Puke.

This small, slow-flowing stream meanders across orchard land and holds a few small rainbow and brown trout. Fished mainly with spinners and wet flies by local anglers.

Pongakawa Stream

Location and access Crossed by SH 2 near Pukehina, east of Te Puke. Reached from SH 2, Benner's Road and Rotoehu Road.

A small, spring-fed stream flowing over pastoral land holding a limited stock of small rainbows. Not highly regarded and generally only fished by local anglers with spinners or live bait.

Location and access Flows north down Otamarakau Valley from Rotoehu Forest. Reached from Otamarakau Valley Road.

Another small stream, but this one is quite highly regarded by local anglers. Contains small rainbows.

Rotorua District

It is thought the Rotorua area was first settled about the middle of the fourteenth century by Maori from the *Arawa* canoe. About 1830, Hans Tapsell from Maketu was the first European to visit Rotorua, followed in 1831 by the missionary Thomas Chapman. The area is world famous for its thermal activity.

The Rotorua district includes more than a dozen lakes within a half hour drive from the city. Most of these lakes are volcanic in nature and owe their present form to lava flows which have blocked their drainage.

Brown trout were first liberated into the Awahou and Ngongotaha streams in 1888 and rainbows ten years later. All lakes hold rainbows and some brown trout, but these are generally in the minority and more difficult to catch. Most of these lakes offer shoreline fishing but a boat is a decided advantage and opens up areas that cannot be accessed by road. Good spawning habitat is scarce in many of the lakes so annual liberations are made from the Ngongotaha Trout Hatchery. Statistics indicate that 50% of anglers fly fish while 74% troll or jig. Most fly fishing is accomplished by lure fishing and much of this is done at stream mouths and at night.

Restrictions
- No licence holder shall fish for any sports fish between 12.00 midnight and 5.00 am.
- Fly fishing only within 200 m of any stream mouth or outlet.
- Lake Rotokakahi (Green Lake) is privately owned and closed to fishing.

- Lead or wire lines can now be used for trolling on all the Rotorua lakes, excluding fly-only areas.
- Down-riggers are illegal.
- Daily bag limit is eight trout but only two brown trout may be taken from Lake Rotorua.

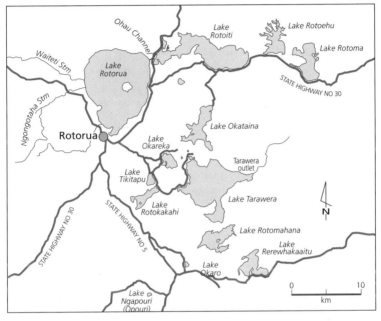

Rotorua Lakes

Location and access Rotorua city lies on the southern shore and access is generally freely available all around the lake.

Season Except for those waters leading into the Ohau Channel, the lake is open for fishing all year.

Boat ramps These are numerous, with the best all-weather ramp at Sulphur Point through the Government Gardens. There are two at Hamurana, two at Ngongotaha, two in Rotorua and one at Hannah's Bay.

Covering 7878 ha, Lake Rotorua is the largest lake in the district but is relatively shallow, at 25 m deep in the deepest part. Apart from the built-up areas, the lake is surrounded by farmland. There have been pollution problems in the past, and in summer, when the lake warms, a bloom of blue-green algae can be troublesome. Weed growth can be prolific in the shallow bays but hopefully, now that efforts have been made to improve the water quality, these problems will diminish. The shoreline and stream mouths are safe to wade.

Good stocks of rainbows averaging 1.5 kg are present in the lake and, to add more interest, trophy browns up to 4 kg are not uncommon.

Fly fishing from the shore

When the lake temperature rises in summer, trout congregate in large numbers in the cooler, oxygenated water of stream mouths. Fishing can be excellent, especially at night from late December through to March. By April, trout begin their spawning runs and although fish can be caught, they do not congregate for any length of time before running upstream. Stream mouths are all shallow, so trout remain wary during the day unless the lake is ruffled by a stiff breeze. Fishing is best when this blows offshore.

Use a floating, slow sinking or sink tip line and a lure to imitate a smelt or bully. Lures to use during the day include smelt patterns, Rabbit varieties, Dorothy, Parsons' Glory, Kilwell No 1, Lord's Killer and Hamill's Killer. At night, try Craig's Night-time, Scotch Poacher, Fuzzy Wuzzy, Hairy Dog, Black Prince and Black Marabou. Some anglers use two flies — a conventional black lure and a luminous Doll Fly.

During bright, sunny, summer days try wading out into the lake and look back in to shore. By using Polaroids, large cruising browns can be spotted and stalked with a small smelt pattern or even a nymph. A favourite spot for this type of fishing is between Hamurana and the Ohau Channel as the cliff background eliminates glare on the water and improves visibility. Cast well ahead of cruising fish.

Spinning can be carried out from shore provided you are 200 m from any stream mouth. Fly casting from an anchored boat is also permitted at stream mouths but give shoreline anglers plenty of room.

Stream mouths

Utuhina Access from Arataua Street. Sunken boulders and logs snag a few deeply sunk lures.

Ngongotaha Access from the end of Beaumont's Road or Taui Street by walking along the beach. Best when the wind blows from the west.

Waiteti Access from Arnold or Operina streets. Wading is possible out as far as 200 m at this shallow mouth. There is also good fishing in the slow-flowing lower reaches either side of the footbridge. Use a slow sinking line and a black lure after dark or a small well-sunk nymph during the day.

Awahou Access from Gloucester Street. Considered to be the most productive stream mouth, it is heavily fished in January and February. Best in west or north-west winds.

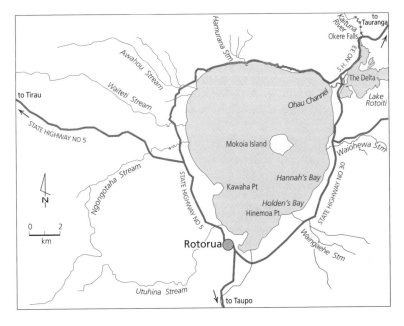

Lake Rotorua

Hamurana There is good fishing at the mouth of this cold spring creek when the lake is warm.

Other small stream mouths include the Waiowhiro, Waikuta, Waiohewa and Waingaehe (Holden's Bay Stream). These will only take two or three rods and fish best with an offshore breeze, a floating line and false casting. Some require permission from landowners. These streams are closed to fishing upstream from the mouth.

Trolling and harling

More than half the trout caught in Lake Rotorua are landed from boats. Apart from the hot summer months when fish gather round the cooler stream mouths, trolling and harling are very productive. Fish can be caught anywhere in the lake, although round Mokoia Island is a favourite area. Other spots worth trying are Kawaha Point, Sulphur Point, Hinemoa Point, the Airport Straight, Whakatane turn-off and in the vicinity of the Ohau Channel outlet. Early morning and late afternoon are the best times. When harling a fly, use a high density fly line. The same flies as recommended for stream mouths can be used for trolling with the addition of Ginger Mick and Green and Yellow Orbit.

When trolling a spinner try black or green Cobra, Billy Hill, Tasmanian Devil, Black Toby or a Flatfish. Blue, green and black are favoured colours. In rough conditions, Lake Rotorua can be treacherous so keep a weather eye open.

Rotorua streams

Season The Ngongotaha, Waiteti, Hamurana and Awahou streams are open all year below the bridges where the Ngongotaha and Hamurana roads cross these streams.

The Utuhina below Lake Road bridge is also open all year. Upstream from these road bridges, the season is 1 December–30 June.

Fishing is not permitted in the Utuhina above the Pukehangi Road bridge nor in the Hamurana and Awahou streams above the Hamurana Road bridge. All other small streams flowing into Lake Rotorua are closed to fishing.

Restrictions Fly fishing only on all these streams except the Utuhina below Lake Road bridge, where spinning is permitted.

Access *Utuhina Stream* Crossed by SH 5 near Ohinemutu. There are a number of accesses available through Rotorua City Council reserves.

Ngongotaha Stream Access off Ngongotaha Valley Road through private property. There are signposted access points.

Waiteti Stream The lower reaches can be accessed from a footbridge near the mouth, the upper reaches through private farmland north of Ngongotaha.

All are spawning streams for Lake Rotorua and hold good stocks of trout either early or late in the season. They are small, clear-water streams and, apart from their lower reaches, fish can be stalked and easily spooked. Although overgrown in parts, some sections offer good small nymph fishing for run fish.

Ohau Channel

Location and access Flows slowly and deeply between Lake Rotorua and Lake Rotoiti. Crossed by SH 30. Much of the land bordering the channel is Maori owned so permission should be sought. The Ohau Channel Camp proprietor will allow access to the camp area except on opening day, when only anglers staying at the camp have permission.

Season 1 October–30 June.

Restrictions Fly fishing only. Fishing is not permitted from an anchored boat within 200 m of the entrance or exit.

Trout live, spawn and migrate through this channel at certain times of the year. Lake Rotoiti trout have very few natural spawning areas so many pass through the channel on their way to spawn in the Rotorua streams. In spring and early summer schools of smelt also migrate through the channel and this attracts trout. Because the water is deep, a sinking line should be used and cast well across and upstream to allow the lure to sink. The most heavily fished section is near the weir at the Rotorua end. The best time to fish the channel is early and late in the season. October, November, May and June are prime months. Rainbow and brown trout averaging 2 kg can be expected, with a few of trophy proportions caught each season.

During the day try smelt patterns such as Grey Ghost, Hawk and Silver, Doll Fly, Dorothy, Yellow and Silver Rabbit and Jack Spratt. At night use the usual night patterns like Black Marabou, Black Prince, Craig's Night-time, Fuzzy Wuzzy, Scotch Poacher and 'lumo' flies. Late in the season, when fish spawn in the Channel, some anglers have success with egg patterns.

The Delta

Location and access This is the exit or mouth of Ohau Channel into Lake Rotoiti. Access from SH 33 at the rest area 1.5 km east of Mourea.
Season 1 October–30 June.

Wading can be tricky as the bottom is uneven. The lip is also deep and drops off suddenly. Stand back 10 m or so from the lip and cast over it with a sinking line. Wait until your lure sinks, then quietly retrieve. April, May and June are the best months. Few anglers fish here at night, although there is no reason for this except perhaps the difficulties in wading. It pays to be in position before dark. Use flies similar to those suggested for the Channel, with the addition of Hamill's Killer, Kilwell No 1 and Mrs Simpson.

Lake Rotoiti

Location and access Lies north-east of Lake Rotorua. SH 30 follows the southern shore and SH 33 the western shore. Large areas of this lake can only be reached by boat.
Season 1 October–30 June. There is an open season for shoreline anglers between landmarks situated at Ruato and Hinehopu extending 200 m offshore. Trolling is not permitted within this area.
Boat launching There are boat ramps at Otaramarae, Waipuna Bay, Gisborne Point and Hinehopu. Otaramarae is the deepest.

Rotoiti is the third largest lake in the Rotorua area and covers 3340 ha. The northern shore is bush-clad.

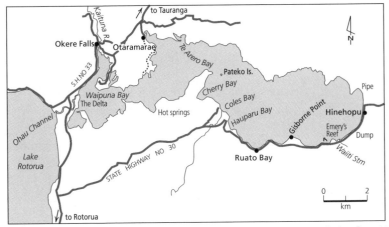

Lake Rotoiti

Fly fishing

Regular releases of Ngongotaha Hatchery 'r' type rainbow fry are made along the shore between Ruato Bay and Hinehopu. When mature, these fish return to their release site to spawn along the shallow, sandy beaches. As a consequence, there is good shoreline fly fishing, especially at night from April to the end of October. Trout weighing over 4.5 kg are not uncommon. Fishing pressure can be intense at times, with some anglers securing their spot well before dark. The same shoreline can be fished during the day but trout are shy and much more difficult. Most fish are caught in shallow water close to shore, so quiet wading, false casting and a slow retrieve are required. Use a floating, sink-tip or slow sinking line, and during the day try Red Setter, Kilwell No 1, Hamill's Killer, Mrs Simpson, Parsons' Glory, Jack Spratt and egg patterns. At night try Scotch Poacher, Black Phantom, Hairy Dog, Black Marabou and luminous Doll Fly. Many anglers use two flies.

When fishing Rotoiti it is wise to have 100 m of backing on your reel as, although some fish are disappointing fighters, others just never stop.

The following shoreline spots are recommended.

Hauparu Bay This is the first bay reached from Rotorua on SH 30. Access is down a driveway opposite the bus stop. A small stream mouth can be located 30 m down the beach to your right. Note that this bay closes to fishing on 30 June as wild fish spawn in the stream.

Ruato (Twin Stream) Bay SH 30 runs the length of this popular bay and the odd logging truck has been caught on the back-cast. Two streams enter the lake, one at either end of the sandy beach, but the larger stream at the eastern end provides the best fishing. An offshore wind is desirable and wading is often unnecessary, especially late at night. Fish are taken close in on floating lines. If the fishing is still slow by 9.30 pm it is probably not worth persisting.

Emery's Reef This spot is opposite Emery's Store. Enter the lake on the right-hand side of the jetty and wade quietly along the shore for 80 m to a large karaka tree on the bank above. There is an old engine block to stand on if you can find it! The reef can be covered by casting out slightly to your left. A cold spring near the reef attracts fish.

Gisborne Point Wade still further along the shore from Emery's Reef to the point. There is another cold spring here close to the shore.

Waiiti Stream SH 30 crosses this stream. Access to the mouth is from the eastern side of the bridge. Fishes best in windy conditions, especially a northerly. Will hold four or five rods.

The Quarry (Dump) The quarry and rubbish collection area are easily seen from SH 30 and access is simple from the road to the lake. The lake shore fishes well in a westerly all along this shoreline, from the quarry past The Transformer and The Pipe to the bluff at Hinehopu. There is good, safe wading.

The Pipe Lies at the far end of the beach past the baches at Hinehopu. Fishes best after rain, when water flows through the pipe from the swamp behind. Wading should be avoided and a slow or medium sinking line used. Cast over the drop-off and wait a while before slowly retrieving. There is also good fishing beyond the pipe to the bush-covered bluff, but wading is required to avoid snagging the bush on the back-cast. Watch for old, slippery, sunken logs along the sandy beach.

A lot of fish are caught by trolling a spinner or harling a fly from a boat. Popular areas include the northern bush-clad shore, Sulphur Bay, Pateko Island, Cherry Bay, Coles Bay and Te Arero Bay. Harling a fly over weed beds on a high density fly line is often more effective than trolling hardware. The cooler months of the year and early morning and late evening are the best times. Try Parsons' Glory, Orange and Green Rabbit, Red Setter and Green Orbit lures and Tasmanian Devil, Cobra, Billy Hill, Pearl or Toby. Black and red are popular colours.

Jigging and ledging are popular along the northern shore. Tie your boat up to an overhanging branch.

In winter, try the Rotoiti hot pools on the edge of the lake but don't forget to jump off the jetty to cool down!

Kaituna River For continuity, this river is described in the Tauranga District although the upper reaches lie in the Rotorua District. See page 100.

 *Lake Tarawera and other lakes*

Location and access Lies south-east of Rotorua. Turn right off SH 30 at Ngapuna and drive 15 km, past Lake Tikitapu and the Buried Village. The Outlet can be reached through the Tasman forestry from Kawerau (permit required from the forestry manager).
Season Te Wairoa Landing (excluding Te Wairoa Stream mouth), Rangiuru Bay between the designated landmarks at Stony Point and Kariri Point, and between the Tarawera Outlet boat ramp and the landmark at the southern end of Te Tapahoro Bay are open for fly fishing all year. Elsewhere, 1 October–30 June.
Restrictions
- Lake Tarawera Outlet is closed to fishing for 150 m downstream. Below this spawning sanctuary, fly fishing only is permitted.
- Rangiuru Bay and within 200 m of all stream mouths, fly fishing only.
- Catch and release for all male trout caught within 200 m of Te Wairoa Stream mouth.

- Catch and release for all wild rainbow trout caught over 65 cm in length.

Boat ramps are located at Te Wairoa Landing, Stony Point Reserve, Kariri Point boatsheds, Rangiuru Bay, Otumutu and Te Tapahoro.

Lake Tarawera has always seemed a dark, forbidding lake to me. It is very deep and dominated by the now dormant volcano Mt Tarawera. Bush-clad hills surround most of the shoreline and in winter Tarawera can be very cold and inhospitable. The lake can cut up rough during a strong southerly or even an easterly — boat owners be warned.

In the past, the lake has been renowned for its trophy rainbows, but now it is unusual to land one weighing over 4.5 kg. However, the measures taken by the Eastern Fish and Game Council, as outlined in the restrictions, will hopefully restore this fishery to its former glory. There is still a reasonable chance of landing a trophy from this lake.

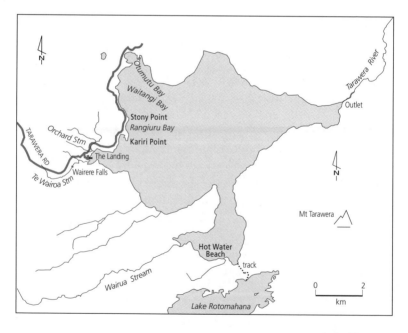

Lake Tarawera

Shoreline fly fishing Stream mouths are favoured spots during April, May and June, but angling pressure can be intense. Some fish can be taken during the day but most are caught at change of light or at night.

Favoured lures for daytime fishing include Kilwell No 1, Red Setter, Hamill's Killer, Leslie's Lure, Green Smelt and Parsons' Glory, in sizes 6 to 8. At night try Scotch Poacher, Black Marabou, Fuzzy Wuzzy, Black Prince and luminous Doll Fly.

The following are favoured spots.

Te Wairoa Stream mouth Follow the track to the right from Te Wairoa Landing for 150 m. The stream mouth holds five or six rods. Care is needed when wading as the drop-off is very deep. Stand back and fish quietly over the lip. At night use a medium-sinking line, but during the day a fast sinker or even a shooting head is best. There is a weed bank to the right and at night or early in the morning fish can be taken on a floating line over this bank. Fishes best in a westerly or south-westerly.

As outlined under Restrictions, jack fish must be released. This can be a problem for anglers fishing the 'heave and leave' method as trout swallow the egg pattern well down the gullet and are often left bleeding following hook removal.

The Landing or Main Beach Turn off the Tarawera Road onto Spencer Road. During an easterly and especially late in the season, anglers crowd this beach shoulder to shoulder as schools of fish move close in to the stirred up waves. Many of the fish caught will be foul hooked and must be released. Use a slow sinking line and a Red Setter or Killer pattern during the day and one of the usual night lures at night.

The Jetties Use a medium to fast sinking line off the jetties but a floater if fishing the tiny stream mouth to the left of the jetty. Best at night and in westerly conditions.

The Orchard Walk to the left from the car park beneath the rocky bluff to a small stream that empties into shallow water. Only holds two rods and false casting with a floating line is required so as not to frighten fish. Start well back as fish move close in during early morning and at dusk. Best in a westerly.

Rangiuru Bay Drive past Spencer Road to Rangiuru Road. This leads to a picnic area and boat ramp by the willows. Wading is necessary; the most popular spot is in the south-west corner. There is a broad sandy shelf out in front of a bush-covered promontory with acacia trees on the skyline. Wade out 40 m and fish over the lip with a medium sinking line. Fish can be taken during the day, but night fishing provides the best sport. Use the usual black night flies dressed with or without Aurora Skirt and a luminous Doll Fly. It pays to carry a landing net as it's a long walk back to shore. Fishes best in a westerly or south-westerly.

Waitangi Bay Access to this spot is from the end of Waitangi Road. Follow a path to the foreshore reserve and round into the bay. As conditions are similar to the Orchard, use a floating line with false casting.

The Waterfall Enters Te Wairoa Bay beyond the Orchard and can only be fished by casting from an anchored boat.

Twin Streams Access by boat between Te Wairoa Bay and the Wairua Arm. Cast from an anchored boat or wade the shelf and fish over the lip.

Wairua Stream mouth Access is by boat to the head of Wairua Arm. Can offer great fishing from April to June but is heavily frequented. Fishes best at night and comfortably holds three rods, although this is a rare event these days. Fish school off the mouth prior to running up the stream to spawn. Cast over the lip where the stream melts into the lake using a medium-sinking line. During the day try Orange Rabbit, Kilwell No 1, Red Setter or a small smelt pattern. At night use Black Marabou, Scotch Poacher, Black Prince, Hairy Dog, Fuzzy Wuzzy or Red Setter. A luminous Doll Fly sometimes works well.

Trolling and harling

Harling a Yellow Rabbit or Parsons' Glory along the lip or over shelves can be exciting early in the season, but when the weather warms, trout go deep and trolling with a wire or lead line is necessary. Fish can be caught anywhere although Humphries Bay is popular. Early morning and late evening are the best times. It is a matter of finding the fish and fishing at the right depth. Favoured spinners include Flatfish, Tasmanian Devil, Toby, Cobra and Zed.

Location and access Turn right off SH 30 at Ruato and travel 6 km along a scenic bush-lined road to the lake.

Season There is an open season for shoreline fishing from land-marks situated at Te Koutu Point and west of Okataina Lodge. Elsewhere, 1 October–30 June.

Restrictions Fly fishing only within 200 m of any stream mouth.

Boat ramp At Home (Tauranganui) Bay.

This beautiful, unspoiled lake is surrounded by native bush. Since the introduction of 'r' type late maturing rainbow fry, this lake, along with Lake Rotoiti, has become the trophy lake for the Rotorua district. Fish weighing over 6 kg have been caught fly casting from the shore and fishing from a boat. You will need 100 m of backing on your reel. As with Lake Rotoiti, there are few spawning streams entering the lake, so fish move into the shallows during the colder months in search of spawning beds.

When fly casting from the shore during the day use a slow or medium sinking line but at night use a floater. Some wading is required but is safe. Fish can be taken anywhere along the shore especially during April, May and June. The best times are early morning, dusk and at night. Prime spots are stream mouths, the Log Pool, Te Koutu (Maori) Point, Rocky Point, Parimata and Kaiakahi Bays. As is usual in the Rotorua lakes, fish go deep during January, February and March and shoreline fishing becomes very difficult.

If fishing from an anchored boat, use a high density or shooting head line and fish deep over weed beds. Popular lures include smelt patterns, Rabbit varieties, Green Hairy Dog, Parsons' Glory and Red Setter. At night pukeko night flies are effective along with a luminous Doll pattern. Some anglers have success ledgering a Muppet or Glow Bug.

When trolling or harling, the secret for success in this lake is to get down deep. Lead or wire lines are generally used, although early in the morning or at dusk fish can be caught harling a fly on a high density line over weed beds. Popular spinners are Toby, Flatfish, Cobra, Penny and Tasmanian Devil.

Location and access Lies between lakes Tarawera and Rerewhakaaitu west of SH 5 near Waimangu. Access is via Rotoehu Forest from Waimangu Valley Loop Road. A forestry permit is required from the Forestry Corporation Information Centre in Long Mile Drive, Rotorua.
Season This lake is open for fishing all year.
Boat launching Boats can be launched from the end of Forest Access Road.

The world-famous Pink and White Terraces were situated on the shores of this lake prior to the eruption of Mt Tarawera in 1886. There is still plenty of thermal activity in the area, with steam rising from cliffs. Rotomahana is an attractive bush-fringed lake dominated by Mt Tarawera. There is a pleasant 1–2 hour walk to the lake from Hot Water Beach on Lake Tarawera.

Most fishing is carried out from a boat, either fly casting, harling or trolling. Fishes best during the cooler months of the year. Rainbows average 2 kg, but due to their high mercury content consumption of high numbers of these fish should be avoided. Generally, trout are in excellent condition and fight vigorously when hooked.

Use lures and spinners as suggested for Lake Okataina.

Lake Okaro

Location and access From Waimangu Valley Loop Road.
Season Open all year.
Boat launching Small boats can be launched from the road.

This small lake offers shoreline and boat fishing for active rainbow trout averaging 1.5–2 kg. This underfished lake is best in the cooler months of the year when the water skiers have gone home.

Lakes Ngahewa and Ngapouri

Location and access Both lie south and west of the Rainbow

Mountain junction off SH 5 and SH 38.
Season Open all year.

Both these small lakes offer small boat or float tube fishing for rainbow trout early in the season.

Lake Rerewhakaaitu

Location and access Turn off SH 38 about 5 km from Rainbow Mountain onto the Rerewhakaaitu road. The best boat ramp is on Homestead Arm via Brett Road. The shingle beach at Awaatua Bay can be used for small craft.
Season Open all year.

This is a shallow, windy lake and the water quality is generally poor. There is plenty of scope for shoreline fishing, with Homestead Arm, Crater Bay, Ashpit Bay, Lone Pine and School Arm popular spots. There is good fishing during the summer and autumn months, with trout around the 2 kg mark not uncommon. Wading is safe. As the lake is relatively shallow, medium or slow sinking lines are used for shoreline fly fishing, casting over weed beds from a boat or harling a fly. Use the same flies and spinners as for lakes Rotorua and Rotoiti.

During summer, recreational campers, jet skis and small yachts may disturb the peace.

Lake Tikitapu (the Blue Lake)

Location and access The Tarawera Road follows the north-eastern shore.
Season Open all year.
Boat ramp Good ramp on the main beach.
Generally holds small rainbows, but the odd fish up to 2.5 kg has been caught. Harling and trolling the drop-off are popular but there is reasonable shoreline fishing at the western end of the main beach during heavy rain! A well-used walking track skirts the perimeter of the lake and the Rotorua Water Ski Club operates here. Being well sheltered and surrounded by native and exotic

forest, it is an attractive and popular picnic spot. Not a highly regarded fishery.

Lake Okareka

Location and access Branch off the Tarawera Road to the Buried Village either just before or at Lake Tikitapu (the Blue Lake).
Season Open all year.
Boat ramps Acacia Bay and the ski club.

This is a most attractive lake and a number of permanent residents commute daily from here to Rotorua. Most of the lake is surrounded by farmland, although there is an area of bush along the northern shore. Rowing and water-skiing are popular recreational pursuits.

The best time to fish this lake is during the cooler months as fish go deep during summer. There is reasonable night fly fishing from the shore at Boyes Beach, especially around the small stream mouth, and the boat ramp in Acacia Bay, where fish were presumably liberated. Wading is safe at Boyes Beach.

Most trout are caught from boats either trolling a spinner or harling a fly on a high density fly line. Popular areas are the northern shore and the eastern end of the lake during May and June. Rainbows in the 1–1.5 kg range can be expected.

Lake Rotoehu

Location and access SH 30 passes the southern shore while Pongakawa Valley Road touches part of the eastern shore.
Season Open all year.
Boat launching There are no ramps, but small boats can be launched off the beach at Te Pohue, Kennedy's and Otautu bays.

As with Lake Rerewhakaaitu, the water quality in this shallow lake suffers in mid- and late summer and weed growth can cause problems. There is some scope for the shoreline angler in October and November, when trout can be caught from the sandy beaches on smelt patterns. In the autumn, try night fishing at the small stream mouth in Te Pohue Bay with a floating line and a night lure.

Most fish are caught from boats either harling a fly over the weed beds or trolling. Rainbows average 1–1.5 kg.

Lake Rotoma

Location and access SH 30 follows the southern shoreline beyond Lake Rotoehu. Manawahe Road runs parallel to the northern shore.
Season Open all year except for the spawning areas in Manawahe Bay and between landmarks at Anaputa Point and Matahi Lagoon. The season to fish these spawning areas is 1 October–30 June.
Boat ramps At Otamatahei Bay, Whangaroa Bay and Merge Lodge.

This deep, clear lake has good water quality and is often difficult to fish for that reason. Anglers fishing from a boat should use a long trace. Except for 'tiger' fish (a sterile cross between a brook and a brown trout), all fish are rainbows and average around 2 kg. About 25 hybrids are caught each year, generally in the evening by harling a fly. Most rainbows are caught by deep trolling or harling a fly on a high density fly line.

The shoreline fly angler should try Oneroa Beach from late evening in May and June as trout gather in this area to spawn. The flies and spinners recommended for Lake Rotoiti will catch fish in Lake Rotoma.

Mangaone Stream

Location Rises from springs in the bush-clad hills east of Lake Rotoma, flows parallel to and north of SH 30 and enters the Tarawera River just south of Otakiri.
Access From SH 30 across private farmland and from Braemar Road, which crosses the lower reaches.
Season 1 October–30 June.

This small, clear stream winds across farmland and holds rainbow trout in the 0.5–1 kg range. Fish can be easily spotted and stalked as the water is clear and the stream bed is pumice and weed. There is a pleasant 3 km of fishing upstream from Braemar Road before the stream enters bush and scrub and becomes completely overgrown. In this stream a few years ago, I hooked a small rainbow which stranded itself by jumping clear of the water straight into a bush.

Ruruanga Stream

Location and access Flows off Mt Maungawhakamana, south of Lake Rotoma, then runs south of SH 30 for a short distance before turning south-east across farmland. Meets the Rotoma–Kawerau road just west of Kawerau before turning north and entering the Tarawera River.
Season 1 October–30 June.

This small stream holds small rainbows and browns and is used by junior anglers from Kawerau as a learner fishery.

Rangitaiki River system

Rangitaiki River

Access to Kaingaroa Forest As the upper Rangitaiki River, the Rangitaiki (Wheao) Canal, Flaxy Lakes, Otamatea River, Otangimoana Stream and Wheao River lie in Kaingaroa Forest, a permit is required from Fletcher Challenge Forests to fish these waters. This can be obtained from the Fletcher Challenge Forests Visitor Centre, Long Mile Road, Rotorua; phone (07) 346 2082. At times in summer, the forest can be closed because of the fire risk. It is strongly suggested that a map of the forest should be obtained as the forestry roads can be very confusing. Free basic camping is available at Te Awa provided there is no fire risk.

Rangitaiki River

Location This large river rises on Lochinvar Station then flows north beneath SH 5 (the Taupo–Napier road) just east of Rangitaiki. From SH 5 the river meanders through Kaingaroa Forest to Murupara then across the Galatea Plains to the hydro lake, Lake Aniwhenua. Further north, the river enters and leaves another hydro lake, Lake Matahina. From the Matahina Dam, the river continues its northerly course across farmland to enter the sea near Thornton. The river has been modified by four hydro-electric power stations. As the river exhibits widely differing characteristics throughout its course its description is divided into three sections: upper, middle and lower.

Upper reaches in Kaingaroa Forest

Access
- From SH 5 (the Taupo–Napier road) bridge. There is a small section of river upstream from the bridge that can be fished with a spinner but generally the banks are overgrown with scrub. Downstream access off SH 5 is via River Road to the Otamatea confluence. Below this confluence, Eastern Boundary Road follows the river to Te Awa camping ground.
- From SH 38 (the Rotorua–Murupara road), take Wairapukao Road, Low Level Road and Wainuki Road to Te Awa camping ground. Eastern Boundary Road follows upstream.

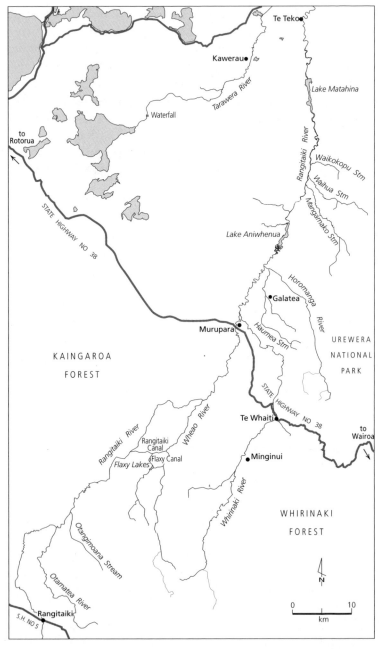

Rangitaiki River system

- From SH 38 just west of the Rangitaiki Bridge near Murupara, take Kiorenui Road to the Rangitaiki (Wheao) Canal. Bush Road leaves the southern side of the canal and gives access to Flaxy Lakes and Flaxy Canal. A branch road off Kiorenui Road, Ngahuinga Road, leads to the Wheao confluence.

Season Above the Otamatea confluence, 1 October–30 June. Below this, the Rangitaiki River is open all year.

There is 25 km of highly regarded river to fish within Kaingaroa Forest. The river is deep and slow flowing in some stretches but there are a few riffles and runs. Although the brownish water is generally clear, trout are not easy to spot, except from a high bank in bright light. With a pumice, shingle, rock and weed riverbed, wading is not too difficult and there are selected spots where the river can be crossed. Some stretches are difficult to fish as the river is overgrown by scrub, tussock and toetoe. It can be tiresome repeatedly retrieving flies from eight foot high toetoe!

Fish rise readily to hatches, even during the day, but watch the rise form as the insects may be emergers. The river holds a good stock of both browns and rainbows with drift dives revealing 98 medium-sized rainbows per kilometre of river and a smaller number of browns. There are a few fish around the 4 kg mark. November to March is the popular time to visit this river although on one occasion I had great sport as late as May, when fish were frantically feeding on a mayfly hatch. Trout can be taken on dry flies, emergers, nymphs, soft hackle wets and even lures fished deeply across and down.

Below the Wheao confluence there is good water all the way to SH 38, although much of the fishing in this section is done with a spinning rod.

Middle reaches

Access From the Murupara–Te Teko road generally across private farmland.

The river becomes very large, deep and slow-flowing in this section. Fishing can be difficult between the willows but there are some stretches that offer reasonable fly fishing and where you are unlikely to be disturbed by other anglers. There is a good rise on calm, warm summer evenings. Most of the fish are caught on spinning gear. Some anglers use a boat to access the river upstream from Lake Aniwhenua.

Lower reaches

Access Roads follow both banks from the Matahina Dam to Thornton.

Below the dam there is fast, heavy water better suited to spinning, but this section of river is not highly rated. Fish tend to be smaller in these lower reaches. Boats are often used for access.

Rangitaiki (Wheao) Canal

Access Kiorenui Road leaves SH 38 just west of the Rangitaiki Bridge near Murupara. Kiorenui Road crosses the canal and roads run on both sides.
Season Open all year.

This canal, which diverts Rangitaiki River water to the Wheao hydro-electric power scheme, is 20 m wide and 8 m deep in the middle. Fish get trapped in the canal by passing through the control gates but there is an abundance of insect life. Trout are hard to spot but there are good numbers of browns and rainbows up to 3 kg. There is a good evening rise in favourable conditions. Try mayfly and caddis imitations.

The penstocks is also a popular spot to fish although the aesthetics are hardly pristine.

Flaxy Lakes

Location and access There are two hydro lakes connected by the Flaxy Canal lying above the Flaxy power house. Bush Road from the Rangitaiki Canal provides access.
Season Open all year.

Hold mainly rainbows, with fish up to 5 kg having been caught. Fish best in the cooler months, especially near the creek mouth at the top end of the lake where trout gather prior to spawning. There is shoreline spot-fishing on bright summer's days but many anglers use a small boat or float tube. Fish can be taken on dry flies and nymphs but a sunk brown or olive Woolly Bugger or Hamill's Killer is most effective.

Lake Aniwhenua

Location Lies on the Galatea Plains north of Murupara, Galatea and the confluence of the Horomanga and Rangitaiki rivers.

Access

- At the southern end there is access from both sides of Rabbit Bridge.
- From Kopuriki Road downstream from Rabbit Bridge on the eastern side.
- From Galatea Road across private farmland.
- At the northern end from Black Road to the free camping area and dam. A track follows the eastern shoreline south from the boat ramp.

Season Open all year.

Boat launching There are two ramps: one at Rabbit Bridge, the other at the camping area off Black Road.

Formed in 1980, this hydro lake, covering 200 ha, averages only 2.5 m in depth, except for some deep holes along the old Rangitaiki riverbed. The eastern shoreline is farmland, while the western shore is scrub-covered and generally unfishable from the shore.

There are large, wild, well-conditioned rainbow and brown trout in these waters, and fish up to 6 kg can be anticipated. It is a lake for the trophy hunter. Although it is easier to fish from a boat or float tube, there is shoreline fishing at both ends of the lake and along the eastern shore. On a bright summer's day, browns especially can be spotted cruising the edges. By mid-summer, this shallow lake has warmed and fish seek the colder, deeper waters of the old riverbed.

In the cooler months, the fishing tends to improve. Fish can be taken trolling a spinner, harling a fly, spinning, fly casting from the shore or night fishing using a large black lure. Fly casting from a drifting boat at night using a sinking line is the most productive method. The top spots are the old Rangitaiki riverbed holes. During the day, nymphs account for most fish caught.

Prior to 1996, net weed was a serious problem, especially for trollers, but in February of that year it mysteriously disappeared. However, trout size and weight diminished somewhat and it became apparent that the weed had harboured thousands of worms — a high protein diet for trout. The net weed has been replaced by oxygen weed and red weed, and although trout feed on the snails living in these, worms are a more valuable food source. Although oxygen weed regresses in winter there are still wild goldfish present, which trout also eat.

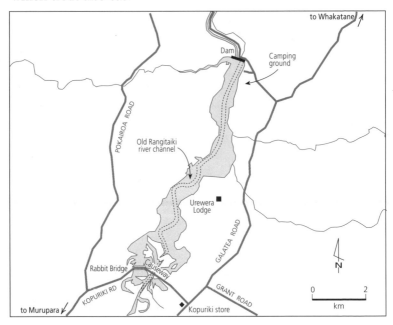

Lake Aniwhenua

Suggested flies to use on this productive lake include Hare and Copper and Dragonfly nymphs, Black and Peacock, Olive and Brown Woolly Bugger, Muddler Minnow and Hamill's Killer lures, and Cicada and Midge Pupa in summer. Dry flies are used but the main source of trout food is sub-surface. When all else fails, a San Juan Worm is worth trying. At night, a Black Marabou with or without Aurora Skirt is a good choice.

Lake Aniwhenua at Christmas.

Rangitaiki tributaries

Otamatea River

Location and access This small feeder stream joins the Rangitaiki River in the southern area of Kaingaroa Forest. Eastern Boundary Road follows upstream for some distance from its confluence about 15 km south of Te Awa camping ground.
Season 1 October–30 June.

A challenging small stream, with very clear water, overhanging vegetation and timid rainbows. The best method of approach is to drop into the river and very quietly wade upstream. Trout are easily spotted on a bright day and just as easily spooked. An accurate first cast is very important, whether with a small nymph or a dry fly. Spooked fish tend to race upstream and scare others, so a couple of fish per day from these waters is very satisfying. Above Airstrip Road the stream is virtually unfishable because of overhanging manuka but there are a few spots where the banks are clearer. Carry a landing net!

Otangimoana Stream

Location and access This small stream enters from the true right bank of the Rangitaiki River downstream from its confluence with the Otamatea. Dry Fly Road from Eastern Boundary Road offers access. The lower stretches can be reached after wading across the Rangitaiki River.
Season 1 October–30 June.

This small, crystal-clear spring creek is also very difficult to fish owing to overhanging scrub, swampy banks and watercress. It is worth a look early in the season.

Wheao River

Access
- To the penstocks from Kiorenui Road and the eastern end of the Rangitaiki Canal.
- To the Rangitaiki–Wheao confluence from Kiorenui and Ngahuinga roads.
Season Open all year.

Once world-renowned as a fly stream, the Wheao has been ruined by a hydro-electric power scheme. Medium-sized rainbows can still be caught below the penstocks at the power house, usually on spinning gear, and there are good stocks of fish just upstream from the Wheao's confluence with the Rangitaiki River. Elsewhere, the river is swift and overgrown and not worth the struggle.

Location and access Rises in the hills of the Whirinaki Forest, flows north by Minginui and Te Whaiti, and eventually joins the Rangitaiki River north of Murupara.

Access *Upper reaches*

- Across the river from Minginui settlement, River Road follows up the true left bank. There is good access from this road. The Whirinaki Track leads further upstream from River Road to the headwaters.
- From SH 38, Minginui Road follows upstream on the true right bank to Minginui. Mangamate camping ground lies off this road 1 km north of Minginui.
- Te Whaiti camping ground lies off SH 38 just north of Te Whaiti.

Middle reaches

- Okui Road (an old logging road) follows north down the true left bank from SH 38, 2.5 km north of Te Whaiti.
- Whirinaki Road runs off SH 38 east of Murupara and crosses the river. There is plenty of wilderness fishing upstream from the Whirinaki Bridge if one is prepared to walk.

Lower reaches

- From Ngatimanawa Road opposite the oxidation ponds in Murupara. A track runs along the river bank.

Season 1 October–30 June.

This is an excellent, clear-water, rock and stone river with a large section of wilderness fishing available. Upstream from Minginui, the shingle riverbed is somewhat unstable and fish stocks are not great in this bush-lined section. There is more stable water upstream from SH 38 although, as one might expect, the best section is the wilderness stretch between the Whirinaki Bridge and Okui Road. It is suggested that anglers make use of one of the many camping spots so they have time to explore this popular river. Trout can be spotted on bright days and good stocks of both rainbow and brown trout averaging a little under 2 kg can be expected.

The lower section is willow-lined in parts and good willow grub fishing is available in summer.

Location Rises in the heavily bush-clad hills of the Urewera National Park, flows in a north-westerly direction and joins the Rangitaiki River just above Lake Aniwhenua.
Access *Lower reaches* Galatea Road crosses the river.
Middle reaches From the Troutbeck Road bridge.
Upper reaches A gravel road runs upstream on the true left bank from the south side of the Troutbeck Road bridge. A track continues upstream from the end of the gravel road. There are two DoC huts further upstream in the headwaters if an overnight stay is planned.
Season 1 October–30 June.
Restrictions Fly fishing only in this river and its tributaries. The bag limit is two trout only although, in my opinion, the upper section should be catch and release.

This relatively small river holds a few good-sized resident fish in some deep pools in the upper reaches and headwaters. However, the main attraction is the spawning run of large fish that enters the river from Lake Aniwhenua during April, May and June. Late spawners are still present in the river when the season opens on 1 October.

The lower reaches, holding small, resident rainbows, cross pastoral land and are shingly and relatively unstable. There are more stable, deeper pools in the middle and upper reaches, where trout can be spotted and stalked. A few patches of scrub along the banks add to the excitement of casting but access to these stretches is generally good. The headwaters are lined by native bush.

Most fish are caught on small, weighted nymphs such as Hare and Copper, Hare's Ear, Pheasant Tail and Half Back. Some anglers use egg patterns like Glow Bug and Muppet. Although the bag limit is two fish, I believe trout landed in this stream should be released so the gene pool for Lake Aniwhenua is maintained. Even a trophy fish can be photographed, measured and weighed before being released relatively unharmed. Some large fish have been landed from this stream in past seasons.

Haumea Stream

Location and access This small tributary of the Horomanga River joins just upstream from the Rangitaiki confluence. Galatea and Haumea roads cross the lower reaches.
Season 1 October–30 June.

Holds a few spawning fish that enter from Lake Aniwhenua late in the season.

Mangamako, Waihua and Waikokopu streams

Location and access These small, clear-water streams drain the Ikawhenua Range, flow north-west and empty into the Rangitaiki River between lakes Aniwhenua and Matahina. All are crossed by Galatea Road in the vicinity of Waiohau School.
Season 1 October–30 June.

All are fun to fish, especially late in the season, when fish numbers swell with spawners entering from the Rangitaiki River. They also hold resident rainbows, and these can be sight fished in the slower-flowing stretches. There is a spawning run of brown trout late in the season. The middle and lower reaches cross pastoral land, where gorse and scrub can be a problem, while the upper reaches are bush-lined. They are boots and shorts rivers where fish fight with amazing energy. Don't neglect to fish the faster runs blind as fish often hold in this type of water during summer.

Lake Matahina

Location and access Lies just south of Te Teko on Galatea Road. Shoreline access is limited but there is an opportunity round the eastern side of the lake near the dam.
Season Open all year.
Boat launching There is a boat ramp at the dam.

Most trout are taken on deeply trolled spinners. The lake is surrounded by exotic forest and sheer, rocky bluffs. Some shoreline fly and spin fishing is also possible from Rototaha Road and at Clear Creek at the western end of Waiohau Bridge, but this lake is not highly recommended for the shoreline angler.

Tarawera River

Location Drains Lake Tarawera, emerges from Tarawera Forest at Kawerau, then flows north to the Bay of Plenty west of Thornton.
Access *Upper reaches* The Outlet is closed to fishing for 150 m downstream from the lake. Below this protected spawning stretch there is very little fishing before Tarawera Falls. This part of the river can be reached by walking downstream from the Outlet. The Outlet is reached by boat or by a forestry road from Kawerau.
Middle reaches Good forestry roads from Kawerau provide access to the river below the falls. Fentons Mill Road parallels the true left bank. A permit to enter the forest must be obtained from the forestry officer at Tasman Pulp and Paper Mill, Kawerau.
Lower reaches Waters below Kawerau have been polluted by the pulp and paper mill and are not worth fishing.
Season Open all year below the falls. Above the falls, 1 October–30 June.

Although this river is not part of the Rangitaiki River system, it is convenient to describe the stretch below the falls in this section. It is medium-sized and fast flowing, and generally best fished with spinning gear. There are some stretches within the forest that invite upstream nymph fishing or even a large deer-hair dry fly in summer. Rainbows averaging 1.2 kg give a good fight in these boisterous waters. The river slows somewhat at Kawerau, where there are some deep holes. Spinning is the favourite method of fishing.

Urewera National Park

Urewera is the largest national park in the North Island, covering 200,000 ha, 90% of which is forest. There are blocks of privately owned land within the park boundaries and permission must be sought from the owners before entering these areas.

The park has two main valleys, the Whakatane and the Waimana, both running from south to north, and two beautiful lakes, Waikaremoana and Waikareiti. Altitude ranges from 150 m to 1300 m and the rainfall exceeds 2540 mm. Snow can fall in winter. There are well-cut tracks around both lakes and into some of the valleys, but anglers visiting the park for the first time are strongly advised to visit the park headquarters at Aniwaniwa, where maps and specific information can be obtained. In general, the park is heavily bush-clad and rugged; it is easy to get lost off the beaten track.

Headwater stream in the Urewera National Park.

Lake Waikaremoana

Location and access Lies in the south-eastern sector of the Urewera National Park. Access from SH 38 from Rotorua and Murupara to Wairoa. This windy, narrow, gravel road skirts the northern and eastern shores.

Season The lake is open all year. Tributaries draining into the lake are open from 1 December to 30 June.

Restrictions Metal cored and wire lines are illegal. Daily bag limit

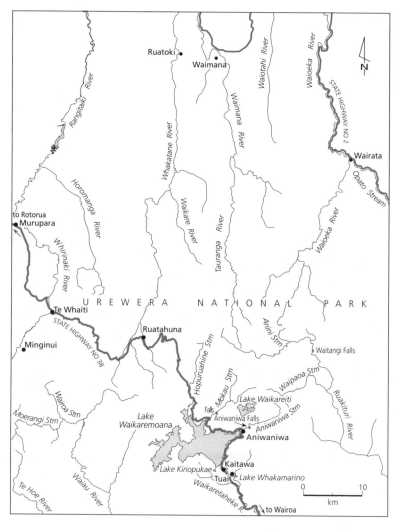

Urewera National Park.

is eight trout with no more than two brown trout. Fly fishing only in the tributary streams upstream from designated marker poles.

Boat launching There are boat ramps at Mokau Landing, Opourau (Home) Bay, Rosie Bay and Onepoto. Dinghies can be launched at the Hopuruahine Stream mouth.

This bush-lined lake, created by a giant landslide 2000 years ago, was harnessed for hydro-electricity generation in 1947. Fortunately the lake's pristine features have been preserved. The lake lies at an altitude of 580 m and is 220 m deep in its deepest part. Although subject to changeable weather conditions, there are numerous arms where boats can shelter in adverse conditions. A well-cut track follows the perimeter of the lake and Park Board huts in many of the arms provide overnight accommodation for trampers. It is necessary to carry cooking equipment and fuel. There is a motor camp at Opourau Bay and camping is also permitted at Mokau Landing and Hopuruahine.

The lake contains mainly wild fish, first liberated in 1896, as well as tagged hatchery fish. Rainbow and brown trout are both present, with an average weight of around 2 kg. The liberation of smelt into the lake in 1948 markedly improved the fishery, and trout up to 4 kg are occasionally landed.

Stalking cruising brown trout during the summer months is very popular. During the day these wary fish prefer small nymphs and bully imitations, but cast well ahead of a cruising fish. Use Polaroid glasses and clothing that blends well with the background. In the evening, they may rise to a Black Gnat or Coch-y-bondhu dry fly.

Most rainbows are taken by trolling a spinner or harling a fly on a high density fly line. Try spinners such as Toby (especially red or black), Cobra or Flatfish, and lures such as Red Rabbit, Green Orbit, Woolly Bugger and Hamill's Killer. Favourite trolling areas include beneath Panekiri Bluff, Te Puna Bay, Waipaoa Bay and Opourau Bay.

In April, May and June, a strong spawning run enters the Hopuruahine River and Mokau Inlet. There is shoreline and boat fishing available at Mokau, with upstream nymph or downstream lure fishing in the Hopuruahine River. Stream mouths are also profitable spots to fish at this time of year. Take neoprene waders as the weather can be very cold, with early snow a real possibility.

Lake Waikareiti

Location and access The lake is reached by walking uphill for an hour on an excellent scenic bush track that begins 200 m from the park headquarters at Aniwaniwa. A track roughly follows the shore to Sandy Bay at the top end of the lake, where there is a Park Board hut.

Season Open all year.

Dinghy hire Dinghies can be hired from park headquarters at Aniwaniwa and are available at the lake.

The lake is not easy to fish as the shoreline is surrounded by heavy overhanging bush and the drop-off is close inshore. White Bull Bay and Sandy Bay offer limited shoreline fishing. The lake holds mainly rainbows averaging 1.5 kg and these wild fish are generally in excellent condition with very pink flesh. Trolling, harling and fly fishing from a dinghy account for most fish caught. Try the same flies and lures as listed for Lake Waikaremoana, with the addition of Red Setter and Parsons' Glory. Few fish are caught on dry flies although a Coch-y-bondhu cast under the beech canopy can be effective in December and January.

The next three small lakes lie outside the park boundary but are best described in this section.

Lake Kaitawa

Location and access Lies south-east of Lake Waikaremoana. Branch off SH 38 to Kaitawa. There is road access to the lake past the power station although there is only foot access to the opposite side. There are no boat ramps but a dinghy can easily be launched.

Season 1 October–30 June.

Restrictions Fly fishing only. Motorised craft are not permitted.

There is limited shoreline fishing on this small, shallow hydro lake. Most trout are taken by fly casting from a dinghy. The lake is regularly stocked and often yields trout of trophy proportions. Holds both browns and rainbows. These respond best at dusk to a Woolly Bugger, Mrs Simpson, Red Setter or Hamill's Killer fished on a sinking line.

Lake Whakamarino

Location and access Branch off SH 38 to Tuai. The lake is past the hydro village. There is a boat ramp next to the flood gate past Tuai School.
Season 1 October–30 June.
Restrictions Fly fishing only. Motorised craft are not permitted.

This is a larger and deeper lake than Lake Kaitawa and offers better prospects for shoreline fishing. Holds both browns and rainbows averaging 2.3 kg but trophy fish up to 12 kg have been taken. As with Kaitawa, blind lure fishing at dusk, night and early morning is the most successful method. Use the same lures as listed for Lake Kaitawa.

Lake Kiriopukae

Location and access Lies near Onepoto. There is a 20-minute walk on a marked track from the Onepoto Bay car park.
Season 1 October–30 June.

This small lake is seldom fished but provided it hasn't dried during a hot summer, brown trout can be caught by spinning or fly casting.

Waiau River and tributaries (headwaters and upper reaches)

Note: the middle and lower reaches are described in the Wairoa section.

Location Drains the rugged bush-clad ranges west and south of Lake Waikaremoana. Flows south-east through the Urewera National Park and eventually joins the Wairoa River at Frasertown.
Access There are a number of routes to the headwaters and upper reaches, all of which require considerable tramping experience and good maps.
• From Okahu Stream at Ngaputahi on SH 38: a two-hour tramp

to Skip's (Whangatawhia) Hut; and a further two hours to Roger's (Te Wairoa) Hut.

- From Mimiha Stream and White's Clearing 8 km west of Ruatahuna, also off SH 38: a five-hour tramp to Parahaki Hut, at the junction of the Wairoa and Parahaki streams; then downstream to Central Waiau (1^1/$_2$ hours) and Te Waiotukapiti Hut (four hours). Te Waiotukapiti is difficult to reach if the river is high.
- From Maranui Arm on Lake Waikaremoana: a difficult ninehour tramp over the Pukekohu Range to Te Waiotukapiti.
- By helicopter!

Season 1 October–30 June.

This long, unspoilt, picturesque river holds a large population of rainbow trout. Fish of 4–5 kg are not uncommon, especially near Te Waiotukapiti. The Waiau feeder streams including the Whangatawhia Stream at Skip's, the Moerangi and Mangakahika streams at Roger's and the Wairoa Stream at Parahaki all offer excellent small-stream wilderness water. The streams are all bushlined and clear and trout can be sight fished in well-defined runs and pools. These waters seldom discolour unless the rainfall has been very heavy and prolonged.

At Te Waiotukapiti, the river becomes moderate in size and crossings should be chosen with care. The water quality is still excellent, however, and trout can be readily spotted. This large river and its many feeder streams would take a month to fish and the upper reaches are highly regarded as a wilderness trout fishery.

Whakatane River

Location This large river rises near Ruatahuna, flows north through the Urewera National Park and Bay of Plenty farmland and reaches the sea at Whakatane.

Access *Upper reaches* From Matatua Road just east of Ruatahuna off SH 38. There is a 40-minute tramp on the well-marked, steep, Whakatane River track from the road end to the river.

Middle reaches From the Whakatane River track, either from the Ruatahuna end as described or from Ruatoki Valley Road off Reid

Road at Taneatua in the Bay of Plenty.
Lower reaches From Whakatane, Taneatua or Ruatoki.
Season Above the Owaka Stream confluence, 1 October–30 June.
Below this point the river is open for fishing all year round.

For the angler intent on stalking trout, the upper and middle reaches well upstream from Ruatoki offer the best fishing. Although fish stocks are only moderate, the bush-lined river has stable pools and runs and is interesting to fish. Both brown and rainbow trout are present and average around 1–2 kg. Above the Waikare confluence, the river is medium-sized and can be crossed quite easily at selected fords. During the summer months, trout respond equally well to weighted nymphs and dry flies fished delicately on a long trace.

Below the Ohora Stream confluence, the river becomes quite large with long, unstable, shingly runs and glides, but still holds moderate numbers of fish.

The lower reaches are very large, deep and slower flowing and more suited to downstream lure and spinning. Try a smelt fly for sea-runners in October and November.

For the adventurous angler, and providing the Whakatane River can be forded, the Konihi tributary entering from the true left bank near the Ohora Hut is worth a visit.

Some years ago, while I was tramping the Whakatane River Valley with family and friends, my quiet evening's fly fishing efforts were rudely interrupted by a genial local threadlining off the back of his horse. He splashed from pool to pool and when a fish was hooked he quickly wound it in and stuffed it into a saddle-bag without even bothering to dismount.

Waikare River

Location and access This moderate-sized tributary of the Whakatane River rises near Maungapohatu and joins the main river at Waikare Junction Hut. Access is difficult and permission must be obtained from Maungapohatu land owners to fish the upper reaches. The lower reaches can be fished from the Waikare Junction Hut by walking upstream.

Although this small, wilderness-type river runs through heavily bush-clad country, it is well worth a look for tramper/anglers. There is very pleasant sight fishing.

Waimana River

Location Drains the Kairaka and Kahikatea ranges of the Urewera National Park, flows north through hill country to Waimana, parallel to and east of the Whakatane River, and then joins this river at Taneatua.

Access *Upper reaches and headwaters* A tramping track follows upstream beyond the Lions' Club Hut.

Middle reaches Turn off SH 2 onto Bell Road, then take Matahi Valley Road.

Lower reaches From SH 2.

Season Open all year below Reid Road bridge. Above this point, 1 October–30 June.

Although this medium-sized river has stable headwaters and well-developed pools and runs, fishing can be patchy. If fishing is poor in one section, try elsewhere as fish seem to move about the river. Holds medium-sized rainbows and browns in moderate numbers.

Fish can be spotted in the bush-clad upper reaches and headwaters but plenty of walking is often required. There is good water in the vicinity of the Lions' Club Hut, below Ogilvie's Bridge and just upstream from Waimana township. In the lower reaches, some holes are 6 m deep and, being close to SH 2, swimming is popular in summer.

In the upper reaches, weighted nymphs take most fish. Near Waimana in the willow-lined sections, willow grub and lace moth imitations are good deceivers in summer. The lower reaches are best suited to spinning and downstream lure fishing, especially when whitebait are running.

A small feeder stream, the Raroa, offers limited fly fishing at Waimana township.

Location and access Flows parallel to, but east of, the Waimana River. The lower reaches are crossed by SH 2 while the middle section can be accessed from Waiotahi Valley Road.

Season 1 October–30 June.

The upper reaches emerge from native bush onto cleared farmland and exotic forest. The most productive stretch to fish is upstream from SH 2 as the upper reaches are thin and barren. Fish stocks are not high but a few of the locals enjoy this stream.

 Waioeka River and tributaries

Waioeka River

Location Drains the Huiarau and Kahikatea ranges in the Urewera National Park, flows generally north to join the Opato Stream at

Headwater tributary of the Waioeka River

Wairata in the Waioeka Gorge next to SH 2, then follows SH 2 to the sea at Opotiki.

Access *Headwaters and upper reaches* Tramping through the bush is required to reach these waters but the effort is well worthwhile.

- Access can be obtained from the end of Wairata Station Road at Wairata but permission should be obtained from Redpath's Farm. Nikau Flat Hut is a day's fishing upstream.
- The Forks Hut at the confluence of the Kahunui Stream and Koranga River can be accessed from the end of Moanui Valley Road. This leaves SH 2 at the foot of Trafford's Hill. From the road end, DoC sign and car park, a well-marked track follows downstream on the true right bank to the Forks Hut.

Middle reaches There are a number of access points from SH 2.

- Aro Aro Bridge: a track to the river lies on the Gisborne side of the car park.
- Mangapumarumaru Stream: there is car parking.
- Girl Guides' Hut: there is a house close to the road.
- Tauranga Track at Tauranga Bridge: there is a ten-minute walk to the river.
- Fisherman's Bend: near the Oponae Stream confluence.
- Wairata Station Road: with permission from Redpath's Farm.

Season Open all year below Cruen Creek confluence (Aro Aro Bridge). Above this confluence, 1 October–30 June.

Restrictions Fly fishing only above the Opato Stream confluence.

Although the Waioeka is a large river in its lower reaches, there is a different style of water in each section. The upper reaches and headwaters offer superb wilderness fishing in native bush surroundings. The water is clear, trout can be sight fished, and these headwater streams are easily crossed at selected fords. Fishing is best combined with tramping unless a day trip by helicopter is planned. There are good-sized rainbows present and a few browns. The Koranga River, and the Kahunui, Makakoere and Tataweka streams, are all well worth exploring. Remember, this is wilderness country and heavy rain and flash floods are not uncommon.

In the middle reaches, the river becomes quite large, with some very deep holes and long shingle beaches and glides easily seen from SH 2. Few fish are visible from the main highway but do not

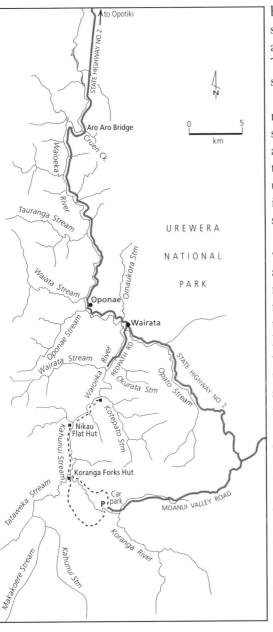

Waioeka River and tributaries

be disappointed as stocks are reasonable away from the road. The water quality is still good.

Below Cruen Creek, most fish are taken on spinning gear and the average size is smaller than in the middle and upper reaches. Fly fishing is restricted by the size of the river.

Fish respond to a wide variety of flies and lures but in summer, green beetle, lace moth and cicada imitations are suggested. Most weighted nymphs will take fish provided they are well presented and fished at the correct depth.

There are a number of small feeder streams in the middle reaches that are worth exploring early in the season. These include the Waiata, Oponae, Omaukora, Okurata, Wairata and Te Pato streams. Fish tend to drop back into the main river during the hot summer months.

Location and access Joins the Waioeka River at Wairata. As this stream follows the road it is accessed from SH 2, although a scramble down a scrub-covered bank may be necessary. There is a picnic area about 1 km from Wairata.
Season 1 October–30 June.
Restrictions Fly fishing only.

This small, boisterous and rocky clear-water stream holds a few good rainbows in the better-developed pools. There is only 2 km of river to fish below a waterfall. Use a well-weighted nymph with an indicator in the more stable water. Because of the turbulence, it is unusual to spot trout so the river should be fished blind.

The Otara River at Opotiki holds a few small rainbow and brown trout, especially in the middle and lower reaches, but is subject to flooding and has an unstable shingle bed. Tends to warm in summer.

The Ruakituri River is described in the East Coast, Gisborne, and Wairoa section, and the Horomanga River is dealt with in the Rangitaiki River system.

East Coast, Gisborne and Wairoa

These three districts lie in the Eastern Fish and Game Council's region. There are three main river systems supporting a significant trout population: the Motu, the Waiapu and the Wairoa river systems. Many East Coast rivers were turned over by colossal floods in 1981, 1985 and 1988. Because of land forms, soil types and clear-felling of native bush, the country is very unstable and prone to erosion after heavy rain in the high country. The tail end of some tropical cyclones often seriously affects these regions and rivers rapidly become silt laden and take time to recover. In the pastoral sections, farm run-off and warm water during the hot summer months adversely affects the trout population. The only rivers offering consistently good fishing have stable headwaters draining native bush-covered hills. These include the inaccessible Motu and tributaries, the Ruakituri and tributaries, and the Hangaroa and Waiau rivers.

The upper Waiau River is described in the Urewera National Park section, so only the lower reaches are considered in this section.

East Coast, Gisborne and Wairoa

The three main tributaries of this large river system, the Ruakituri, Waiau (middle and lower reaches) and Hangaroa rivers, all offer exciting fishing.

Wairoa River

Location Formed by the confluence of the Hangaroa and Ruakituri rivers at Te Reinga Falls, this extensive waterway empties into the sea at Wairoa township.
Access From Frasertown on SH 36, the back road to Gisborne via Tiniroto.
Season Open all year below Te Reinga Falls.

The Wairoa River is large, rather slow flowing and sluggish, often silt laden and best suited to spin fishing. Contains both brown and rainbow trout with the latter predominating.

Waiau River (middle and lower reaches)

Note: the upper reaches are described in the Urewera National Park section.

Location Emerges from the heavily bush-clad ranges of the Urewera National Park to flow in a south-easterly direction across cleared pastoral land. Joins the Waikaretaheke River near Patunamu Forest and empties into the Wairoa River at Frasertown.
Access *Middle reaches* Turn inland near Raupunga on SH 2 and follow on Putere Road.
Lower reaches Accessed from SH 38.
Season Above the Waikaretaheke confluence, 1 October–30 June. Below this confluence the river is open all year.

This medium to large river supports good stocks of both brown and rainbow trout which can be stalked along the water's edge on bright sunny days. The fishing is best upstream from Otoi, with well-developed pools and runs and patches of native bush to enhance the

146

scenery. In summer it is well worth fishing the broken water blind with a well-hackled dry fly or a weighted nymph. Although trout average around 1 kg, fish up to 3 kg are not uncommon.

Spinning is the best method of fishing the lower reaches, where the river becomes larger and slower flowing.

Ruakituri River and tributaries

Location Drains the rugged, bush-clad hills north of Lake Waikaremoana, flows south-east and joins the Hangaroa River at the spectacular Te Reinga Falls.

Access *Headwaters*

- From Waimaha Station at the end of Taumata Road west of Rere, via a farm track and a three-hour bush tramp on Rua's Track to the Anini Stream.
- From Papuni Station. This lies at the end of Ruakituri Valley Road and Papuni Road. Ruakituri Valley Road leaves SH 36 at Te Reinga. After obtaining permission, take the farm track (paper road) to the road end at Lockwoods and the car park. It is a four-hour tramp to Waitangi Falls.
- Access to the Waipaoa tributary is gained by fording the main river below Papuni Gorge and tramping upstream on the true right bank from Ruakituri Reserve. Papuni Station claims riparian rights so the true left bank of the Ruakituri River is closed to fishing upstream from Makokomuka Ford as far as the Urewera National Park boundary at Flanagan's Creek.

Middle and lower reaches Ruakituri Valley Road follows upstream at first on the true left and later on the true right bank to Erepeti Bridge. Above this bridge, Papuni Road continues on the true left as far as Papuni Station. There are numerous access points from this road but please ask permission to cross private farmland unless access is easy and obvious. There are a few camp sites in the valley with no facilities and some local farmers rent out their shearers' quarters to anglers.

Note: Do not attempt to fish through the Erepeti Gorge immediately above the Erepeti Bridge unless the river is low.

Season 1 October–30 June.

Restrictions Fly fishing only. The bag limit above Waitangi Falls is

Ruakituri River

two fish and only fish between 30 and 60 cm can be taken. Below the falls, eight fish can be taken provided these are longer than 30 cm. There is no maximum length restriction below the falls. Choppers are not permitted to land anglers within the park boundary.

This relatively inaccessible medium-sized river offers superb fly fishing for over 30 km. There is another 20 km of water in the headwaters and tributaries for active anglers proficient in bush-craft and prepared to tramp.

Above Waitangi Falls, there are trophy rainbows up to 5 kg but anglers need to be fit, able to scramble round rocky bluffs and confident in fording rivers. Trout can be spotted but some of the pools are overgrown, deep and difficult to fish. Anglers intent on fishing above Waitangi Falls will need to camp. If the Anini tributary is reached from Rua's Track, the best fishing lies downstream from where the track crosses the river.

The Waipaoa tributary upstream from Papuni Station is a delight to fish and again holds mainly rainbows, averaging 1.8 kg. This clear-water stream, flowing through partially cleared native bush and pastoral land, has well-developed pools and runs upstream for 10 km from its confluence with the Ruakituri. As with a venture above Waitangi Falls, anglers should strongly consider tramping and camping to enjoy the best of this stream. The Papuni Gorge holds fish, as does the slow-flowing stretch of river above Papuni Station, but anglers must respect the riparian rights of the station.

For anglers keen on nymphing, the stretch of river between the Erepeti Bridge and the Makokomuka Stream is hard to beat. Trout stocks are very high and fish average around 2 kg. Browns and rainbows are present in equal numbers. They are not easy to spot, however, unless the river is low or fish are feeding on the edges of runs. The water often has a hint of colour, and as this is rather unstable papa country any rain usually results in a silt-laden river, which may take three days to clear. The riverbed is papa, boulders, stones and silt, and wading anglers should be wary of the slippery beds of papa and deep slots in the rock. There are well-defined pools but many fish hold behind rocks in the fast runs. There are seldom any casting obstructions. The river can be crossed at the tail of most pools but a wading stick is helpful.

Below Erepeti Bridge, there is again excellent water all the way downstream to below Ruakituri School. The river is willow-lined in this section and trout are very difficult to spot. It is worth fishing all the likely looking water with an attractor pattern dry fly or well-weighted nymph.

Most trout are caught in the Ruakituri on well-weighted caddis and mayfly nymphs. The deeper runs should be fished with two nymphs and an indicator. On summer evenings there is often an active splashy caddis rise on some of the more quietly flowing pools. Try an Elk Hair or a Goddard Caddis in these conditions.

Trout fight hard in this river and rainbows will often test a 4 kg tippet. As the fish often have a muddy flavour, catch and release is no hardship.

Hangaroa River

Location Rises north of Rua's Track in the eastern part of the Urewera National Park, and emerges from the native bush to follow the western boundary of Marewa, Tahora and Waimiha stations. Generally flows south-east from Waimiha to Hangaroa, then to Te Reinga, where it joins the Ruakituri River above Te Reinga Falls.

Access Taumata Road from Rere leads to Tahunga and Waimiha Station. Most good water can be reached from this road across private farmland or from the Waimiha Station farm track.
Season 1 October–30 June.
Restrictions Fly fishing only from the base of Te Reinga Falls.

The best water lies upstream from Tahunga, where trout can be spotted and stalked. Below Tahunga, the water quality deteriorates. During hot summers, the lower reaches become warm and fish tend to move upstream to seek the shade of the bush. The stretch of water on Waimiha and Marewa stations should be visited in these conditions.

There are long, slow-flowing reaches on this river and fish may cruise so look for trout facing downstream. Rainbows averaging 1.8 kg predominate, with browns more common in the lower river. Generally, fish are not fussy and will take small nymphs and dries carefully presented on fine tippets.

Within limits, spotting a fish, getting into position without being seen and making an accurate cast are more important than the artificial presented.

Waikaretaheke River

Location Drains lakes Waikaremoana, Kaitawa and Whakamarino (Tuai). Has been severely modified for power generation. Joins the Waiau near Patunamu Forest.
Access SH 38 from Waikaremoana to Frasertown follows the river downstream.
Season Above the Piripaua power house, 1 October–30 June. Below the power house, the river is open all year.

A fast-flowing, overgrown river not easy to fish except with a spinning rod. Holds an average stock of rainbows.

Mangapoike River

Location Flows in a south-westerly direction to join the Wairoa River at Opoiti north of Frasertown.

Access From Mangapoike Valley Road, which leaves SH 38 just south of Frasertown.
Season 1 October–30 June.

This small stream supports a small population of rainbows but in recent years the water quality in summer has been marginal for trout.

Putere Lakes

Location and access Turn inland from SH 2 at Raupunga south of Wairoa. Waireka Road leads to the lakes near Otoi.
Season Open all year. Bag limit is eight fish.

These three small lakes — Rotonuiaha, Rotoroa and Rotongaio — are surrounded by farmland. All hold trout, with late maturing hatchery 'r' type rainbows liberated. Because of water warming in summer and farm run-off, however, eutrophication has impaired the trout habitat. Most fish are taken on spinning gear.

Tiniroto Lakes

There are a number of small lakes at Tiniroto that hold small rainbows. The largest, Rotokaha, is easily seen from SH 36 just south of Tiniroto. These are best fished from a boat or float tube as the shoreline is swampy and rush infested. Eutrophication is a problem in summer and over recent years the water quality has been poor. Open all year but not recommended.

Nuhaka River

Location and access Flows in a southerly direction, parallel to and west of the Kopuawhara River, to enter Hawke's Bay at Nuhaka near the Mahia Peninsula. Turn off SH 2 onto Nuhaka River Road 5 km north of Nuhaka.
Season 1 October–30 June.

Supports a small stock of rainbows but poor water quality over recent years has not helped this fishery.

Kopuawhara River

Location and access Rises in Wharerata Forest north of the Mahia Peninsula and flows south to enter the sea at Oraka Beach. Travel east from Nuhaka to Opoutama, then north on Mahanga and Kopuawhara roads. A permit should be obtained from the Forestry Corporation before entering the forest.
Season 1 October–30 June.

Because the water quality has been good in this stream trout have been stocked in the past. It is doubtful whether it is self-sustaining, however, but there are small rainbows present.

Wharekopae River

Location and access Rises from the eastern slopes of the Huiarau Range, flows east to Rere and then north-east to join the Waipaoa River near Te Karaka. Access from Rere, west of Gisborne.
Season 1 October–30 June.
Restrictions Fly fishing only.

This small stream traverses isolated, hilly sheep country. The roads are windy and narrow. The river silts easily and the water quality in summer is marginal for trout. It does hold a few browns but these are very difficult to spot. Rere Falls is a good picnic spot.

Motu River and tributaries

This large river system drains some of the most inaccessible country in New Zealand. The river is protected by a National Water Conservation Order and is popular for rafting, the most suitable method of transport along some sections. The Motu is unusual in that the upper reaches are accessible for trout fishing whereas the middle reaches below the Motu Falls are very difficult to reach. It is an excellent self-sustaining fishery, despite its large eel population.

Only two of the tributaries are worth describing, but other inaccessible side streams do contain trout, the Mangatutara being one.

Location Drains the northern Huiarau Range and the rugged Raukumara Range between Gisborne and Opotiki. After meandering across cleared farmland near Matawai the river descends the spectacular Motu Falls. It then follows a northerly course through inaccessible, bush-clad, gorgy terrain to enter the sea southwest of Te Kaha.

Access *Upper reaches* From Matawai on SH 2, take the road north to the settlement of Motu. There is access to the river from this road across private farmland. The Motu Falls Road is washed out beyond Waitangiruru Station.

Middle reaches By rafting or tramping through 'tiger' country or from SH 35 10 km south of Omaio and then upstream by jet-boat.

Season 1 October–30 June.

Only the upper farmland section between Matawai and Motu can be recommended as a fishery. The river is flood-prone and may remain discoloured for three or four days at a time owing to the muddy banks and the riverbed silt.

In bright, clear conditions, brown trout averaging 1–2 kg can be spotted and tempted with dry flies and nymphs. However, as the

Headwater stream of the Motu River

153

clear grassy banks are often elevated, it can be difficult to approach fish without spooking them. The river is medium-sized here and selected crossings can be accomplished. Because of the relative lack of bank vegetation, glare on the water can be considerable, but this can be overcome by one angler spotting for another.

The rough, gorgy water below the Motu Falls is best fished by active anglers using spinning gear. When rafting this river, it is worth taking a trout rod and an eel line. Only experienced rafters should tackle this trip as one section is grade 5.

Further downstream below the confluence with the heavily silt-laden Mangatane River, the water deteriorates to such an extent that fishing is hardly worthwhile.

Of the Motu tributaries, only the Waitangirua and Takaputahi are described.

Waitangirua Stream

Location and access Permission and directions must first be obtained from Waitangirua Station on the Motu Falls Road. One should only attempt this steep, papa clay farm track over the hills with a 4WD and chains. After rain, the track becomes impassable and very dangerous. It is 8 km to the stream but the views are spectacular. It is best to take overnight camping equipment. Private access can also be obtained via Whatatutu and Okaihau by following down Jackson Stream.
Season 1 October–30 June.

This small stream is not for the faint hearted. Upstream from the back whare, it is a rugged boots and shorts wilderness-type fishery. Holds a good population of brown trout averaging 2 kg, with an occasional fish up to 3.5 kg. Fish are easy to spot, especially in the upper reaches, as the dense bush eliminates glare. However, the stream was ravaged by a flood in 1996, causing landslides and trees to fall into it. There is a full day's fishing upstream from the back whare provided you don't mind climbing over a 100 m bluff.

Downstream, where the land has been cleared, the fish population is smaller but there are still a few good trout to sight fish. There is a full day's fishing down to the Motu junction. The stream is well replenished from the Motu but heavily poached in the lower farmland section.

Takaputahi River

Location and access Flows in an easterly direction to enter the Motu north-east of Toatoa. Turn off SH 35 about 10 km east of Opotiki on the road signposted Waiaua and Toatoa. From Toatoa, the Takaputahi Road leads to the river, where basic camping is available at the Whitikau camp site. Toatoa can also be reached from Matawai on a long, tortuous one-way metal road which has been used in the past for car rallying.
Season 1 October–30 June.

This medium-sized river flows at first through partially cleared pastoral land and then enters heavy bush further downstream before joining the Motu. There are some very deep, stable holes but the trout population tends to vary from year to year. Fish can be spotted and stalked along the edges, especially away from the road, although the water is mildly peat stained. Brown trout average over 2 kg and trophy fish are occasionally landed. It is not an easy river to fish unless one is relatively fit and agile. Crossings can be made at the tail of most pools.

Waiapu River and tributaries

Waiapu River and tributaries drain the Raukumara Range in the vicinity of Mt Hikurangi, west of Ruatoria. After flowing generally north-east, the Waiapu enters the sea 15 km south of East Cape. The Waiapu and the Mata River downstream of the Waingakia confluence have little good holding water. Floods, an unstable, shifting shingle riverbed and silt-laden water are not conducive to good trout habitat. Some of the tributaries are more stable and hold fish but many of these are relatively inaccessible. Although releases have been made into the Waitahaia, Mangaokura, Oronui, Waingakia and Raraparariki by helicopter, recurring floods have wiped out many of these fish. Only two tributaries are worth fishing unless one is also hunting. The Waingakia and Waitahaia both hold rainbows averaging 1.3 kg and are worth visiting.

Waingakia Stream

Location and access Turn off SH 35 at Aorangi south of Ruatoria, travel inland to Makaraka School, cross the Mata River bridge and follow the narrow Horehore Road up the true left bank of the Mata to the road end. The Waingakia seeps out under boulders into the Mata River.
Season 1 October–30 June.

Unstable shale and eroded cliffs dominate this valley, but the river has a few stable pools and runs. Rainbows can be caught on fly or spinner and, despite the harsh environment, are generally in good condition and fight well. Stocks are not high, however, and the bag limit of eight fish is frankly ridiculous for such a stream.

Waitahaia River

Location and access This tributary lies inland from Te Puia Springs. Turn off SH 35 south of Tokomaru Bay and travel inland to Mangatarata, Huiarau and Owhena on Ihungia Road. Access to the river is through private farmland and most farmers will be amazed at your request and readily grant permission. The river follows a deep valley.
Season 1 October–30 June.

In bright conditions, trout can be sight fished but only fit, agile anglers in boots and shorts should attempt to fish this stream. A lot of walking is required.

The Raukokore and Kereu rivers, which enter the sea between Waihau Bay and Te Kaha, also hold a few rainbows but because of their unstable nature are not recommended.

Hawke's Bay Fish and Game Council region

On the western aspect of this interesting region, the headwaters and tributaries of the Mohaka and Ngaruroro rivers drain the remote, bush-clad, mountainous country of Kaweka and Kaimanawa Forest parks. In northern Hawke's Bay, small rivers traverse steep hill country which is somewhat prone to erosion, while in the south, rivers have cut deep gorges in the soft limestone rock. Across the fertile Heretaunga Plains, the rivers are wide, shallow and shingly and the smaller streams and tributaries can become too warm for trout and sometimes dry up completely in long, hot summers.

There are four main river systems in Hawke's Bay: the Ngaruroro, Mohaka, Tukituki and Tutaekuri. Lake Tutira is the only lake of significance to anglers.

Daily bag limits
- Esk River and the Mohaka River tributaries — one sports fish.
- Ngaruroro River above Kiwi Creek — catch and release.
- Ngaruroro River between the Whanawhana cable and Kiwi Creek — one sports fish.
- Mohaka below SH 5 (excluding tributaries), lakes Tutira and Waikopiro, and Lake Opouahi — four sports fish.
- Lake Kuripapango (the larger of Twin Lakes) — no limit.
- All other waters — two fish.

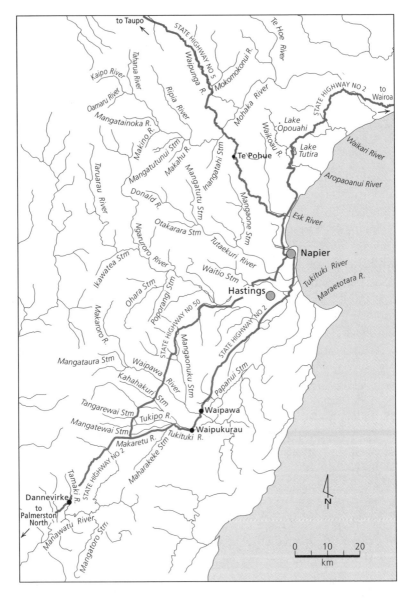

Hawke's Bay

Mohaka River

Location The headwater tributaries, Oamaru, Kaipo and Taharua, join near Poronui to form the Mohaka River. The main river flows south-east through Kaweka Forest Park for over 20 km before meeting the Ripia River near Pakaututu. The middle reaches then turn and flow north-east from Pakaututu to eventually reach the sea south of Wairoa at the small settlement of Mohaka.

Access *Upper reaches* Access is not easy as a private fishing lodge on the Taharua River prevents access through the old Poronui Station. There is a paper road across the farmland but this is difficult to follow.

- For the tramper/angler there is a five- to seven-hour tramp over Te Iringa Saddle from Clement's Access Road off SH 5 to Oamaru Hut.
- A five- to six-hour tramp over Waitawhero Saddle from Boyd Hut and airstrip down Oamaru Valley to Oamaru Hut. Then an hour's walk downstream to the Taharua confluence, where the Mohaka begins.
- By fixed-wing aircraft from Taupo to the Oamaru or 'Footy Field' airstrips. This is the easiest and most economical access.
- By arranging to raft the river with a commercial operator from Taupo.

Middle reaches
- From Pakaututu north of Puketitiri. Just before Pakaututu Bridge turn left onto the Hot Springs–Makahu road. This leads to the Blue Gums camping area at the road end with access to the river. A tramping track follows further upstream.
- From Pakaututu Bridge over the Mohaka River.
- SH 5 (the Taupo–Napier road) crosses the river 45 km north of Napier. McVicker's Road follows upstream on the true left bank before crossing the river. Waitara Road follows downstream on the true right bank to Fisherman's Bend and the DoC camping ground at Glenfalls.
- Pohokura Road, from Tutira on SH 2 north of Napier, leads eventually to the river opposite the Te Hoe River confluence.

- Willow Flat Road leaves SH 2 near Kotemaori.

Lower reaches SH 2 crosses near the mouth at Raupunga.

Season Above the Mangatainoka confluence, 1 October–30 April. Below this confluence, but excluding all tributaries, the river is open for fishing all year.

Restrictions Daily bag limit upstream from SH 5 bridge is one fish. Below this bridge the bag limit is four fish. The bag limit in all tributaries is one fish.

This large river, protected by a national water conservation order in its upper reaches, offers a wide variety of fishing and is the most popular fishing river in Hawke's Bay. However, access, to the upper reaches, is difficult because of private ownership and the rugged terrain that the river traverses. It holds an excellent stock of brown trout in the upper reaches above Pakaututu and mainly rainbows in the middle reaches below Pakaututu. These average 1.4 kg. However, there are trophy fish in this river and trout weighing 3 kg are not uncommon.

The wild and scenic upper reaches are best fished by adventurous tramper/anglers. The river banks in this section below the Taharua confluence are very overgrown by fallen manuka scrub and beech bush interwined with bush lawyer and are truly an angler's nightmare. The river can be forded but rocks and stones are often slippery and there are gorgy sections. There is seldom any need to wade until a fish is spotted and then only to get into position. Trout are very receptive to a wide variety of dry flies, nymphs and spinners. As with many wilderness rivers, the trout here are not very sophisticated and a careful approach with an accurate first cast — avoiding drag — is generally more important than the choice of fly pattern. With stable scrub- and bush-covered banks, this upper section seldom discolours after rain and when it does can become fishable again in a day or so.

The river becomes larger in the middle reaches between Pakaututu and Glenfalls but still offers excellent water for the fly angler. There are some very deep holes and fast runs but the river can still be crossed in carefully selected places. This stretch is the most heavily fished. Trout can be spotted if feeding on the edges of a run but it is worthwhile fishing blind with dry flies, heavily weighted nymphs or a well-sunk Woolly Bugger. When spinning, use a well-weighted lure, especially in the deeper holes.

The lower reaches also hold fish but the river becomes very large, slower flowing and rather unattractive to fish.

Oamaru River

Location This headwater tributary flows north-east down the Oamaru Valley from the Waitawhero Saddle to join the Kaipo River near Oamaru Hut.

Access As for the upper Mohaka River.
- A five- to seven-hour tramp from Clement's Access Road.
- By fixed-wing aircraft to the Oamaru airstrip.
- Private access through Poronui.

Season 1 October–30 April.

Only the first 2–3 km of river are worth fishing upstream of Oamaru Hut. Below the hut and downstream to the Taharua confluence there is excellent, stable water holding a good stock of brown trout with an occasional rainbow to enliven proceedings. Fish can be spotted and stalked but are wary. Some lie sheltered in the rocky slots. Wading and crossing can be tricky as there are deep, slippery slots and scalloped channels in the bed-rock, especially just upstream from the Taharua. The river seldom discolours with rain, and the fishing can improve when the river is rising. Trout suddenly appear from the depths of pools and slots to feed actively on dislodged mayfly and caddis nymphs. The tussock banks do not obstruct the back-cast.

By April these upper reaches hold good numbers of fish, with many having arrived from the lower river intent on spawning.

Kaipo River

Location and access Rises near Te Iringa Saddle and flows down through native bush to join the Oamaru River near Oamaru Hut. Access as for the Oamaru River.

Season 1 October–30 April.

This small bush stream holds browns and is worth exploring for 1–2 km above its confluence with the Oamaru River. Casting soon becomes difficult owing to overhanging trees and scrub, but trout can be sight fished and often present an intriguing puzzle.

Taharua River

Location Rises from springs on the pumice plateau south of SH 5 (the Taupo–Napier road) and flows south through farmland (the old Poronui Station) to join the Oamaru River and form the Mohaka.
Access Over the last few years access has become very difficult owing to a private fishing and hunting lodge closing off the stream. There is a paper road that crosses the upper reaches and one could possibly walk upstream through the manuka scrub from the Mohaka but this is not easy. The commercial operators of the lodge would hardly be overjoyed!
Season 1 October–30 April.

This is a small, clear stream meandering across farmland with patches of manuka scrub growing along stable grassy banks. It has been likened to an English chalk stream. The stream has a pumice, stone and weed bed and holds only browns as rainbows in the Mohaka cannot negotiate the falls near the Mohaka confluence. The trout population is self-sustaining. The stream can flood and become silt laden after heavy rain and may take three days to clear. Fish average 1–2 kg and rise well to a gently presented Coch-y-bondhu or manuka beetle imitation during the green beetle hatch in November and December. An accurately presented size 14 Hare and Copper or Pheasant Tail nymph is equally effective. Strong downstream winds often make fly fishing difficult in this open valley. A landing net is very useful on some sections of the river.

Mangatainoka River

Location Flows east through both Kaimanawa and Kaweka Forest parks to join the Mohaka River 6 km from the road end at the Pakaututu thermal springs reserve.
Access By tramping up the Mohaka Valley from the road end. A marked trail leads up the true right bank.
Season 1 October–30 April.

This small, clear, stony bush stream offers excellent wilderness brown trout fishing to anglers prepared to walk and camp. There are no fish above the falls 3–4 km upstream from the Mohaka confluence. Dense bush overhanging the stream provides an abundance of insect life. Fish can be easily spotted and the stream is safe to cross. It rarely becomes discoloured except after prolonged heavy rain.

The Makino and the Makahu are two small tributaries that join the Mohaka downstream from the Mangatainoka. The Makino is not recommended, and although the Makahu holds trout in a few stable pools, it floods readily and is generally unstable.

Ripia River

Location Flows south-east from its source on Lochinvar Station to join the Mohaka River just downstream from Pakaututu Bridge on Puketitiri Road.
Access By walking upstream from the Mohaka confluence or from SH 5 by permission from Carter Holt Harvey through Awahonu Forest. The headwaters are very difficult to access.
Season 1 October–30 April.

This small, stony, clear-water stream flows through scrub, bush and exotic forest. Trout can be spotted and the stream crossed at the tail of most pools. Holds browns and rainbows averaging 1–2 kg. As with many similar streams, fishing improves away from civilisation so active anglers should walk for an hour or so upstream before fishing. Trout will accept attractor pattern dry flies, small weighted nymphs and even lures sunk deeply and fished through pools.

Inangatahi Stream

Location and access Rises near Puketitiri, flows north-east and empties into the Mohaka from the true right bank just upstream from the SH 5 bridge. Access is across private farmland over the bridge on McVicar's Road. Permission may not be easy to obtain.
Season 1 October–30 April.
This small, flood-prone stream flows through deep gorges and

cleared unstable farmland and readily discolours after rain. At times it holds a few good fish while at others it is barren. Both rainbow and brown trout can be spotted on a bright day.

There is three to four hours' fishing upstream from the mouth.

Waipunga River

Location Rises near the Wheao headwaters in Kaingaroa Forest and flows south to meet SH 5 (the Taupo–Napier road) 15 km east of Rangitaiki. It then follows SH 5 for 20 km before turning east, south of Tarawera, to join the Mohaka River.

Access *Above the falls* A permit should be obtained from the Fletcher Challenge Visitor Centre, Rotorua (phone 07 346 2082) before fishing above the falls. Turn off onto Pohokura Road where SH 5 first meets the river. Then turn left before the bridge down Koromika Road, which runs upstream on the true right bank. A scramble through swamp and scrub may be required to reach the river.

Below the falls SH 5 (the Taupo–Napier road) follows, crosses and recrosses the river for 20 km but bush and scrub make access difficult in parts.

Season Above the falls (excluding tributaries), 1 October–30 April. Below the falls, the river is open for fishing all year.

Above the falls, this small, clear stream holding only brown trout meanders through swamp, tussock, toetoe and scrub in a relatively open valley. There are some well-developed pools at the bends in the river where fish can be spotted in bright conditions. However, they are very wary and require a cautious approach and an accurate presentation first time. As the pools are small, one should fish short to eliminate drag but this naturally gives the fish a good chance of seeing the angler. Crossings are possible but the riverbed stones are very slippery. Fish stocks are not high and catch and release in this section is recommended. This is a testing stretch of water especially if the prevailing downstream wind impedes casting.

Below the falls, the river flows through bush and scrub for 20 km and tends to be more swift and boisterous. It is very rough immediately below the falls but lower down the valley there are picnic areas and other clearings presenting reasonable access to the river. There is more shelter from a downstream wind below the falls. Fish are difficult to spot unless rising so the water should be fished blind with a deer hair attractor dry fly or weighted nymphs and an indicator. Both rainbow and brown trout are present below the falls and some well-conditioned rainbows can be a real handful when hooked. It is wise to carry a landing net despite the scrub. One needs to be reasonably fit to fish this river successfully. I have seen a rainbow weighing 3.6 kg taken from the Waipunga River.

Mokomokonui River

Location This small Waipunga tributary drains the southern boundary of Urewera National Park. It flows south to join the Waipunga just south of Tarawera on SH 5.
Access A loop road a few kilometres south of the Tarawera Hotel leads off SH 5 to the junction of the two rivers. This road crosses the Waipunga to Tataraakina Station. The lower reaches can be fished by walking up the gorge but the station owners are reluctant to allow access to the middle and upper reaches.
Season 1 October–30 April.

This river has been severely affected by floods over the past few years and many pools have filled with shingle. As a result the river discolours easily after rain and takes time to clear. It holds mainly rainbows with a few large browns in the inaccessible bush-clad upper reaches.

Te Hoe River

Location Drains the heavily bush-clad ranges south of the upper Waiau River to join the Mohaka River at the settlement of Te Hoe.
Access A permit should be obtained from Carter Holt Harvey Forests, Napier (phone 06 835 6390).
Upper reaches The headwaters can be reached through Kaingaroa Forest. The upper reaches can be accessed by a long tramp south from Roger's Hut on the Waiau headwaters.
Lower and middle reaches Turn off SH 2 at Tutira store and follow

the winding, metalled Pohokura Road to the Mohaka–Te Hoe confluence. The Mohaka River must be forded to reach Te Hoe and this can be very difficult except in low-water summer conditions.

Restrictions Fly fishing only. This regulation also applies to the Hautapu tributary.

Season 1 October–30 April.

Te Hoe is a medium-sized, isolated tributary of the Mohaka and fish numbers can be very unpredictable. In the past, it has been severely affected by floods with the riverbed completely turned over and the pools filled with shingle. It has recovered to some extent but only fit anglers experienced in the New Zealand bush and back country should attempt to fish this rather rough and boisterous river. It is best to walk for an hour after fording the Mohaka before fishing. It holds rainbows and browns averaging 1.2 kg and these can be sight fished.

The Hautapu tributary also holds fish but anglers contemplating fishing this river should tramp and camp out for a few days. Beware of wet weather as the Mohaka may rapidly become impassable on the return journey.

 *Tutaekuri River and tributaries*

Tutaekuri River

Location The headwaters drain the Kaweka Range; the middle reaches cross the Heretaunga Plains through the outskirts of Taradale; the lower reaches enter the sea in conjunction with the Ngaruroro River just south of Napier.

Access *Upper reaches* Side roads including Flag Range Road, off the Taihape–Napier road.

Middle reaches From Puketapu and Dartmoor roads west of Taradale.

Lower reaches From behind Taradale, where there are many access points. SH 2 crosses just above the mouth.

Season Above the Mangaone Stream confluence, 1 October–30 April. Below this confluence, open all year except May.

The middle reaches of this medium-sized river are wide and shingly although there are a few stable pools in the upper reaches. The best fishing is in the lower reaches during October and November, when schools of rainbow trout follow whitebait, smelt and elvers upstream. A smelt fly or a silver or gold spinner can produce great sport during these conditions. In the hot summer months, weed becomes a problem in the lower reaches. In the middle reaches, the best water is where the river runs deep against a stable bank covered in willows or other vegetation. It is worth prospecting for such water as although fish stocks are not high in the unstable sections, some good fishing can be obtained in the more stable pools.

Donald River

Trampers entering Kaweka Forest Park from Mangatutu find the Donald River holds a few small rainbows. Access is from Lotkow Road and Hut. The river is unstable and flood prone, and best suited to spinning.

Mangatutu Stream

Location and access Off Waldon and Waihau roads after passing through Dartmoor. Also from Price, Cockburn and Hawkston roads.
Season 1 October–30 April.

This small stream holds only a few fish and is best fished early in the season before it dries.

Mangaone Stream

Location Drains Te Waka Range, flows generally south and joins the Tutaekuri River at Dartmoor west of Napier.
Access *Upper reaches* Rotowhenua Road off SH 5, 5 km south of Te Pohue.
Middle reaches From Puketitiri Road at Rissington and Glengarry Road 5 km before Rissington, across private farmland.
Lower reaches From Puketapu Road at Dartmoor.

Season 1 October–30 April.
Restrictions Fly fishing only.

Although this small to medium-sized river offers over 30 km of fishable water, access is not easy, especially to the upper reaches, where the river runs through deep gorges. It holds mainly rainbows averaging 1 kg with a few browns in some of the deeper holes. It is a clear-water stream and pleasant to fish, although stocks are not high. Best fished early in the season before low water and weed growth become a problem, particularly in the lower reaches. Fish can be spotted in the upper and middle reaches but in the lower reaches the water should be fished blind.

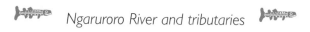

Ngaruroro River and tributaries

Ngaruroro River

Location Drains Kaimanawa and Kaweka Forest parks and flows parallel to and east of the Rangitikei River in its upper reaches as far south as the Taihape–Napier road at Kuripapango. Here the river turns east, leaves the Ruahine mountains and flows over the Heretaunga Plains to share a mouth with the Tutaekuri River.

Access *Upper reaches*

- By fixed-wing aircraft to Boyd Hut on the headwaters of the river.
- By walking upstream from Kuripapango, where the Taihape–Napier road crosses the river. The first two fords can be deep and difficult so care should be taken unless the river is very low.
- If the river is unfordable, take the high level trampers' track to Cameron Hut (four to five hours for tramper/anglers only).

Middle reaches

- Through Fernhill on the Ohiti Road to Whanawhana. There is a commercial jet-boat operator in this area who can take you further upstream to the Taruarau confluence.
- A number of other roads offer easy access to the middle and lower reaches.

Lower reaches From Fernhill Bridge a good track runs down the true left bank. Pakowhai Road crosses the river further downstream.

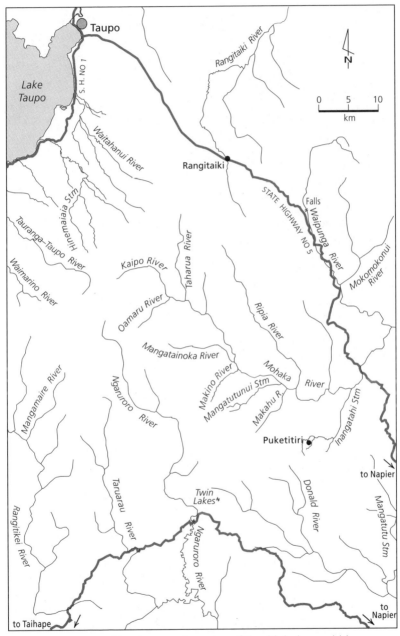

Headwater tributaries of the Mohaka and Ngaruroro

Ngaruroro River

Season
- Above the Taruarau confluence, 1 October–30 April.
- Below the Taruarau confluence excluding tributaries, open all year except for the month of May.
- Between Chesterhope and Fernhill bridges, open all year.

Restrictions In the headwaters above Kiwi Creek, catch and release and fly fishing only. Between the Whanawhana cable and Kiwi Creek, only one fish can be taken and this must be between 35 and 55 cm in length.

For ease of description, this large river is described in sections.

Headwaters and upper reaches The headwaters flow across exposed open tussock country in Kaimanawa Forest Park. There are usually a few fish both above and below the Boyd airstrip but fishing improves considerably 5 km downstream near Panako (Gold) Creek. Here the river enters patchy manuka scrub with a few easily negotiated short gorges but the pools are well developed and stable. The river is smaller than the upper Rangitikei and crossings can be made at the tail of most pools. Clear water affords great visibility so fish are easy to spot and stalk and just as easily spooked. Holds a good stock of rainbows averaging 1.3 kg with an occasional fish weighing up to 4 kg. Rafting is popular on this stretch of river down as far as Kuripapango.

The river upstream from Kuripapango is very gorgy with steep cliffs, and difficult to negotiate in anything but low-water conditions. It is only suited to active anglers confident with river crossings. However, there is good fishing all the way to Cameron Hut and beyond. In this section it is a medium-sized river with some very deep pools.

An occasional fish can be sight fished but likely looking water should be fished blind with heavily weighted nymphs or an attractor pattern dry fly.

Middle reaches Below Kuripapango on the Taihape–Napier road, the river enters a very difficult gorge and only becomes fishable again in the vicinity of Whanawhana. Here the character of the river changes with open shingle banks, long glides, shallow runs and willows. There are some stable pools, especially where the river runs up against a bank, but the river can alter considerably during a flood. Favoured spots include the Ohara and Otamauri stream mouths at Whanawhana, and the Ohiti Stream mouth past Fernhill. Rainbows average 1 kg and respond to all types of fly fishing and spinning.

Lower reaches The river becomes larger in the lower reaches with long glides and short runs. Fish are difficult to spot and weed becomes a problem in summer. However, there is some entertaining smelt fly fishing in October and November when the whitebait are running. Most trout are taken on spinners in these lower reaches.

Without doubt, the inaccessible upper reaches upstream from Kuripapango offer the most exciting fishing in this large river.

Taruarau River

Location Rises in Kaimanawa Forest Park between the Rangitikei and Ngaruroro watersheds. It then flows south through Ngamatea Station, is crossed by the Taihape–Napier road, and flows east through Timahanga Station. The confluence with the Ngaruroro is very difficult to reach except by jet-boat.

Access Both Ngamatea and Timahanga stations are very reluctant to grant access so the Taihape–Napier road bridge is the easiest option. Tramper/anglers can reach the river in three to four hours by tramping south over the Comet Range.

Season 1 October–30 April.

Restrictions Only trout measuring between 35 and 55 cm can be taken. The bag limit is two fish.

Deep gorges and dense manuka scrub severely limit access to this excellent small stream, which holds well-conditioned rainbow trout averaging 1.4 kg. These can be spotted and will accept a wide variety of dry flies and nymphs. In the upper reaches on Ngamatea Station the river meanders across open tussock grassland but soon enters very deep gorges after leaving Ngamatea.

The small Ikawetea tributary joining the Taruarau River 2 km downstream from the Timahanga farm bridge also holds some nice rainbows in its lower section.

Location Rises in the Ruahine Range, then flows north-east to join the Poporangi Stream before entering the Ngaruroro River opposite Whanawhana.

Access *Middle and upper reaches* Turn off SH 2 at Longlands; take Maraekakaho, Kereru then Big Hill roads.

Mouth and lower reaches Take the Matapiro–Whanawhana road. The braided Ngaruroro River can normally be crossed on foot with care.

Season 1 October–30 April.

Rafting hazard on the Ngaruroro

The upper and middle reaches run through a deep gorge, making access difficult. All reaches fish best early in the season before the summer heat reduces water flow and fish drop back downstream. This is a small stream holding mainly rainbows averaging 1 kg which can be sight fished under sunny conditions.

Location Rises from springs near Swamp Road and enters the Ngaruroro River upstream of Chesterhope Bridge.

Access From Pakowhai Road by walking over the stopbank opposite Pakowhai store. Or from Chesterhope Road, which crosses the stream. Permission is required to cross private land.

Season 1 October–30 April.

Restrictions Bag limit is now two sports fish.

This deep, cold-water, spring-fed 'ditch' is difficult to fish but holds a good stock of well-conditioned rainbows averaging 1 kg. Watercress and weed add to the difficulties of fishing but casting is generally unobstructed as the creek flows over pastoral land. Early morning and late evening are the best times to fish and trout rise quite readily during these periods. It is best to fish small caddis and mayfly imitations — either nymphs, emergers or dry flies. A landing net can be useful to lift fish over the weed.

Twin Lakes (Lake Diamond and Lake Kuripapango)

Location and access Take Castle Rocks Road from Kuripapango on the Taihape–Napier road. From the car park it is a 25-minute walk to the western lake.

Season Open all year. There is no bag limit.

Only the larger, western lake (Kuripapango), which holds a large stock of small Loch Leven brown trout, is fishable. The eastern lake is unfishable as it is surrounded by swamp, manuka scrub and rushes. Fishing access is good on the western lake providing the water level is not too high. Fish take dries and small nymphs, but if these fail, try a small olive Woolly Bugger. There are patches of weed in some areas.

Tukituki River and tributaries

Tukituki River

Location Rises in the Ruahine Range, flows south-east to

Taruarau River rainbow

Waipukurau, then turns north-east to eventually enter the sea at Haumoana, near Hastings.

Access *Upper reaches* From the end of Mill and Tukituki roads off SH 50 south of Ongaonga.

Middle reaches Many roads meet and cross the river although permission is required to cross private farmland to reach some stretches. Middle Road follows the true left bank from Patangata to south of Hastings. Walker Road leads to the Tukituki–Waipawa confluence and access is also available from the Tamumu and Patangata bridges.

Lower reaches The river flows just east of Havelock North and Te Mata Peak and there are many access points. River Road follows the river from the Waimarama Road bridge to Haumoana.

Season In the Tukituki wildlife refuge, and between the confluence of the Tukipo River and the Mount Herbert Road extension, the river is open to fishing all year. From the SH 50 road bridge near Ashcott to the sea, open all year except for the month of May. Elsewhere, 1 October–30 April.

A popular medium-sized river flowing across pastoral land and offering almost 70 km of fishing water for brown and rainbow trout. Fish average 1.2 kg but each season trout around the 4 kg mark are taken. Most of these are sea-run browns that enter the lower and middle reaches early in the season chasing whitebait, elvers and smelt. Apart from a stretch near Patangata where the riverbed is slippery papa rock, the river has a shingle bed and can be safely waded and crossed. Willows line the banks along some stretches and there are cliffs and deep pools in the middle reaches.

The upper reaches above Waipukurau are best early in the season before the shallow shingly runs become too warm. Late in the season, a spawning run improves the fishing.

The middle reaches fish well most of the year but in summer, when the water warms, weed growth can be an exasperating problem. There is a good evening rise to mayfly and caddis but fish are difficult to spot during the day. However, good rainbows can be taken on a small, dark sedge wet fly fished across and down on a floating line.

Try a smelt fly below Waimarama Bridge in October and November as large browns enter the river at this time.

The most popular stretch of river lies between the Tamumu and Patangata bridges.

Waipawa River

Location Drains the Ruahine Range and flows south-east to join the Tukituki River near Waipawa.

Access *Upper reaches* From Springhill and Makaroro roads off SH 50 and Caldwell Road off Wakarara Road.

Middle reaches From Stockade Road off Ongaonga Road.

Lower reaches SH 2 crosses the river in the Waipawa township.

Season Above the SH 2 bridge, 1 October–30 April. Below the bridge as far as the first overhead power cables of Rathbone Street, open all year except for the month of May.

This medium-sized, willow-lined, shingly tributary of the Tukituki River fishes well for most of the year.

There are sufficient deep holes under willows where fish can escape the hot summer sun. Holds mainly rainbows averaging 0.5–1 kg but there are some larger browns. The river is easily waded and crossed but trout are hard to spot and anglers generally fish this river blind during the day with dry flies and small weighted nymphs. There is often an active evening rise for caddis, and small soft hackle wet flies or caddis emergers can be very effective around dusk.

Makaroro River

Location and access *Upper reaches* From Wakarara Mill Road.

Middle reaches From Springhill Road.

Lower reaches and the Waipawa confluence From Makaroro Road off SH 50.

Season 1 October–30 April.

This small tributary of the Waipawa fishes best either early or late in the season. It is a typical small Hawke's Bay stream, being shingly and willow-lined, although the upper reaches become gorgy and inaccessible. Holds small rainbows but is not highly valued.

Mangaonuku Stream

Location Flows south from its spring-fed source near Poporangi to join the Waipawa.

Access From the Waipawa–Tikokino road, Brow Bridge on Tikokino Road and Stockdale Road from Ruataniwha for the Waipawa confluence.

Season 1 October–30 April.
Restrictions Fly fishing only.

Some surprisingly large trout have been taken from this small stream. This may be due to the water quality as, being mainly spring fed, it rarely discolours. Holds rainbows and browns and fishes best early and late in the season. Some sight fishing is possible in optimum conditions.

Tukipo River

Location and access *Upper reaches* From SH 50 between Ashcott and Takapau.
Middle reaches From Balfour Road off SH 50.
Lower reaches From the Ashcott–Waipukurau road through private farms, and the Pukeora Bridge.
Season 1 October–30 April.
Restrictions Fly fishing only.

Another small, shingly, willow-lined stream that holds mainly rainbows averaging 1 kg. They are hard to spot but fish the likely looking water with a size 14 Pheasant Tail nymph on the dropper and a similar sized Parachute Adams as an indicator. Again, best early or late in the season.

Maharakeke Stream

Location This spring-fed tributary joins the Tukipo River just west of Waipukurau.
Access Crossed by SH 2 south of Waipukurau, and Hatuma Limeworks Road follows up the true right bank.
Season 1 October–30 April.
Restrictions Fly fishing only.

This small, clear, spring creek has become weed infested and very difficult to fish. In years gone by it had an excellent reputation as a classic fly stream but the local freezing works are thought to be responsible for eutrophication. It is still worth a look, however.

Watch for fish cruising the slow water.

Two other tributaries, the Makaretu River west of Waipukurau (fly fishing only) and the Mangatewai Stream, hold fish but are not highly recommended.

Maraetotara River

Location Rises on Mt Kahuranaki, flows for 18 km in a northerly direction east of Havelock North and reaches the sea at Te Awanga.

Access The Havelock North–Waimarama road crosses the middle reaches. There is access to the upper reaches from Maraetotara Valley Road across private land but permission must be obtained. Permission is also required to access the lower reaches from the road to Ocean Beach.

Season 1 October–30 April.

Restrictions Fly fishing only.

Poor land management practices have unfortunately caused deterioration of this once highly valued spring creek. Bank clearing leading to silt and fertiliser run-off is thought to be the main culprit. Above the dam only brown trout are present, but rainbow were introduced below the dam in 1998.

Above the road bridge and below the dam the river is still overgrown in parts, but this provides food and cover for fish and offers anglers a real challenge. In some sections, a flick or bow and arrow cast is all that can be achieved but fishing to sighted trout in short rock pools can be exciting. The deep pool immediately below the falls always holds fish but these are safe even for the adventurous angler.

Below the bridge the river meanders across farmland, but because of the clear water fish are not easily deceived. A careful approach, long fine tippets, an accurate gentle presentation and small flies should bring success. Careful observation of feeding fish and seining the stream with a small net should guide you in the selection of dries, lightly weighted nymphs or emerger patterns. It is hard not to start with size 16 Parachute Adams dry flies, Pheasant Tail nymphs or CDC Emergers.

Waikari River

Location At Putorino, north of Lake Tutira.
Access *Headwaters* 5 km before reaching Putorino, turn left off SH 2 onto Matahoura Loop Road then second right onto Heays Access Road.
Middle reaches Turn right past Putorino onto Waikari Coast Road then first left onto Glenbrook Road.
Season 1 October–30 April.

Severe floods in the 1980s ravaged this small, isolated stream. Despite being very gorgy in parts there are some deep holes, making fish difficult to spot. Holds both rainbows and browns but stocks are not high. Should be fished in boots and shorts early in the season.

Lake Opouahi

Location and access Turn left off SH 2 past the Tutira store onto Matahoura Road then onto Pohokura Road.
Season Open all year.
Restrictions No power boats permitted.

This deep, 2 ha lake holds *Savelinus fontinalis* (brook trout), a residual population of rainbows and recently introduced 'tiger' trout (a sterile cross between brown and brook trout). It is best fished from a rowboat or float tube by spinning, deeply harling a streamer or casting with a high density fly line. Lead lines are permitted. Try Woolly Bugger, Red Rabbit, Mrs Simpson or Red Setter lures or spin fish with a well weighted Toby or Cobra spinner. Fishes best in the cooler months of the year.

Waikoau and Aropaoanui rivers

Location and access *Upper reaches* From Pohokura Road off Matahoura Road, which leaves SH 2 past the Tutira store.

Middle reaches Crossed by SH 2 just north of Devil's Elbow.
Lower reaches Turn off SH 2 onto Aropaoanui Road at the summit of Tongoia Hill.
Season 1 October–30 April.

These are relatively small rivers, with the Waikoau being a tributary of the Aropaoanui River. Both flow through deep gorges but the streams are easy to cross and wade. Both hold a small population of brown and rainbow trout. Fish are not easy to spot.

Lake Tutira

Location and access SH 2 follows the western shore 38 km north of Napier. There is a boat ramp halfway along this shore. A car track at the northern end of the lake runs to a locked gate. A causeway at the southern end between lakes Tutira and Waikopiro provides easy vehicle access. A walking track makes angling access simple along the eastern shore but the western shore is overgrown by willows and scrub. There is a basic camping ground.
Season Both lakes, with the exception of Sandy Creek, are open all year.
Restrictions Boats and float tubes are allowed but motors are prohibited. Artificial fly and lure only permitted.

Tutira is 200 ha in area and is stocked annually. It now holds Loch Leven browns and 'r' type rainbow trout. In the cooler months there is some good shoreline fishing. In summer, the majority of fish are caught from a boat or float tube as fish tend to go deeper in the warmer months of the year. Algal blooms can still be a problem when the water warms. Trolling, harling and casting over weed beds are the principle methods used. Fish are very difficult to spot from the shore. The western shore is willow-fringed and can only be fished from a boat. However, the other shores are clear for casting. Wading is easy and safe except for the northern end of the lake, which has a close, steep drop off.

Use a slow sinking or floating line and try damsel and dragon fly imitations including Olive and Brown Woolly Bugger and Hamill's Killer. Size 8 to 10 lures, such as Parsons' Glory, Red Setter and

Rabbit patterns and small, lightly weighted nymphs slowly retrieved between the weed beds will also pick up fish. Trolled black and gold Toby spinners can be very effective at times.

The adjoining Lake Waikopiro also holds fish. These lakes are very popular and heavily used for recreation in summer.

Esk River

Location Rises in the Maungaharuru Range, flows south through very hilly terrain and eventually meets SH 5 near Eskdale, 15 km north of Napier.

Access *Upper reaches* Turn off SH 5, about 2 km before Te Pohue on the Napier side, onto Ohurakura Road then right onto Berry Road, which takes you across a ford. Permission to cross private farmland is required. There is a good two hours' fishing before an impassable gorge blocks progress.

Middle reaches The Ellis–Wallace road leaves SH 5 just past Eskdale and follows the river upstream.

Lower reaches SH 2 crosses near the mouth just past the SH 5 turn-off.

Season 1 October–30 April.

Restrictions Only one fish between 35 and 55 cm can be taken above the Ellis–Wallace road bridge.

This once highly regarded small stream has deteriorated over the years from unwise farm management practices and the planting and harvesting of exotic forest in the headwaters. The river nows floods easily and becomes heavily silt-laden after rain. When clear, fish can be spotted in the middle and upper reaches but stocks are very low. The upper and middle reaches flow through hilly Hawke's Bay sheep country and anglers need to be prepared for a long day's walk. There are rainbow and brown trout present and these can be carefully stalked with dry flies and nymphs. A cicada or grasshopper pattern in summer will surprise some fish.

The lower reaches become sluggish, tidal and unattractive to fish but some large sea-run browns are taken most years on smelt patterns.

Lake Te Pohue, on SH 5, at Te Pohue has been stocked with trout. Perch are also present. Best fished with spinning gear as shoreline access is difficult.

Tongariro–Taupo Conservancy

Ova from European brown trout (*Salmo trutta*) were brought to the South Island from Tasmania in 1867 and to Taupo in 1886. Rainbow trout (*Salmo gardnerii*) ova from Sonoma Creek, a tributary of the Russian River in San Francisco Bay, were obtained in 1883, hatched in a pond in the Auckland Domain and liberated in Lake Taupo in 1897. All the rainbow trout in New Zealand have originated from this one shipment.

Food sources in Lake Taupo were initially plentiful and included the striped kokopu (small native greyling), koura (native freshwater crayfish), inanga (whitebait) and cockabully. Liberated trout thrived and by 1910 fish weighing 9 kg were being caught. In the early 1920s the food supply became depleted and trout lost condition, so the government introduced netting to reduce stocks. In 1934 a smelt (*retropinna*) was introduced from Rotorua as a food source. This was very successful and smelt now constitute the main food supply for Taupo trout.

In 1926, due in no small way to the co-operation of the local Maori tribes, the 1926 Maori Land Claim Adjustment Act was passed into law. This entitles anglers holding a current Taupo trout fishing licence to a 20 m wide right of way along the shores of Lake Taupo and the banks of most Taupo rivers.

Lake Taupo

Season Lake Taupo is open all year. A separate Taupo licence is required.

Restrictions Only the important ones are listed. Anglers must obtain a copy of the regulations from local sports stores or DoC and be familiar with these when fishing Taupo. There is no excuse for ignorance!

- No licence holder may fish for any sports fish between 12 midnight and 5.00 am.
- A maximum of two lures or flies may be used at any one time.
- In fly-only waters, weighted flies must not be tied on a hook longer than 17 mm or deeper than 5.5 mm (about size 10). Bead heads are legal within the above size limitations.
- Strike indicators must be made from natural or synthetic yarn only. They can be dyed and impregnated with floatant.
- In fly-only waters it is illegal to use split shot, sinkers, weights, bubbles, fly spoons or artificial floats.
- Spinning is not permitted in any of the streams or rivers flowing into Lake Taupo. It is permitted in the Tokaanu tailrace below the main road bridge (SH 41). It is not permitted within 300 m of any stream mouth.
- Treble hooks on spinners are illegal.
- All bait fishing is prohibited.
- It is illegal to harl or troll within 300 m of any stream mouth, the only exceptions being the Waikino and Otupoto Falls in the western bays.
- For boat owners, a permit must be obtained from local stores or fly shops before using a public boat launching ramp.
- Lead and wire lines are permitted.
- Down-riggers are permitted but the cable must be no longer than 40 m and lines must be unweighted.
- Set rods on boats are only legal provided every person on the boat is licenced.
- Fly fishing from an anchored boat is only permissible at the following stream mouths: Tongariro, Tauranga–Taupo, Waikino and Otupoto Falls. A float tube or kick boat is classed as a boat.
- Daily bag limit is three trout.
- Size limit is 45 cm minimum.

Etiquette I cannot stress too strongly that anglers intent on fishing the Tongariro–Taupo Conservancy should first read the chapter entitled Conservation and Etiquette. At times the fishing pressure in the Taupo area can be very intense and unpleasant confrontations between anglers are to be avoided at all costs.

Lake Taupo, New Zealand's largest lake, is 40 km long, 30 km wide and covers more than 600 square kilometres. It has an average depth of 120 m, the deepest point being 160 m, and lies at 360 m above sea level.

This fishery fully deserves its worldwide reputation, as it offers a wide variety of superb angling water. Rainbow trout in Taupo have some characteristics common to steelhead in that they treat Lake Taupo like a sea. Perhaps some steelhead genes were acquired from the Russian River, where there is a good run of steelhead? The average weight of trout caught varies from year to year but is usually around 1.6 kg. Fish weighing over 4 kg are not uncommon, and although the majority of these are brown trout, trophy rainbows are still caught. Most fish landed by fly anglers are caught on lures or streamers (wet flies) and nymphs, although there is some dry fly fishing available in the surrounding streams. Boat fishing accounts for large numbers of fish taken.

The movement of trout in the lake follows the smelt life cycle, and the spawning run. Between April and September, 60 per cent of trout in Lake Taupo run up rivers and streams entering the lake

Summer stream mouth fishing, Western Bays, Taupo

to spawn. Naturally, river fishing and stream-mouth fishing are very popular during these months. Spent fish (kelts or slabs) return to the lake between October and December, at much the same time that smelt school into the shallows and river mouths to spawn. Trout then feed voraciously on smelt to regain condition. These are the months when shoreline smelt fishing and stream-mouth fishing become very popular. After January, shoreline fishing becomes unproductive but stream-mouth fishing, especially at night, remains good. From the end of May, when river water temperatures equal lake water temperatures, fish feed in the deeper waters of the lake and only enter stream mouths briefly prior to running up to spawn. Deep trolling then comes into its own. Fry enter the lake nine to twelve months after spawning when 15–20 cm long. These fingerlings reach maturity in 2–4 years, and so the life cycle continues.

Fly fishing at stream and river mouths

This information pertains to all stream- and river-mouth fishing, not just Lake Taupo.

Trout feed along the lip, where the river delta drops off into deeper water, and along the edges of the current, where it merges with the lake water. When fishing, it is important to stand back a few metres from the lip as fish usually take the fly during the retrieve just as it passes over the lip. Wading is usually necessary and waders are essential to protect against the cold — especially at night and in the cooler months. In shallow mouths thigh waders may be sufficient, but chest waders are needed for deeper water.

At shallow mouths, false casting above the water is recommended as excessive water disturbance, even at night, frightens feeding fish. Most Taupo stream mouths can be fished with medium sinking or floating lines. A weight forward line will enable a longer cast to be made, an important factor when fishing pressure is high. Generally, a strong onshore wind makes fishing difficult, although at times, when the current parallels the shore, the hot spot may be 50 m along the beach. A light onshore breeze is usually conducive to good fishing.

There is no substitute for experience as each stream or river mouth has its own characteristics. When the fishing is slow, a number of options are available. Try changing position, but before doing so always ask other anglers and do not force your way into a prime spot unless there is an obvious gap or you are joining the end of the line. Sometimes fish may not be feeding along the lip, or casting pressure may have driven them further out. It may be worth wading deep and fishing the tail of the rip. Do not fish in front of other anglers, however, unless permission has been granted. Other tactics when the fishing is slow include changing lines, trying a smaller fly or changing fly patterns. Some flies do not swim well and set up unusual vibrations in the water. Altering the speed of your retrieve is another tactic worth trying. Sometimes fish simply stay out in deep water until very late. At night, if no fish have been caught by 9.00 pm, it is worth spreading the 'bad news' to other anglers or even talking about how nice it would be in a warm bed. You will be amazed how many anglers will agree and leave soon after. Hopefully, the fish will then come into the rip.

At small stream mouths, wading and false casting on the water may only drive feeding fish further out. It can also be very beneficial to periodically rest the mouth and allow spooky fish to return and begin feeding close in again. It may be difficult, however, to convince other anglers to co-operate with these suggestions.

Fishing is generally better on dark, moonless nights or when the barometer is rising after the passing of a front. There are always exceptions, however.

During the day, when fish are smelting through the rip, action can be fast and furious or totally frustrating. Trout can be seen gorging on smelt and, although many of these fish are kelts, fishing is invariably fascinating. If trout are ignoring your fly, try a small pattern such as a size 12. When all else fails, a nymph fished along the edge of the current can bring surprising results.

There are many successful lure patterns to use, but during the day try some of the older ones such as Grey Ghost, Green Smelt, Taupo Tiger, Jack Spratt or a Doll Fly. The more modern Mylar bodied patterns can be deadly at times. When fish are feeding like crazy even dropping your fly on the water in front of them will result in a strike. However, finding a good lure pattern when the fishing is tough is the real challenge.

At night, most black flies that swim well will take fish. This includes Hairy Dog, Black Prince, Black Marabou, Craig's Nighttime and Fuzzy Wuzzy. Some anglers fish two flies, one with a luminous body. When all else fails, try a daytime smelt pattern.

Smelt fishing along the beaches

Walking the beaches on a hot, bright day searching for smelting fish is my favourite form of fishing at Taupo. November and December are the best months. Wear shorts, sandshoes, hat, Polaroids and sunscreen. At times, schools of fish break the surface, throwing caution to the wind in their efforts to round up and feed on the tiny spawning fish.

A quick cast and a fast retrieve is required, using a floating line and a small smelt fly. In very calm, bright conditions, casting directly at fish frightens them. Try stalking with a slow sinking line and only retrieving when a fish approaches. This is an exciting way to fish, especially in the company of another angler, as one can spot for the other.

Shoreline smelt fly fishing, Western Bays, Taupo

From the end of March to the end of November, the vast majority of Taupo trout intent on spawning enter the rivers and streams flowing into the lake. By July the rivers are full of fish. By September many are spent and drift back downstream to the lake to recover. A run of fish usually enters a river as a fresh recedes and makes its way upstream over the next few days. The run may be spread over several kilometres of river and the rest of the river may be very quiet. Thirty days is the average time for a run of fish to reach the Whitikau tributary of the Tongariro River, although some make it in 18 days while others may take 80 days. Some fish spawn in the main stream itself. Most hens are caught soon after they enter the river and are moving upstream but jacks are more aggressive when guarding their territory and will snap at a lure or nymph at any time. After a period of fine weather try further upstream, but soon after a fresh try the lower reaches. It is important to change location on the river if the fishing is poor.

Trout tend to lie in the deeper parts of pools or under banks where there is maximum cover and protection. Each pool has a favoured lie, some having more than one. To be successful, an angler must cover the lie being fished at the same depth that the trout are holding. Usually this means dredging the bottom of the river. Trout will often move some distance sideways to intercept a lure or nymph fished at their depth but will seldom bother with lures that pass high overhead.

Downstream lure

In the smaller streams and rivers, a 6 or 7 weight rod and a reel holding a medium sinking line of similar weight can be used, but in the larger Tongariro River an 8 or 9 weight rod and a high density or shooting head line should be employed. Use a short tippet of 2–2.5 m with a breaking strain not less than 3.5 kg in the larger rivers, lighter in the smaller streams. The lure should be cast across or even slightly upstream on a long cast, the line mended two or three times as the lure sinks and the lure retrieved through the lie. The take usually occurs at the end of the swing and there is nothing as exciting as a fat, fresh-run rainbow smashing the fly. Subtle variations can be made with regard to casting, mending the line, covering each section of the pool and altering the speed of the retrieve. A downstream lure tends to be more successful when fished through a fresh run of fish. Fishing becomes hard during periods of low flow, clear water and bright sunny days. It pays to use smaller lures in these conditions.

Favoured lures in sizes 4–10 include Rabbit flies, Red Setter, Hairy Dog, Mrs Simpson, Mallard patterns and Woolly Buggers. Some anglers fish egg patterns on a sinking line.

Upstream nymph

The same weight rod can be used to fish nymphs and lures but, obviously, floating lines matching the rod weight are required to fish nymphs. On the larger rivers, where a long drift is important, I prefer a weight forward floater.

For the smaller streams, one weighted nymph with or without an indicator can be used, but on the Tongariro River most anglers use two nymphs and an indicator. The proximal nymph is often used simply as a weight while the distal nymph can be unweighted. It is unwise to use too heavy a rig as it can be very unwieldy and intimidating to cast. After a couple of blows to the back of the head from ultra-heavy nymphs the unfortunate angler can suffer mild concussion and be only too willing to return home. However, as mentioned earlier, it is pointless drifting your nymphs a metre or so over the fish's head. They must sink well down through the lie. The total length of the trace should be 4–4.5 m and the nymphs can be tied 30–50 cm apart. The strength of the trace will vary according to the water being fished but, generally, a simple knot-less length of nylon in the 2.5–4 kg range is preferred.

An indicator of wool or synthetic yarn soaked in floatant is usually tied to the first metre of leader by a simple overhand knot. The distance of the indicator from the nymphs is determined by the depth of water being fished. As a general rule, the distance should be one-and-a-half times the depth. However, if the nymphs are not touching the bottom of the river, the distance can be increased. To help the leader sink, some anglers reduce the surface tension by washing the leader in soap solution or detergent or running it through sand. Others use Fuller's Earth.

A long cast upstream with a long drift is very important in the Tongariro River as this ensures your nymphs have plenty of time to sink and drift deeply through the lie. Allow the nymphs to float down naturally, as drag will cause them to rise. Although contact should be maintained with the nymphs, some slack line can be an advantage as a perfectly straight-line cast will be affected by drag. The indicator should be watched like a hawk and any suspicion of sinking, deviating or slowing should immediately be acted upon by striking. All water can be explored with nymphs and pocket water should not be neglected. If you are first on a pool at dawn, the fish may well be sitting in shallow water, so try the edges first.

Favoured nymphs include Hare and Copper, Half Back, Pheasant Tail, White Caddis and Bug Eye. Egg patterns include a variety of Muppet and Glow Bug creations. The most common and successful rig for the Tongariro River is a well-weighted Bug Eye or Bead Head with an unweighted egg pattern.

 Favoured locations around Lake Taupo

Trout can be caught anywhere in Lake Taupo. Stream mouths are top locations, but many rocky points around the lake can also provide good fishing. Trout tend to cruise the blue line or drop-off, the junction between inshore shallows and deeper water. Before selecting a location to fish, make certain there is not a strong onshore wind.

Stream and river mouths

Mangakura Stream A small stream entering the lake 1 km north of the Waitahanui mouth. Is worth exploring when fish are smelting, and at night. You are unlikely to be disturbed by another angler.

Waitahanui River mouth The most famous river mouth on Lake Taupo, not because of the number of fish caught but because of the 'picket fence' or line of anglers easily viewed from the main highway. This is not the place for a beginner, as a long cast with a medium sinking line is essential if one is to compete with other anglers. After a westerly storm, the current will be forced along the beach and 200 m of the rip can be fished without wading. The mouth is also well known to anglers as a place to catch trophy brown trout, usually at night during February and March.

Otupata Creek Drains Rotongaio Lagoon. There is good smelt fishing south along the beach at the foot of White Cliffs all the way to Hatepe. The mouth is worth trying at night.

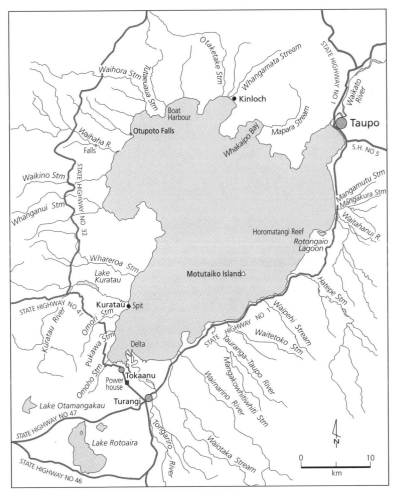

Lake Taupo

Hatepe Stream mouth When other rivers run dirty after rain, try this mouth. The Hatepe often remains clear as it drains the hydro dams. You can drive to the mouth. A favourite spot when fish are running.

Waitetoko Stream mouth A very small stream with a shallow mouth entering Manowharangi Bay. Suits a floating line at night.

Tauranga–Taupo River mouth Before wading and fishing this mouth at night, anglers are strongly advised to inspect it during the day. It is very deep and can be dangerous for wading, but there is good fishing off the spit. Many anglers fish it from an anchored boat positioned so they can cast over the deep lip with a fast sinking line. The fishing can be excellent, especially at night.

Waipehi Stream mouth There is a delightful rest area beneath the kowhai trees at this small stream mouth. It is shallow and rocky but trout often come in very close at night so deep wading is unnecessary. Fishes well all year but use a floating line.

Waimarino River mouth Take the rough track off SH 1 just south of the Waimarino bridge to the mouth then walk north along the beach. The drop-off can only be fished when the lake is low, as a long wade out may be needed in order to reach it. At this point the

Relaxed fishing, Taupo stream mouth

current is barely perceptible and a few changes of position may be necessary before the hot spot is reached. Use a fast or medium sinking line, cast over the lip and wait a few minutes before retrieving. If the lake level is above normal carry a landing net, otherwise fish will need to be beached 100 m behind you. Fishes well all year but beware of a strong nor'easter. Some anglers fish this mouth with large Glow Bugs using the 'heave and leave' method, while others have success fishing Booby flies.

Waiotaka Stream mouth Turn off SH 1 onto Frethey's Road and the yacht club car park and walk south along the beach to the mouth. This medium-sized stream has a shallow mouth, best fished with a floating line. Has a reputation for large browns that feed at night on tadpoles and frogs washed out of the surrounding swamp after heavy rain. This mouth can be 'hot' at times.

Tongariro River mouth The Delta is a prime fishing spot, but can only be reached by boat. The severe floods of 1998 changed the Main mouth. The selection of which mouth to fish is governed by wind direction. The boat should be anchored with the transom barely hanging over the lip. Use a fast sinking or high density line, cast out as far as possible over the lip and wait a few minutes before retrieving. Be very careful if you decide to land as wading along the deep soft pumice lip can be hazardous. In favourable conditions, fishing at the Delta can be quite superb.

Tokaanu tailrace From November to February, when the smelt are running, the screens at the Tokaanu power house impede upstream progress. Schools of these tiny fish gather in confusion and are easy prey to marauding trout. At times, good fly fishing can be had from the banks of the tailrace, especially upstream of the main road bridge. Weed can cause difficulties at times but the tailrace has a reputation for large trout.

Fish can also be caught at the mouth of the tailrace and from Tokaanu Wharf close by. The tailrace is open all year but fishing is not permitted between the power house and a marker located approximately 110 m downstream. Spinning is permitted below the SH 41 bridge.

Tokaanu, Omoho (Slip), Pukawa and Omori stream mouths All can be reached from SH 41 between Tokaanu and Kuratau. They should be fished at night with floating lines. False casting is recommended, and there is room for only two or three rods at each mouth. Little wading is needed. Most fish well all year. Fishing the streams is not permitted.

Kuratau River mouth This shallow delta is safe to wade and the fishing can be excellent when trout are smelting. Use a floating line during the day and at night.

The Kuratau Spit, a few hundred metres south of the mouth, is well worth fishing as the lip runs close inshore.

Whareroa Stream mouth Can be accessed by car from the Kuratau hydro road, which runs off SH 32. This is another relatively shallow mouth which fishes well along the beach during the smelting season. Large browns can be caught at night 50 m south of the mouth, especially when the current parallels the shore.

Whanganui Stream mouth This is in the most inaccessible of the western bays and generally access is by boat. There is a rough private road through Wharerawa Block on SH 32 but this is unreliable and has been completely washed out at times, becoming impassable even for 4WDs. Over the past few years, and especially when the lake has been low, boats have been unable to shelter in the river mouth. During the smelting season, there is very good stream mouth and beach fishing. Use either a floating or slow sinking line. If action is slow at the rip, try either end of the beach. Usually there is good night fishing at the stream mouth, but like all Taupo stream mouths it can be dead at times.

The Whanganui Stream is open to fishing from 1 December to 31 May. A long wade upstream or a scramble through scrub takes you to the pool below the falls. There are usually a few fish in this pool although casting against the down-draft created by the falls can be taxing.

Waikino Stream mouth This stream gushes out of a rocky cleft between the Whanganui and Waihaha bays. There is a peg in the rock on the north side of the current where a boat can be tied up. Use a high density line to reach the fish that can be clearly seen feeding deeply in the current. At times, night fishing can be hot, even off the rocky shelf to the south, but it is a long way from home if the wind gets up.

Waihaha River mouth Access is by boat; the nearest boat ramp is at Kinloch. The bay can be reached by walking through bush down a steep track from the end of Waihaha Road off SH 32. Although this mouth changes frequently during storms it is usually deep enough to shelter a boat. Private camping can also be arranged with the owners. Fishing is best when the river current flows in the direction of Whakatonga (Richwhite) Point. During smelting, there is good beach and river-mouth fishing and also interesting fishing off the point itself. It is useful if a friend sits up high on the point and spots.

The river is navigable for small boats up as far as Tieke Falls. There are usually a few fish in the falls pool. The season for the river is 1 December–31 May.

Otupoto Falls Enters the lake at the southern end of Waihora Bay. The usual method of fishing is trolling through the current but fly casting from a boat is also popular.

Waihora River mouth Access is by boat from Kinloch but there is an excellent sheltered harbour close by in Boat Harbour at Kawakawa Point. There is good night fishing at this mouth and fish cruise and smelt along the beach in November and December. A few large browns often lie deep in the lower reaches of the river but these are very wary and difficult to catch.

Tutaeuaua (Chinaman's) Creek This small stream enters the southern end of Kawakawa Bay. Access is generally by boat but there is a private 4WD track off Whangamata Road to the cliff top. From there a walking track leads down through the bush to the beach. The stream mouth is ten minutes' walk along the beach to the north. The usual methods apply to this shallow mouth, including false casting, resting it periodically and fishing with a floating line. Wading is usually unnecessary. Holds two rods comfortably and fishes best at night.

Otaketake Stream mouth This tiny stream can only be reached by wading round a rocky point at the western end of Whangamata Bay when the lake is low.

Whangamata Stream mouth Reached by walking west along the beach from Kinloch. Fish the mouth with a floating line at night.

Mapara Stream mouth This small stream enters the eastern end of Whakaipo Bay. The mouth is very popular and heavily fished, especially at night. A strong southerly or westerly wind will make it unfishable. Use a floating or sink-tip line and the usual night lures.

The eastern shoreline of Whakaipo Bay, south of the Mapara mouth, also fishes well when trout are smelting.

Trolling and harling Lake Taupo

See the beginning of this chapter for the principal regulations.

More trout are taken from Lake Taupo by anglers fishing from boats than by any other method. Small boats can be launched from most beaches. Public boat ramps for larger craft can be found at the Waikato River outlet, Acacia Bay, Kinloch, Kuratau Spit, Waihi, Tokaanu Wharf, Motuoapa and Four Mile Bay or Wharewaka. Permits are required before using these ramps.

In Maori the lake is sometimes called Taupo-hau-rau (lake of a hundred winds) because of the strong southerly that can blow up unexpectedly. A short, steep chop of 1.5 m can be very troublesome even for a 5 m boat and a 60 hp outboard. Anglers are strongly advised to carry the same safety equipment as if fishing offshore at sea.

The VHF radio network for Taupo operates on channels 61, 6 and 8. Weather forecasts provided by the coastguard are broadcast at 0915, 1215, 1615 and 2015. Cellphones can also be useful.

Trout can be caught anywhere in the lake, even in the middle, but favoured trolling locations include Whanganui Bay, Kawakawa Bay, Whangamata Bay, Whakaipo Reef, Mine Bay, Rangitira Point, off the Waitahanui River mouth (more than 300 m), and Horomatangi Reef off Rotongaio.

From September to February, when trout are smelting near the surface, harling a smelt fly on a fly rod rigged with a high density line can be very effective. Boat speed must be kept to a minimum either by using a small auxiliary outboard motor or slowing the boat with a sea anchor. Let out the whole fly line and 20 m of backing so the fly sinks sufficiently. The trace should be 5–6 m long. Following the blue line or drop-off is recommended.

Flies to use include Parsons' Glory, Ginger Mick, Orange, Yellow and Green Rabbit, Taupo Tiger, Grey Ghost, and Green and Yellow Orbit in sizes 4 to 6.

In the autumn and winter, trout feed in much deeper water and wire and lead lines and down-riggers come into their own. A wire line sinks deeper than either a lead line or a down-rigger restricted to 40 m, but has a nasty tendency to tangle. A down-rigger provides more sport as once a fish is hooked and breaks clear of the rigger, it can be played on a light, unweighted mono-filament line. Fish hooked on a wire line often initially feel like a piece of weed. Many variations can be tried, with some anglers using only a colour or two of lead line incorporated into their monofilament line. If using monofilament it pays to use 8 kg strength and let out 80–100 m. Do not turn the boat too sharply when trolling and be aware of other boats in your area. If a fish is hooked and boated, turn and troll back through the same area. Don't forget to take a landing net.

Spinners to try include Toby and Cobra variations, Flatfish and Zed spinners or different colours and sizes.

Spinning in Lake Taupo

Spinning is only permitted in the lake and in the Tokaanu tailrace below the main road bridge. Remember to keep 300 m away from stream mouths. No weight can be added to the spinner. Only a single hook is legal.

Taupo rainbow caught smelt fly fishing

Few anglers use this method on Taupo but it is an ideal way for a beginner to start fishing. Fish can be caught anywhere in the lake and a silvery coloured spinner is very effective when trout are smelting.

Rivers flowing into Lake Taupo

Waitahanui River

Location Rises from springs in the northern end of Kaimanawa Forest Park and flows generally west to enter Lake Taupo a few kilometres south of Taupo township.

Access *Headwaters* From forestry roads behind Iwitahi on SH 5. Although permission is required from the Forestry Corporation it is hardly worth the trouble as the river is deep, overgrown and impossible to fish.

Upper reaches Access to the upper pools is from Blake Road, which leaves SH 1 south of Waitahanui Bridge. There are walking tracks along the banks.

Middle reaches Mill Road, also from SH 1, leads to the middle pools.

Lower reaches From SH 1 either side of the main road bridge.

Mouth From a walking track off SH 1 north of Waitahanui Bridge.

Season Above Te Arero Stream confluence, 1 December–31 May. Below Te Arero Stream confluence, the main river is open all year. For the Mangamutu tributary joining the Waitahanui immediately above the main road bridge, 1 December–31 May.

Because this medium-sized river is spring-fed, it seldom discolours after rain. The riverbed is rock, stone and fine pumice, and above the middle reaches the banks are scrub-covered. Below Waitahanui Bridge, fishing pressure is usually very intense, especially after fresh-run fish have entered the river. Most anglers fish this section with a heavy sinking line and lure, although some anglers nymph the pools either side of the bridge. In some sections in bright conditions when the water is clear, fish can be spotted. Around Easter and after a good southerly storm, many fish can be seen under the main road bridge.

The middle and upper pools offer a different challenge. While there are 7 km of river to fish and some pools are relatively straightforward, others are overgrown by manuka scrub and are very difficult to fish. The river is swift in parts but there are some excellent, deep holding pools. Downstream lure fishing with a high density line and upstream nymphing methods are equally popular. The river can be waded, but some runs are deep and swift and care should be taken. Angling pressure is much lower in these reaches of river and the surroundings are very tranquil and pleasant. The usual lures and nymphs, as described in the introductory section on fishing Taupo rivers, can be used.

Hatepe (Hinemaiaia) Stream

Location Drains the western boundary of Kaimanawa Forest Park between the Waitahanui and Waipehi watersheds, flows north-west and enters Lake Taupo at the village of Hatepe on SH 1.

Access The headwaters and upper reaches have been severely modified for hydro-electricity generation and are not worth exploring.

Middle pools, Waitahanui River

Middle reaches An access track runs upstream on the true left bank off SH 1 on the south side of the Hatepe bridge. This takes you to the limit of fishing, 300 m below the dam and marked by a sign.
Lower reaches Downstream from the SH 1 bridge or upstream from the mouth.
Season Above the main road bridge, 1 December–31 May. Below this bridge the river is open all year.

Above the bridge, this small stream has some moderately deep holes and good lies against the banks although overhanging vegetation can impede casting in some sections. Hooked fish have every chance of escaping by diving under sunken logs and tangling round snags. Fluctuations in water flow from hydro-electric operations have caused bank erosion and deterioration in recent years. However, at times there is still good nymph and downstream lure fishing. Some trout can be spotted but many lie protected and hidden under the banks.

'Picket fence' at the Waitahanui stream mouth

Below the bridge, the water is better suited to downstream lure fishing. Roll-cast or float your line downstream and retrieve slowly and deeply against the banks.

The Hatepe (Hinemaiaia) hydro dams also hold fish but are hardly worth visiting. The top dam holds brook trout but silting of the dam has ruined the fishery. Permission to fish can be obtained from Taupo Electricity in Manuka Street, Taupo. Access is from Hatepe hydro road, south of Taupo Airport. The middle dam holds small rainbows. Access is from a side road near Hatepe.

Tauranga–Taupo River

Location Rises in Kaimanawa Forest Park, flows north-west, initially through native bush, then exotic forest and, lastly, pastoral land, to enter Lake Taupo near Te Rangiita.

Access *Headwaters* From Kiko Road, which leaves SH 1 south of the main road bridge over the Tauranga–Taupo River. As there is usually a locked gate on Kiko Road a lot of walking is required to fish this section of river unless a mountain bike is used.

Upper reaches The river can be explored from the Ranger's Pool simply by walking upstream and into a gorge.

Middle reaches (above SH 1 bridge) Quarry Road leaves SH 1 opposite the Te Rangiita store on the north side of the bridge. From Quarry Road, take the first unsealed branch road to the right. This is a private road and the owners charge an access fee from time to time. A permit can be obtained from the Te Rangiita store if required. There are numerous rough branch tracks off this road that lead to the river but the road ends in a car park at the location of the old Crescent Pool. A 4WD is an advantage as these tracks are often rough and partially underwater. From the car park, walking tracks follow upstream on the true right bank to the Cliff Pool. Here the river can be crossed, as the main track now follows up the true left bank as far as the Ranger's Pool. However, recent floods have damaged the track in some sections. There is also an access track to the lower section behind the service station south of the main road bridge.

Lower reaches and mouth From Heuheu Parade just south of the main road bridge.

Season Above the Ranger's Pool and the Mangakowhitiwhiti Stream, 1 December–31 May. Below the Mangakowhitiwhiti Stream the river is open for fishing all year.

This medium-sized river suffered severely during the 1998 floods and the well-known Crescent Pool has been lost. The river simply cut through and isolated the Crescent, which is now almost dry. However, although most of the other pools changed they have remained more or less in their old locations. Fish can be caught throughout the whole river right up to the falls in the headwaters.

The upper reaches and headwaters should be fished in summer after 1 December.

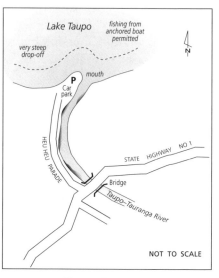

Taupo-Tauranga River mouth

There is sight fishing for both recovering and resident rainbows but anglers need to be reasonably fit to fish this section. Trout will take dry flies and nymphs but a lot of scrambling and walking is required as there are some gorgy sections to get through.

By far the most popular and heavily fished section is the middle reaches. A few resident fish remain after the spawning runs but the time to fish this river is between the end of March and the end of September and preferably after a fresh. With luck, the river will be full of fighting fresh-run rainbows and the fishing can be very exciting. Although some fish can be spotted, the majority hide under banks, logs and riffles or lie deep in pools. This is an easy river to fish as crossings can usually be made without difficulty and wading is safe. As the banks are mostly clear for casting, all sections of water can be covered. Fish are caught equally on nymphs and

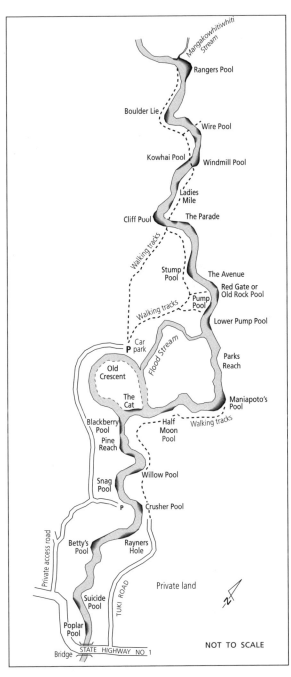

Mangakowhitiwhiti Stream

Rangers Pool

Boulder Lie

Wire Pool

Kowhai Pool

Windmill Pool

Ladies Mile

Cliff Pool

The Parade

Walking tracks

Stump Pool

The Avenue

Red Gate or Old Rock Pool

Walking tracks

Pump Pool

Lower Pump Pool

Car park

P

Flood Stream

Parks Reach

Old Crescent

The Cat

Maniapoto's Pool

Blackberry Pool

Half Moon Pool

Walking tracks

Pine Reach

Snag Pool

Willow Pool

P

Crusher Pool

Private access road

Betty's Pool

Rayners Hole

TUKI ROAD

Private land

N

Suicide Pool

Poplar Pool

Bridge

STATE HIGHWAY NO 1

NOT TO SCALE

Taupo-Tauranga River

lures although lure fishing becomes hard when the river is low and clear. Do not neglect to fish for trout lying under banks of blackberry. They will take both lures and nymphs. At times, this river seems almost barren of fish but a shower or two of rain and the action returns once more. The lies are not difficult to recognise. In the deeper pools, the lie is usually toward the tail of the pool where the current is less strong. Most fish can be beached on the shingle toward the tail of runs and pools so a landing net is not required. There is a good two days' fishing on this river up to the Rangers Pool but you will seldom fish it on your own.

Waimarino River

Location Drains the western boundary of Kaimanawa Forest Park, and flows north-west by Korohe Pa to enter Lake Taupo north of Turangi.

Access *Upper reaches* Unless a friend drops you off at Korohe Pa from Korohe Road, a lot of walking is required, as parking your vehicle on SH 1 is recommended.

Middle reaches This stretch of water lies between SH 1 and Korohe Pa. SH 1 crosses the river and a vehicle access track leads up the true left bank for a short distance. The top section is accessed from Korohe Road, which leads to Korohe Crossing.

Lower reaches Can be accessed from the SH 1 bridge or alternatively from the mouth. A shingle vehicle track runs from SH 1 down the true left or southern bank, albeit some distance from the river, and one can then walk north along the lake shore to the mouth.

Season Above Korohe Crossing, 1 December–31 May. Below Korohe Crossing the river is open all year.

In the upper reaches of this small river, trout can run up to the falls in the vicinity of Te Pahatu trig. There are usually a few resident trout but early in the season most fish will be recovering spawners. There are some delightful pools and runs for anglers prepared to walk and scramble. The banks of scrub, native bush and exotic forest do not impede casting although drag can be a problem when fishing short pools. The river is easy to cross and fish can be spotted.

In the middle reaches, there are a few pools upstream from SH 1 that hold run fish, more so after a fresh. These are easily sighted and can be taken on nymphs, especially early in the day. Some anglers also have success by fishing a downstream lure under the banks of toetoe, scrub and grass. It is hard to bypass a Red Setter or Orange Rabbit but if the river is high or slightly discoloured, try a green-bodied lure.

The lower reaches are more overgrown and there is less holding water, but after rain fish can be taken on a lure well sunk and fished downstream by roll-casting.

Waiotaka Stream

Location Runs parallel to and south of the Waimarino.
Access The upper reaches, running through Hautu Prison farm, are now closed to anglers.
Middle reaches From SH 1 there are two signposted access tracks. Alternatively, take the first road right north of the Tongariro River bridge out of Turangi. Do not be tempted to go to Hautu Prison but continue on until Hautu Ford across the Waiotaka is reached. A walking track leads downstream from the ford on the true left bank.
Season Above Hautu Ford (there is a marker 100 m upstream), 1 December–31 May. Below this marker the river is open all year.

Although this small to medium-sized stream is fast flowing and overgrown by scrub in parts there is good fishing for run fish, especially after rain. The pool immediately above the ford is very popular with guides and beginners as there is every chance of catching a fish. There is not a lot of holding water in this river but fish sheltering in deep water under banks can be tempted by a lure fished downstream. Nymphing is generally more difficult because scrub along the banks may prevent an accurate cast and a good long drift. It is wise to carry a landing net as a hooked fish will turn and run downstream very rapidly. There are few spots where a fish can be easily beached and underwater snags present problems. It is generally not over-crowded by anglers.

Tongariro River

Location Drains the Kaimanawa ranges by way of its major tributary, the Waipakahi River, and Lake Rotoaira by way of the Poutu River and canal. The upper reaches have been modified for hydro-electric power generation. The main river flows generally north through the outskirts of Turangi to enter Lake Taupo 10 km north of that township.

Access In July 1998, two major floods one week apart severely affected this world-famous river and, as well as changing many pools, also washed out numerous access tracks. Some of these have been repaired while others may never be restored to their original condition.

Upper reaches (*above the Fence Pool*) Access becomes difficult for anglers walking upstream as there are few tracks through the bush and the river gorges. For anglers intent on fishing this section it is best to raft downstream from below the hydro dam. Access to the dam and Beggs Pool from SH 1 is by way of Access 10 and Kaimanawa Road.

Middle reaches (*between the Fence Pool and SH 1 bridge*) There are numerous access points:

- At Poutu Bridge on SH 1 south of Turangi there is a rough vehicle track that now only goes as far as the Breakaway car park. Pools upstream from this point can only be reached by walking. A branch off this track to the left leads to the re-formed Dreadnought Pool. Be careful when turning out of this track back onto the main highway as visibility is poor.
- A walking access track off SH 1 about 100 m south of the Red Hut car park leads to both Waddells pools.
- Red Hut car park is clearly signposted. A swingbridge crosses the river to access tracks that lead both up- and downstream on the right bank.
- Marked access track to the Duchess Pool off SH 1.
- National Trout Centre Hatchery. Gate closure times are marked but one can either park inside in the car park or outside the

gate. Tracks lead to Barlows, Birch, Silly and the Duchess pools on the true left bank.

- Admirals Pool Road, signposted off SH 1, leads to Kamahi, a new Admirals Pool and the Stag on the true left bank.
- Kutai Street, off Taupahi Road, leads to the Hydro Pool.
- The access to the Major Jones car park, footbridge and pool are signposted from Taupahi Road. It is prudent to lock your car and leave nothing of value inside. Tracks run up- and downstream from this footbridge.
- Arahori Road, off Taupahi Road, leads to the Island Pool.
- Te Aho Road, off Taupahi Road, leads to Judges Pool.

Lower reaches (downstream from the main road bridge)

- An access track leads downstream on the true left bank immediately below the main road bridge. There is a marked access track on the true right bank from the end of Herekiekie Street which runs off Grace Road north of the bridge.
- A vehicle track leaves Tautahanga Road at the back of Turangi township to the true left bank. This has been severely damaged by the floods and is washed out below Bain Pool. Foot access only is now possible below this.
- Bain Pool car park on the right bank can be accessed off Grace Road. The track downstream to the Reed Pool has been damaged but will probably re-form simply from anglers walking downstream.
- Access further downstream on the left bank via Hirangi and Awamate roads has been severely affected, with the lower end of Awamate Road still under water. There is still foot access, however, for those anglers prepared for a long walk.

Season Above the Fence Pool, 1 December–31 May. Below the Fence Pool the river is open for fishing all year.

Tongariro Pools

The major floods in July 1998 significantly altered this large river to the point where some anglers used to fishing it for years virtually gave up in disgust. They were the third and fourth largest floods on record. The Whitikau, Boulder and Fan pools have not only been destroyed but the boulder itself has disappeared from the

Boulder Pool. However, there are compensations as new pools have been formed and much of the silt and ash from the Ruapehu eruptions has been flushed out of the river. The Dreadnought Pool, famous in Zane Grey's time, has re-formed. The naming of the Tongariro Pools is steeped in history and although some of the pools have gone, new pools close to the original locations have been given the old names. Some new pools have been given the title 'upper' or 'lower' depending on their location and with reference to the major pool.

The term 'lie' is frequently used when describing a pool. It simply indicates where trout lie or are expected to lie in the pool. When trout run up the river to spawn, they often run at night and rest during the day in a lie. This is usually a deep, slower-flowing, sheltered section of the pool where fish can conserve their energy. The following is a brief outline of the main pools and the changes that have occurred. Remember, 'true right' and 'true left' refer to the river when looking downstream.

Big water on the Tongariro River

Middle reaches

Fence Pool It is a 25-minute walk upstream from the Breakaway car park to this pool. The Fence has been fishing well from the true left bank. There is a lie on the true right toward the tail of the pool that can be nymphed but the river crossing can be very difficult.

Sand Pool This pool has remained unscathed and is still deep and swirly, making it difficult to get a good drift. Best fished from the true left bank. The tail of the pool can still be crossed in low water by tall anglers but now that the Whitikau Pool has gone there is no great advantage to be gained.

Blue Pool This very large, long, deep and stable pool is still fishing well although it has changed. The lie runs the length of the pool and is over against the cliff. The middle section is difficult to wade as there is deep water on the outside of a large log. No longer can an angler wade down the centre of the pool and fish! A long cast is still required to cover the lie, with the lower section easier to reach. It is a 20-minute walk from the Breakaway car park.

Big Bend Pool This pool lies well above the bend and offers good fishing from both sides of the river. The lie on the right side is toward the tail but it is a 35-minute walk upriver to this pool from the Red Hut swingbridge.

Fan Pool The old Fan Pool has disappeared and been replaced by a pool further upstream. On the true left, a swift sidestream needs to be crossed before fishing but the pool looks promising.

Breakaway Pool This pool has suffered from the floods and does not hold the numbers of fish that it used to. However, there is a good lie toward the tail of the pool on the right bank, and the left bank still fishes reasonably well. Angling pressure is now much lower.

Cliff Pool Has entirely changed and now runs hard against the cliff on the left bank. It is deep and smooth and slow flowing toward the tail. Can only be fished from the right and this means a 20-minute walk upriver from the Red Hut bridge and the crossing of a small side creek.

Dreadnought Pool The original pool lay just upstream from the Poutu confluence. This new pool lies further upstream and is fishing very well, especially from the left bank. The right bank is covered with bush and scrub. You can drive to this pool with a 4WD

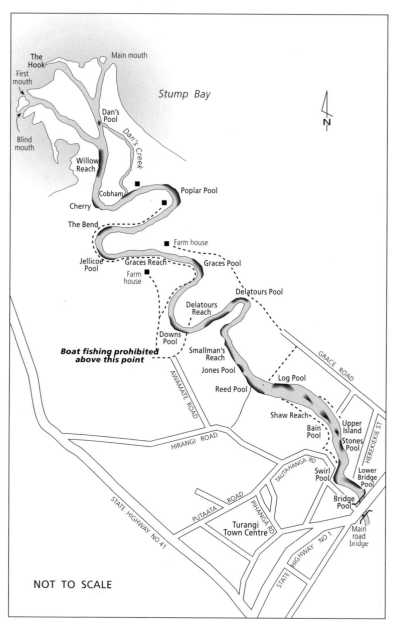

The Hook
First mouth
Blind mouth
Main mouth

Stump Bay

Dan's Pool

Dan's Creek

Willow Reach

Cobham
Cherry
Poplar Pool

The Bend

Farm house

Jellicoe Pool
Graces Reach
Graces Pool
Farm house

Delatours Pool

Delatours Reach

Downs Pool

Boat fishing prohibited above this point

Smallman's Reach

Jones Pool

Reed Pool

Log Pool

GRACE ROAD

AWAMATE ROAD

HIRANGI ROAD

Shaw Reach

Bain Pool

Upper Island

Stones Pool

HEREKIEKIE ST

TAUTAHANGA RD

Swirl Pool

Lower Bridge Pool

PUTAATA ROAD

PIHANGA RD

Bridge Pool

Main road bridge

STATE HIGHWAY NO 41

Turangi Town Centre

STATE HIGHWAY NO 1

NOT TO SCALE

Lower Tongariro River

by taking the left branch of the Breakaway access track at Poutu Bridge. It has become very popular because of the easy access and good-looking water.

Poutu Pool Still lies against the cliff at the mouth of the Poutu River. It is a deep, stable pool and can be accessed by crossing the Red Hut swingbridge and walking upstream.

Upper Waddells Pool This new pool is best fished from the left bank and is yielding some good bags of fish. It is an easy pool to fish and in my opinion will become very popular.

Waddells Pool This pool runs against a cliff on the right bank and can only be fished from the left bank. There is a foot track to both Waddells pools off SH 1 about 100 m south of the Red Hut car park.

Red Hut Pool Has changed considerably but still fishes well from the right bank. Cross the swingbridge from the Red Hut car park and walk down to the river.

Lower Red Hut Pool This rather small new pool just downstream from the Red Hut Pool is also promising and recently yielded a beautiful 3 kg rainbow hen to a visiting angler. Again, fishes well from the right bank.

Shag Pool Still deep and swirly so it is not easy to get a good drift. Walk downstream from the Red Hut bridge and fish it from the right bank.

Unnamed pool — Upper Duchess? This new, promising pool is best fished from the left bank but the lower reaches on the right can be nymphed until deep water runs against a cliff. Access to the right is difficult as one needs to drop down steeply through the bush. Walk upstream from the Duchess Pool for the left bank.

Duchess Pool Has completely changed and is now swifter and shallower than previously. Can be fished from either bank. At present the easiest access to the left bank is by walking upstream from the National Trout Centre Hatchery.

Silly Pool Has improved with the flood and can be fished from both sides although a cliff restricts fishing the right side mid-way up the pool.

Birch Pools These have virtually joined up since the flood and are not easy to define. Best fished from the left although the tail can be nymphed from the right. Access is from the National Trout Centre Hatchery.

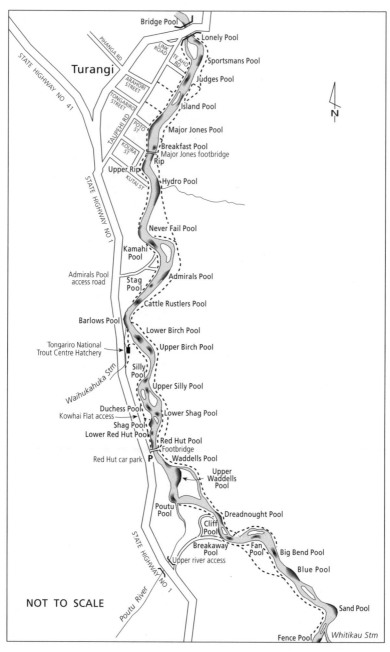

Bridge Pool

PIHANGA RD

LINK ROAD

Lonely Pool

TE AHO RD

Sportsmans Pool

Turangi

ARAHORI STREET

Judges Pool

TONGARIRO STREET

POTO ST

Island Pool

STATE HIGHWAY NO 41

TAUPEHI RD

Major Jones Pool

KOURA ST

Breakfast Pool

Major Jones footbridge

Upper Rip

KUTAI ST

Rip

Hydro Pool

STATE HIGHWAY NO 1

Never Fail Pool

Kamahi Pool

Admirals Pool access road

Stag Pool

Admirals Pool

Cattle Rustlers Pool

Barlows Pool

Lower Birch Pool

Tongariro National Trout Centre Hatchery

Upper Birch Pool

Waihukahuka Stm

Silly Pool

Upper Silly Pool

Duchess Pool

Kowhai Flat access

Lower Shag Pool

Shag Pool

Lower Red Hut Pool

Red Hut Pool

Footbridge

Red Hut car park **P**

Waddells Pool

Upper Waddells Pool

Poutu Pool

Dreadnought Pool

Cliff Pool

STATE HIGHWAY NO 1

Breakaway Pool

Upper river access

Fan Pool

Big Bend Pool

Blue Pool

NOT TO SCALE

Poutu River

Sand Pool

Fence Pool

Whitikau Stm

N

Middle Tongariro River

Barlows Pool Can now be fished from either bank although a cliff on the left restricts fishing from that bank. The left bank is fished from the Trout Centre while the right bank can be accessed by walking 20 minutes upstream from the Major Jones swingbridge or a similar walk downstream from the Red Hut swingbridge.

Cattle Rustlers Pool Fishes best from the right bank but some nymphing is also possible from the left. Has also changed significantly.

Admirals Pool This has changed location and now lies further upstream. Best waded and fished from the left bank to a lie against the right bank. You can drive in on Admirals Pool Road.

Kamahi Pool This pool is now good from both banks. Access to the left bank is from Admirals Pool Road. The right bank can be fished by walking upstream from the Major Jones swingbridge.

Never Fail Pool This small pool should be fished from the right as it runs against a cliff. Cross the Major Jones swingbridge and walk upstream. There is a branch off the main track to the pool.

Hydro Pool This is still a very productive pool, especially for large browns, but the left side of the pool has filled in with stones and become more shallow. Wading is now easier from the left bank and the lie against the right bank can be easily covered with a good cast. Fish are still taken from various high perches along the right bank. Access is from Kutai Street, or walk upstream from the Major Jones swingbridge for the right bank. Angling pressure is usually very high on this pool. It pays to fish at dawn for trophy browns.

Major Jones Pool This long, deep, stable pool is still the largest on the river and although some changes have occurred the fishing is very much the same as before the floods. A long cast from the right bank is still required to satisfactorily cover the lies. The tail can still be nymphed although the lies have changed.

Island Pool This pool has improved and is still fished from the left bank after crossing the side stream. The side stream itself also holds fish.

Judges Pool This long pool offers excellent water from both banks although lure fishing is best from the right side. It is a long pool which slows and shallows out toward the tail and can be crossed in low water. Nymphing is good from the left bank, with access from

Te Aho Road. Walk downstream for 15 minutes from the Major Jones swingbridge to fish the right bank. There is a side track on the left through a small creek.

Sportsmans Pool This is still fished from the left bank. Walk downstream from Judges Pool.

Lonely Pool Although it changed a couple of years before the 1998 floods, this pool remains in its new location against the cliff. Fishes best from the left by walking down from Judges or up from the main road bridge. Scrub on the back-cast can be a nuisance.

Lower reaches

Bridge Pool This is now smaller and extends upstream under the Tongariro River bridge. Access to the left bank is from a track at the car park. Access to the right bank is from the Herekiekie Street track or through scrub by the bridge.

Lower Bridge Pool This excellent, popular new pool is heavily fished and easily observed downstream from the main road bridge. Access is on the left from the track at the car park and on the right from the Herekiekie Street track. Best in my opinion from the left bank.

Swirl Pool Has also changed since the floods and become long and narrow. Best from the right bank.

The Stones Pool This is now a small pool near the stop bank. Not very productive to fish.

Upper Island Pool This has also changed and is best fished from the left bank as the lie runs on the right side of the pool. Access is from the track off Tautahanga Road and then by wading through a small side stream.

Bain Pool This large, deep pool is best fished from the right although a willow stump is a bother on the back-cast when fishing downstream lures. Access via a car park down a shingle road off Grace Road.

The 1998 floods were so severe that the pools below Bain Pool lost definition and the river has become a somewhat featureless, snag-infested, slow-flowing canal. The stony riverbed is now silt-covered, the banks show evidence of having been under water and the walking tracks have been obliterated. Many of the willows have either died or have been swept into the river. Some stretches are so snag-infested that a fly shop located on the bank would make a handsome profit. The vehicle track is washed out beyond Bain Pool so the left bank downstream from here is only accessible by walking.

Shaw Reach If you can identify this reach it is best fished from the left.

Log Pool This is one of the better lower-river pools, with enough definition to determine where it begins and where it ends. Can only be fished from the left because of trees along the right bank. Walk down through the willows from Bain Pool.

Reed Pool It is very difficult to determine where the lies are now located in this once very popular and productive pool. It can still be nymphed from the left bank but, just as before the floods, fishing is best from the right. However, snags are a major problem for lure anglers with a long cast, especially as most fish appear to hold close to the left bank.

Below the Reed Pool, the river is one long canal and not worth describing in detail. The pool definition may well return in time but the floods have caused so much havoc that the lower end of Awamate Road is still under water and the farmhouse has been evacuated. Snags continue to be a problem all the way down to the Poplar Pool. No lies could be defined and no fish were landed when I last walked the river. No doubt it will gradually improve as it obviously has done in the past.

It is wise to be acutely aware of etiquette before fishing the Tongariro River. Angling pressure can at times be very heavy and some anglers become very protective of their stretch of water. It is important to move either downstream or upstream with every few casts and not hog one section of river.

The river can be crossed in a few spots by fit, competent anglers well aware of the riverbed geography but this is a large swift-flowing river and risks should be kept to a minimum. It is not an easy river for the novice as generally a long cast, often with well-weighted nymphs, is required to cover the lies. However, trout use the main river for spawning as well as access to the tributaries. Although the important pools have been described, fish often lie elsewhere such as in pocket water or close to the banks, especially early in the morning. Try some unusual spots away from other anglers.

The middle reaches upstream from the SH 1 bridge are more picturesque, with patches of manuka scrub and native bush growing along the banks. Below this bridge, the river is more open with gravel banks lined by willows.

In summer, when angling pressure is at a minimum, good dry fly fishing on mending fish can be obtained. The Major Jones Pool has a reputation for summer fishing. Try an Elk Hair Caddis or a soft hackle wet fly towards evening. Large browns also enter the lower river in January. These will accept dry flies during the day or a well-sunk green Woolly Bugger fished across and downstream.

In conclusion, this world famous river still maintains its reputation. Trout average a little under 2 kg but there is always the chance of a trophy fish. There is no better place to be than the Tongariro River when the action is hot, but during spells of dry, sunny weather, the fishing becomes very slow.

Poutu River

Location and access SH 1 crosses this small river a few kilometres south of Turangi. A walking track follows upstream on the true left bank from the bridge.

Only a short stretch of water immediately above the bridge, and the pool below the falls a few hundred yards upstream, are worth exploring when fish are running in to spawn. The banks are overgrown with bracken and blackberry.

Waipakihi River

Location and access Drains Middle Range in Kaimanawa Forest Park and flows west to become the Tongariro River. Access from the Desert Road to Hell's Gate, or the Kaimanawa access road (Access 10) and a two- to three-hour tramp over the Umukarikari Range.

Although there are some likely looking pools in this headwater river, flooding and an unstable gravel bed keep trout stocks low. It is only worth a look if you are tramping in the vicinity. The gin-clear mountain water allows fish to be easily spotted. Trout cannot run upstream from the Tongariro River because of the hydro-electric power scheme.

The lower reaches of the Tongariro River

Rivers flowing out of Lake Taupo

Only the large Waikato River, severely modified for power generation, drains this large lake. The section of river between the outlet and the Huka Falls lies in the Taupo area. It is open for fishing all year but access is very difficult due to its gorgy nature, overhanging scrub and the lack of public access roads. Anglers intent on fishing this difficult water should also be very alert to sudden changes in water level. Few survive being swept over Huka Falls. The upper Waikato River is described in the section on the Eastern region.

Location and access SH 46 circles the southern shores where the Rotoaira Fishing Camp is located. Te Ponanga Saddle Road from Turangi and SH 47 skirt the northern shore.

Season 1 September–30 June.

Restrictions As the lake is privately owned, anglers must obtain an entry permit from the Rotoaira Fishing Camp in addition to a Taupo licence and abide by the owners' regulations.

Boat launching From the Rotoaira Fishing Camp. Small boats can be launched at the Wairehu Canal.

This moderate-sized natural lake has a swampy, difficult shoreline so nearly all fishing is done from boats. Harling a fly, casting from a boat or trolling a spinner can all be productive as the stocks of rainbows are high. It's best fished from April to June when fish should be in good condition and average 1–2 kg. Hydro-electric development has not improved this fishery but there is still excellent sport at times. I suggest trying lures such as Red Setter, Rabbit patterns, Kilwell No 1, Hamill's Killer and Woolly Bugger.

Trout can also be taken at the mouth of Wairehu Canal or from the groynes at the Poutu River end of the lake.

Lake Moawhango

Location and access Lies east of Waiouru on New Zealand Army land. Permission from the Waiouru Army Camp must be obtained. There is a gravel vehicle track to the lake.

Season Open all year.

This shallow hydro lake lies in windswept, barren tussock country. In the past, it has held browns, rainbows and brook trout (*S. fontinalis*). Sight fishing is difficult and most fish are landed on spinning gear.

Kuratau Lake

Location and access This hydro dam lies off SH 32 on Kuratau Road.

Season 1 October–30 June.

A small hydro lake with limited shoreline fishing because of swamp, brush and weed. Fish can be taken from the dam itself by using a sinking line and a Woolly Bugger or Hamill's Killer. It is best fished from a boat or float tube. Holds a good stock of rainbows and a few browns. Is underfished.

The Kuratau River upstream from the dam holds small rainbows but the river is mostly overgrown and unfishable.

Waihaha River (above Tieke Falls)

Location and access Crossed by SH 32. Access from either side of the bridge.
Season 1 October–30 June.
There is plenty of river to fish both upstream and downstream from the bridge. The water is slightly peat stained in this small stream and fish usually cannot be spotted. Downstream there are deep slots in the rocky stream bed that hold fish, while upstream there are a few stable, slow-flowing pools. Holds small rainbows.

Lake Otamangakau

Location and access Lies on the opposite side of Te Ponanga Saddle Road to Lake Rotoaira, off SH 47. Two access roads are signposted for the Whanganui Intake, Te Whaiau Dam, Otamangakau Dam, Boat Ramp and Wairehu Control Gate. There are basic camping facilities and a boat ramp.
Season 1 October–30 June.
Restrictions Bag limit is one fish.
The 'Big O' is probably as well known to overseas anglers seeking a trophy fish as it is to locals. This shallow, fertile hydro lake was formed in 1971 by diverting the headwaters of the Whanganui River, is 150 ha in area and lies on an exposed tussock and scrub plain. The view of the mountains close by in the Tongariro National Park compensates for its rather stark environment. The lake is subject to fluctuating levels and although this does not affect the fishing to any great extent it hardly adds to its charm as

the shoreline can become muddy and slippery. When the lake level is high, shoreline access becomes more difficult.

The lake holds browns and rainbows averaging over 2.5 kg but each year a trout weighing between 6 and 7 kg is landed. There is a reasonable stock of fish in the lake, but because there is so much food some of these fish survive to a ripe old age while continuing to grow. Some trout have been found to be eight years old and to have spawned five times. Food consists of mayflies, caddis, snails, midges, dragon- and damselflies and various terrestrials, especially cicadas. There are no smelt or bullies in this lake.

While the majority of fish are caught from boats or float tubes there is some excellent shoreline fishing in summer for sighted trout. Wading is safe but there are some swampy areas. The lake level can affect the shoreline fishing but large browns cruise the channels between the weed beds and these can be stalked on a bright, sunny summer's day. On a hot, windy day in late January or February, cicada fishing can be most exciting. When fly fishing from a boat or float tube use a sinking line, a small nymph and a slow retrieve. It pays to carry at least 100 m of backing on your reel as I have seen at least one angler 'cleaned out' by a trophy rainbow.

Trolling accounts for some fish but weed growth in the warmer months becomes a problem. When fly fishing try the following nymphs: Black and Peacock, Hare and Copper, Pheasant Tail, Zug Bug, Damsel- and Dragonfly, and Half Back.

Suggested lures include Woolly Bugger, Hamill's Killer, Mrs Simpson, Red Setter and Rabbit patterns. Although the majority of fish are taken sub-surface, they can be caught on dry flies such as Coch-y-bondhu, Royal Wulff and Parachute Adams.

This lake has a well-earned reputation for trophy fish but they are not easy to catch and many hours' fishing are usually required for success.

Taranaki Fish and Game Council region

This region is divided into the Wanganui District, the Waimarino District, and the Taranaki, Stratford and Hawera districts.

Wanganui District

There are very few quality waters holding trout in this district. The lower Mangawhero River is a worthwhile fishery for spin anglers, but for convenience this river is described in the Waimarino District.

Lake Wiritoa

Location and access Turn off SH 3 about 3 km south of Wanganui at the Lake Wiritoa turn-off. It is a short drive to the lake.
Season 1 October–20 April and 10 July–30 September.
Restrictions Bag limit is two fish.

This small lake is stocked with rainbow trout and perch. One has to compete with water-skiers and jet-boats so early morning and late evening are the best times. Most fish are taken on spinners.

Virginia Lake at the northern end of Wanganui, on SH 3 at St Johns Hill, is also stocked with rainbow trout. It is open all year for anglers under 19 years only.

Turakina River

Location Rises south-west of Waiouru and flows in a southerly direction to enter the sea 25 km south of Wanganui.

Access Only the upper reaches are worth fishing and these can be accessed either from Wanganui or Taihape. Turn left off SH 1 about 5 km north of Taihape to Mataroa. Then drive a further 18 km to Colliers Junction and the upper reaches of the Turakina.
Season 1 October–30 June.

Flowing through unstable papa country, this small to medium-sized river readily becomes silt-laden after rain. There are patches of native bush in reserves along the river but generally the stream flows over pastoral land. Holds a limited stock of browns that are not easy to sight fish.

Lake Namunamu

Location and access This 13 ha natural lake lies west of Hunterville on Ngaruru Station off Turakina Valley Road. From Wanganui, take Kauangaroa Road through Fordell, then Mangatipona Road. Turn left at Braemore Junction onto Turakina Valley Road and travel for another 2 km. There is a 20-minute uphill walk to the lake. The lake can also be accessed from Hunterville.
Season Open all year.
Restrictions Bag limit is two fish only.

This small lake has bush-clad shores and good water quality. It is stocked with rainbow trout that are best caught from one of the four dinghies provided. It pays to carry in your lunch, water, life jackets and fishing gear and make a picnic for the day. In summer, use a high density fly line or spinning gear as the fish will lie in deep water. Olive and Brown Woolly Buggers, Red Setter, Rabbit patterns and Kilwell No 1 will all take fish. Even a Green Beetle imitation may be useful cast along the bush edge. Please remove any rubbish as this lake is only available courtesy of the landowner.

Waimarino District

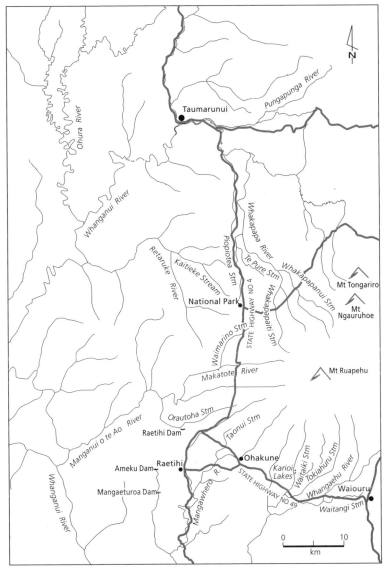

Waimarino District

This sparsely populated district is bounded by Taumarunui in the north, Ohakune and Raetihi in the south, Whanganui National Park in the west and Tongariro National Park in the east. Many of the rivers originate from the melting snows of the three volcanoes Ruapehu, Tongariro and Ngauruhoe. The district offers good fishing in a wide variety of water. Apart from tributaries of the Whangaehu River, all the streams are feeders of the Whanganui River. The upper Whanganui, Whakapapa River and Piopiotea Stream are described in the section on the Auckland–Waikato region.

There are a number of small feeder streams in the Waimarino District that hold trout and are worth exploring. Some, like the rugged Waimarino and Makatote, run in very deep gorges but offer exciting fishing for active and experienced back country anglers who don't mind swimming through some of the pools in a wet suit.

Since 1991 worm and creeper fishing have been permitted in this district.

Bag limit on the Manganui o te Ao and tributaries and at the Raetihi hydro dam — two fish. Unless stated, all other waters four fish.

Lower Whanganui River

Location and access Roads follow down both banks from Taumarunui for 15 km until the river enters inaccessible bush-clad country in Whanganui National Park. Further downstream there is road access at Whakahoro, Pipiriki, Jerusalem and the mouth in Wanganui. The river is popular for kayaking, rafting and canoeing.
Season Excluding the tributaries, the river is open all year.

Below Taumarunui and the Ongarue River confluence, water quality in this large river deteriorates. The river becomes brownish in colour and often runs silt-laden, but does hold a reasonable stock of brown and rainbow trout that can be taken on a spinning rod. Since Wanganui has adopted land-based sewage treatment, a few fish have been caught near the mouth but this is huge water and not very interesting to fish.

Retaruke River and Kaitieke Stream

Location Both these rivers rise on the Central Plateau west of National Park and flow in a westerly direction to enter the Whanganui River at Retaruke.

Access Turn off SH 4 just south of Owhango onto the Whakahoro–Kaitieke road. It is 15 km to the confluence of the two rivers. Roads follow the Retaruke River both upstream and downstream from the confluence but permission should be sought to cross private farmland.

Season 1 October–30 June.

Above the confluence there is 8 km of very pleasant water to fish on the Retaruke River with well-established stable pools and runs. The riverbed is gravel and rock, the banks grass, scrub and patches of bush, and casting is generally unobstructed. Some fish can be spotted on a bright sunny day but the water is slightly tannin stained. Now holds a reasonable stock of brown and rainbow trout although volcanic ash and mud slides in the past have seriously affected the fish population. Fortunately, the river is restocked by trout running upstream from the Whanganui River. There are a few very deep holes. Most fish respond to sunk nymphs or spinners. Below the confluence, there is 20 km of rather heavy water more suited to spinning. Access is not always easy on this section of river. The lower reaches of the Kaitieke are reputed to hold trout but I have yet to see one. There is 3 km of pleasant water to fish before the river gorges. I would suggest looking either early or late in the season as this stream could well be a spawning stream for the Whanganui River.

Manganui o te Ao River

Location Along with its three feeder streams, the Waimarino, Makatote and Orautoha, this river rises, as the Mangaturuturu, on the slopes of Ruapehu and flows west to join the Whanganui west of Raetihi.

Access Turn west off SH 4 about 4 km north of Raetihi on the

Ohura Road. This road has three branches.

Upper reaches From Pukekaha Road.

Middle reaches and Ruatiti Domain From Ruatiti Road.

Lower reaches From Makakahi Road. At Ruatiti Domain there are basic camping facilities as well as a notice board outlining the property boundaries of the various landowners. Permission should be sought before crossing private farmland.

Season For the main river and tributaries, 1 October–30 June.

Restrictions Bag limit is two fish.

This very popular, medium-sized river is protected by a national water conservation order passed in 1989 mainly because the threatened blue duck population is unusually high here. Ash from the Ruapehu eruption severely affected the trout population but recent drift dives near the Mangaturuturu confluence revealed 43 large trout per kilometre. Both browns and rainbows averaging 1–2 kg are present, although the slightly brownish coloured water generally prevents sight fishing, and there are a few large fish in the deeper holes. The upper reaches cut through some very deep gorges making access quite difficult but there is 15 km of water with reasonable road access.

As the riverbed is very rocky and slippery in parts, wading and crossing can be difficult and tedious unless you have a wading stick. This is a very scenic river with clumps of bush along the banks and rocky cliffs overhanging many pools.

Trout compete with the blue ducks for nymphs so it is not surprising that most fish are caught on well-weighted nymphs. However, there can be an evening caddis or mayfly rise and spin anglers may find a Black Toby successful. This river is recommended for its scenic qualities, its relative isolation and its nymph fishing.

The Waimarino tributary offers a short section of attractive water alongside SH 4 at Waikune and through the grounds of the old prison, but further downstream on Erua Road the stream is overgrown and very difficult to fish.

The Makatote can be reached by rock climbing below the Makatote viaduct, but this is for the adventurous angler with a wet

suit!
Orautoha Stream

Location and access Rises near SH 4, flows parallel to Ohura Road and joins the Manganui o te Ao River close to the Pukekaha turn-off. Access is from Ohura Road across private farmland.
Season 1 October–30 June.

The upper reaches are small but the lower 5 km of stream are swelled by water entering from the Raetihi hydro dam. Holds browns up to 2 kg but the water quality is not good and prevents sight fishing. Best early in the season before recovering spawners drop back downstream. Flows across farmland and is easily seen from Ohura Road.

Taonui Stream

Location Rises from springs on the lower slopes of Ruapehu, flows on a south-westerly course and joins the Mangawhero River halfway between Ohakune and Raetihi.
Access From SH 49A and from Old Mangawhero Road near the Mangawhero confluence.

Having a second angler to spot can be helpful when there is glare on the water

Season 1 October–30 June.

This small, spring-fed stream holds fish throughout its length of 8 km, but is mostly fished in the 4 km below the railway line, where manuka scrub gives way to farmland. It is easy to sight fish on this stream and patches of bush and willow present few problems on the back-cast. Pools are stable and although the number of large brown trout is not high, the average weight is around 2 kg. They are shy, however, so a careful approach and an accurate first cast are essential. This can be difficult in this stream as the first cast often frightens fingerlings, which then rush madly upstream scaring everything in their path. Best early in the season before the larger fish become spooky.

Mangawhero River

Location Rises on the southern slopes of Ruapehu, then flows 70 km south through Ohakune to join the Whangaehu River near Kauangaroa.

Access *Upper reaches* From the Turoa Skifield road in Tongariro National Park.

Middle reaches From Ohakune township, Pakahi Road, SH 49 and Old Mangarewa Road.

Lower reaches From the Parapara highway (SH 4).

Season Above the SH 49 golf course bridge, 1 October–30 June. Below this bridge the river is open all year.

Fishing is hardly worthwhile in the national park where the river is small, overgrown and swift. The best water lies in the middle reaches below Ohakune. The river winds its way across farmland for 10 km before leaving the central plateau and entering a gorge. Unfortunately, the water quality has not been improved by carrot washing, and fish are very difficult to spot in the brownish flow. There are pools, riffles and willows and generally this section of the river is easy to blind fish with dry flies or nymphs.

The lower reaches provide another 15 km of fishable water both above and below the Raukawa Falls at Kakatahi. The best water lies in the 10 km stretch above the falls and below a gorge. The river has a mudstone, silt and rock bed. Try a large attractor dry fly and cover the deep, rocky crevices.

Below the falls the river becomes quite large. This section of river is best for spinning.

There is a good stock of browns averaging 1.5 kg in this river despite the dubious water quality.

Tokiahuru Stream

Location Rises from springs and snow-fed waters in Karioi Forest on the south-eastern slopes of Ruapehu. Flows south-west to join the Whangaehu River south of Karioi.
Access *Upper reaches* Through the New Zealand Forestry Corporation headquarters on SH 49.
Middle and lower reaches From Whangaehu Valley Road and Oruakukuru Road. The river flows alongside Karioi Domain.
Season Above SH 49, 1 October–30 June. Elsewhere, open all year.

This fast-flowing, overgrown, cold, clear mountain stream holds strong rainbows and browns averaging around 2 kg. The stream often remains fishable when neighbouring streams are discoloured. Forest gives way to farmland at the railway line and fishing is best below the Waitaiki confluence in the 4 km of water before the stream joins the Whangaehu River.

Above SH 49 a chainsaw in the backpack could come in handy as there are few opportunities to cast in the heavy manuka scrub. There are fish in this section, but when hooked they have every chance to escape downstream as it is almost impossible to follow. In the 4 km stretch recommended, well-weighted nymphs bring best results, but carry a landing net as fish are lively and beaching opportunities are rare.

Waitaiki Stream

Location Flows parallel to but west of the Tokiahuru and joins this stream 4 km above the Whangaehu confluence, south of Karioi.
Access From Karioi Station Road and Whangaehu Valley Road.
Season Above SH 49, 1 October–30 June. Below SH 49, open all

year.
This fast-flowing river is similar to the Tokiahuru, and heavily weighted nymphs are the preferred option. There is not a lot of fishable water as scrub and willows cover the banks. Best between the two confluences.

The Whangaehu River is polluted by Mt Ruapehu's crater lake, but the Tokiahuru and Waitaiki rivers are free of the dirty water further downstream. Other small tributaries of the Whangaehu also hold fish. The Waitangi Stream, which flows across farmland alongside SH 49 between Tangiwai and Waiouru, is worth a look.

Raetihi hydro dam

Location and access Turn west off SH 4 4 km north of Raetihi onto Ohura Road, then right after 2 km onto Middle Road. Travel 750 m and turn left on to a rough track leading to the dam and power house.
Season 1 October–30 June.
Restrictions Bag limit is two trout.

This small 1 ha hydro lake holds browns averaging around 1 kg. Pines surround the lake making casting with a fly rod difficult. Fish can be taken during the day on small nymphs and a fine trace but fishing improves in the evening, when there is often a good caddis rise.

The Karioi Lakes and Ameku Dam have not been stocked since 1993 and at present are not worth fishing.

Taranaki, Stratford and Hawera districts

Many streams drain the high rainfall and melting snows from Mt Taranaki (Egmont). Most have short steep courses and fluctuating water flows. While the headwaters are rocky and rough with bush-covered banks, the middle and lower reaches traverse highly productive dairy farms. Unfortunately bank clearance, enrichment from fertiliser run-off, cowshed and dairy effluent and, in the case of the Kapuni River, petrochemical poisoning have caused considerable deterioration of some streams. Four streams have been dammed for hydro-electricity generation. Many long-term residents and anglers speak wistfully of bygone days when limit bags of good-sized browns taken on opening day were common.

Efforts have been made to restock some rivers but when there is insufficient food, trout simply migrate out to sea. Water quality must be improved and buffer zones along rivers re-established before the trout population will increase. Resident fish must restock the streams with their own progeny; further liberation of hatchery fish into the rivers is a pointless exercise.

More than 30 streams flow off Mt Taranaki and all carry limited numbers of brown trout. Only those with reasonable fish stocks are described. The Stony (Hangatahua) and the Waingongoro rivers are exceptions in holding rainbows.

The streams are a delight to fish, being small and contained and well serviced by a network of roads. Because many of these streams are lightly tannin stained sight fishing can be difficult. The Stony and the Okahu are two exceptions in having very clear water. Permission to fish should always be sought from local landowners as the Queen's Chain does not apply to a number of the streams. This district is unique in that an old Taranaki tradition of live bait fishing with creeper is permitted in most waters. Creepers are Dobson Fly larvae, found under rocks along the stream margins, and are fished upstream on a bare hook in similar fashion to an artificial nymph. It is excellent bait early in the season but not so effective in the warmer summer months.

The prevailing westerly weather should be taken into consideration before embarking on a day's fishing in Taranaki.

Restrictions Daily bag limit: all waters originating from the slopes of Mt Taranaki, two sports fish. Catch and release only in the Mangaoraka Stream between the bridges on Te Arei Road West and Corbett Road. Also in the Kaiauai Stream upstream from the Alfred Road bridge, in the Stony River between the bridges on SH 45 and Mangatete Road and in the Kapuni Stream upstream from

the Skeet Road bridge. Elsewhere four fish.
Lake Mangamahoe

Location and access The turn-off is well marked on the New Plymouth–Inglewood road before Egmont Village. A road skirts the western shore.
Season Excluding the Waiwhakaiho inlet this lake is open to fishing all year.
Restrictions Including the inlet, fly fishing only.

This small, picturesque lake has been created for power generation by damming the Mangamahoe Stream. It lies in a beautiful setting with tree ferns growing around the perimeter and a tree-framed view of Mt Taranaki. It is a grand picnic spot. Being a wildlife refuge, the lake is home to a variety of water fowl. While the eastern shore is overgrown and difficult, the western access from the road is simple and casting is unobstructed.

Browns and 'r' type rainbows have been regularly liberated into this lake and fish can sometimes be seen cruising the shallows. During the day try small lightly weighted nymphs, soft hackle wets or lures such as Woolly Bugger, Mrs Simpson or Hamill's Killer. During the green manuka beetle hatch, a Coch-y-bondhu works well, as does a black lure at night when fish come in close. It is rarely necessary to wade. This is an ideal lake for junior or novice anglers.

 *Waiwhakaiho River and tributaries*

Waiwhakaiho River

Location Drains the north-western slopes of Mt Taranaki and flows on a northerly course to enter the Tasman Sea close to New Plymouth.
Access *Upper reaches* From Alfred Road near the New Plymouth Gliding Club, and Egmont Road.
Middle reaches From the New Plymouth–Inglewood road just beyond the turn-off to Lake Mangamahoe.
Lower reaches From Devon Road, Rimu Street and William Street in New Plymouth.
Season Above Rimu Street extension, 1 October–30 April. Below

the extension this river is open all year.

The upper reaches of this medium-sized river fish well early in the season. Pools and rocky runs are well formed, the riverbed is composed of boulders and stones and casting is generally not a problem. Use a wading stick for river crossings. Holds around 5–10 takeable browns per kilometre of river and most are caught by blind nymph fishing. Conditions suit dry fly fishing, mostly in the evening. The river flows across farmland with patches of bush and scrub lining the banks. The lower reaches often fish well early in the morning before the power station discharge begins. The river's proximity to New Plymouth means it is heavily fished.

Kaiauai Stream

Location The Kaiauai Stream joins the Waiwhakaiho River 1.5 km up Alfred Road.
Access *Upper reaches* From Hill Road via Albert Road across private farmland.
Middle and lower reaches From Alfred Road also across private farmland and from the Alfred Road bridge.
Season 1 October–30 April.
Restrictions Above the Alfred Road bridge, catch and release only and artificial fly or spinner only.

There are some deep holding pools in this small stream and, although fish numbers have dropped in recent times, there are some good-sized browns present. Sight fishing is difficult in the brownish water but blind nymph and dry fly fishing can provide good sport.

The Mangawara Stream also offers some interesting small-stream fishing although fish stocks are not great.

Lake Rotomanu

Location and access Lies near the Waiwhakaiho River mouth in New Plymouth. Clemow Road leads to the lake. Access is good to the whole lake shore.

Season Open all year.

This small lake is great for junior anglers and is regularly stocked

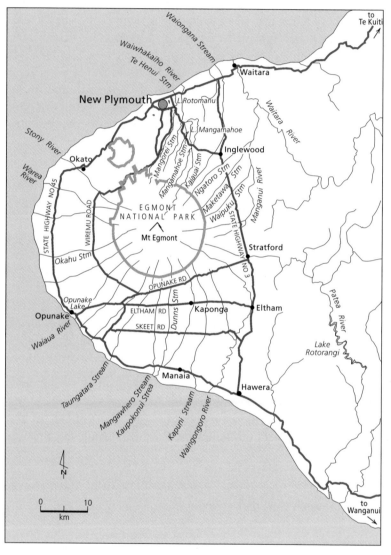

Taranaki District

with rainbow trout. Perch are also present.

Waiongana Stream

Location The upper reaches flow through the outskirts of Inglewood and the stream enters the sea just west of Waitara.
Access Crossed by SH 3 and Devon, Te Arei and and Manutahi roads.
Season 1 October–30 April.

The middle reaches of this small stream near Lepperton are worth fishing, with creeper and spinner being popular. Holds browns in the 0.5–1 kg range. Is overgrown in parts.

Mangaoraka Stream

Location and access This is a small tributary of the Waiongana and can be accessed from Te Arei Road West and Corbett Road.
Season 1 October–30 April.
Restrictions Between the Te Arei and Corbett road bridges, catch and release only and artificial fly or spinner only.

This small stream winds across dairy farms and offers interesting blind nymph fishing. Fish stocks are not high.

Stony (Hangatahua) River

Location Drains the western slopes of Mt Taranaki and enters the sea north-west of Okato.
Access *Upper reaches* From Wiremu, Mangatete, Saunders and Puniho roads.
Middle reaches Via the New Zealand Walkway System opposite Okato Domain. Crossed by SH 45 (the New Plymouth–Opunake road) just south of Okato.
Lower reaches Turn west off SH 45 at Okato Tavern. From Kaihihi and Brophy roads walk across farmland to the river.
Season Above the SH 45 bridge, 1 October–30 April. Below the SH 45 bridge, open all year except for the month of May.
Restrictions Between the SH 45 and Mangatete road bridges —

artificial fly or spinner only and catch and release.

This highly valued, medium-sized river is protected by a local water conservation notice. The Stony holds the clearest water of any of the ring-plain streams and sight fishing is possible, especially in the middle and upper reaches. The river is safe to wade and cross and, although scrub grows along the banks in some places, casting is not difficult. The most disappointing aspect is the lack of trout, in part owing to recurrent severe flash-floods. Drift dives reveal three to six large browns per kilometre of river in the middle reaches. However, there are some nice rainbows in the pocket water of the upper reaches and a few large sea-run browns enter the deep holes of the lower river late in the season. The latter respond to well-sunk nymphs, egg patterns or Woolly Buggers.

Warea River

Location and access Drains the western slopes of Mt Taranaki, flows west and enters the sea south of Okato and the Stony River mouth. SH 45 crosses the lower reaches while Warea Road runs upstream parallel to the river.
Season Above SH 45, 1 October–30 April. Below SH 45 this river is open all year except for the month of May.

This is a productive little stream holding brown trout up to 1.5 kg. Best early in the season, with nymph and creeper preferred.

Okahu Stream

Location and access Is crossed by SH 45 south of Rahotu. Access from Ngariki Road.
Season 1 October–30 April.

This clear-water stream is smaller than the Stony River but similar in that sight fishing is possible. However, it only holds a small population of browns.

Waiaua River

Location Drains the south-western slopes of Mt Taranaki. Flows south-west by Opunake, where the lower reaches are dammed for power generation, forming Opunake Lake.

Access There is a large area of accessible water from Ihaia and Lower Eltham roads but please ask permission before crossing dairy farms.

Season Above SH 45, 1 October–30 April. Below SH 45, open all year except for the month of May.

Holds mainly browns but there is an occasional rainbow present as well. There is plenty of good water upstream above SH 45, with both creeper and nymph fishing effective early in the season. Below Opunake Lake, the river holds many small browns and these are fun to fish with a dry fly or small nymph.

Opunake Lake

Location and access This shallow hydro lake was formed by damming the Waiaua River and lies on the outskirts of Opunake township. Access from Layard and Domett streets and a track from the Opunake side of the SH 45 bridge.

Season Open all year.

This small lake is regularly stocked with browns and 'r' type rainbows. Most fish are taken on live bait or spinners and the lake is great for junior anglers. There is a boat ramp in Layard Street. Fish up to 3 kg have been caught, with the hot spot being the tail waters of the inlet race.

Kaupokonui Stream and tributaries

Location Flows south off Mt Taranaki just west of Kaponga and Manaia.

Access *Upper reaches* From Eltham Road.

Middle reaches From Skeet and Upper and Lower Glenn roads.

Lower reaches From SH 45 or across farmland from Manaia Road.

Season Above SH 45, 1 October–30 April. Below SH 45, open all year except for the month of May.

This stream and its two tributaries, Dunn's Stream and Manga-whero Stream, offer good dry fly, nymph and creeper fishing for browns up to 2 kg. It is popular with local anglers, with the most productive water being above and below the Skeet Road bridge. Dunn's Stream has in the past had a reputation as an excellent dry fly stream but fish numbers have gone down in recent years. Algal growth can be a problem in the lower reaches during summer.

Kapuni Stream

Location Drains the southern slopes of Mt Taranaki and flows south just east of Kaponga to enter the sea near Manaia.
Access *Upper reaches* From Palmer Road above Neill Road inter-section and from the Palmer Road bridge; also from Opunake Road.
Middle reaches From Eltham and Skeet roads.
Lower reaches From SH 45.
Season 1 October–30 April.
Restrictions Catch and release and fly fishing only upstream from the Skeet Road bridge.

This small stream is very pleasant to fish although stocks are not great and the browns tend to be small. Sight fishing is possible in ideal conditions. Has been polluted in the past by the petrochemical industry.

Waingongoro River

Location Flows off the eastern slopes of Mt Taranaki, then turns south just west of Eltham to parallel SH 3 (the Stratford–Hawera highway) on its western aspect.
Access Generally across farmland from side roads west off SH 3.
Upper reaches From Finnerty and Cornwall roads and road ends within Eltham township.
Middle reaches South of Eltham from Rogers, Skeet, Normanby, Forbes, Paora and Wirihana roads.
Lower reaches From SH 45 (South Road).
Season Above SH 45, 1 October–30 April. Below SH 45, open all

year except for the month of May.

This medium-sized river has become more popular since 'r' type rainbow trout were released into the lower reaches. The upper reaches, in the vicinity of the Cardiff Walkway, can be sight fished for small browns. Below the weir at Eltham, the water becomes lightly tannin stained making sight fishing difficult.

The middle reaches south of Eltham are the most popular. Here there are some deep holes and although the river is overgrown in parts there is plenty of water to fish.

The lower reaches are overgrown by willows in some stretches. This is not an easy river to fish but there are good stocks of browns and rainbows up to 2 kg. Upstream nymph, spinning and creeper fishing early in the season account for most of the fish taken.

Lake Rotorangi

Location Lies east of Eltham and north-east of Hawera.
Access From Eltham.
Upper reaches Anderson or Rawhitora roads to the top end of the lake.
Middle reaches Tawhiti and Tangahoe Valley roads.
Lower reaches Ball Road.
Season Open all year except May from the dam face to the Mangamingi ramp.
Boat launching Upper reaches at Glen Nui. Lower reaches at Mangamingi.

This new, narrow, 49-km-long hydro lake was formed by damming the Patea River. Although there is considerable bush cover along the banks, eutrophication in summer detracts from this fishery and trout tend to go into deep water. Most fish are caught from boats in the cooler months of the year either by harling a fly or trolling a spinner. There is very little worthwhile shoreline fishing. The lake holds browns, rainbows and perch and is best in the upper reaches above Glen Nui.

Patea River

Location Rises from Mt Taranaki west of Stratford. Flows south to Lake Rotorangi and eventually enters the sea at Patea.

Access Near Stratford from Juliet Street, Swanson Road and the East Road bridge. Further downstream from Skinner and Bird roads.

Season Above Lake Rotorangi, 1 October–30 April. Below Patea Dam, open all year except the month of May.

Only the upper reaches in the vicinity of Stratford are worth fishing, although since the formation of Lake Rotorangi some good-sized browns have been caught immediately below Patea Dam. Between Stratford and Toko, drift dives have found 20 takeable brown trout per kilometre of river. However, the water quality is poor and fish cannot be spotted.

Manganui River and tributaries

Location The main river and tributaries drain the north-eastern faces of Mt Taranaki. The main stream flows east off the mountain, then turns north about 3 km from Midhurst (on SH 3). It continues in a northerly direction east of Inglewood and eventually joins the Waitara River east of Lepperton.

Access *Upper and middle reaches* From Tariki, Croydon, Manganui and Mountain (SH 3) roads.

Lower reaches From Everett, Bristol and Junction roads.

Season 1 October–30 April.

Although the water is peat stained, making sight fishing difficult, there is good brown trout fishing in this river and its tributaries. There are some very deep holes which yield some large fish to well-sunk nymphs or creepers, especially early in the season. The banks are for the most part stable, as bush clearance has not been total. Fish stocks are reasonable and the river can be crossed between pools.

Tributaries worth exploring include the Waipuku Stream, which joins the main river 3 km upstream from the Tariki Road bridge, the Maketawa, 8 km south of Inglewood, and the Ngatoro, 4 km south of Inglewood. Both the latter tributaries are crossed by SH 3 although the Maketawa Stream can also be accessed from

Junction and Upper and Lower Norfolk roads. The Maketawa Stream offers some interesting sight fishing for wary browns.

It would take years to fish all the other small streams and tributaries flowing from Mt Taranaki that hold brown trout. The countryside is attractive and in clear weather views of the mountain are quite spectacular. A number of small lakes and dams in the district also hold trout and perch but these are not recommended as worthwhile fisheries.

The rivers between Hawera and Wanganui, further south, do

not hold trout.

Wellington Fish and Game Council region

There are four main river systems in this large region. In the north, the Rangitikei River flows south and west from its source in the rugged Kaimanawa Mountains with a number of its tributaries draining the Ruahine Range. In the south, the Hutt River and its tributaries drain the Rimutaka Range south into Wellington Harbour. Between these two river systems lie the Manawatu and Ruamahanga rivers. The Manawatu River and its feeder streams drain northern Wairarapa and southern Hawke's Bay before turning west through the Manawatu Gorge to Palmerston North. The Ruamahanga River drains the Tararua Range and dominates the southern Wairarapa.

In such a large region there is a wide variety of fishing water available, from isolated headwater tributaries in the mountains to the Hutt River flowing alongside a motorway in a large metropolitan city.

Brown trout were first introduced in 1874 and rainbow trout about 1898, although the latter are now present in any numbers only in the Rangitikei and Waiohine rivers.

While some angler accesses have been signposted it always pays to ask permission from local landowners if there is any doubt. Rarely will permission to fish be denied providing the correct approach is adopted.

Daily bag limit All waters upstream of the boundaries of the Ruahine, Tararua and Rimutaka conservation parks, two trout or salmon. Elsewhere, unless stated, there is no limit.

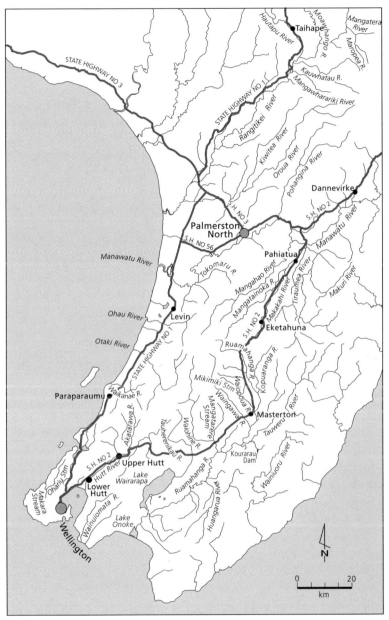

Wellington Fish and Game Council region

Rangitikei River

Location Drains the Middle and Island ranges of Kaimanawa Forest Park and flows generally south to the Taihape–Napier road. The river then flows parallel to but east of SH 1 from Taihape to Bulls, eventually reaching the coast west of Palmerston North.

Access

Upper reaches

- A rigorous two-day tramp over Umukarikari to Waipakahi Hut and Junction Top.
- A similar tramp to the Waipakahi Valley and then over Middle Range on the Thunderbolt Track. Both these tramps are for experienced trampers.
- From Waiouru over New Zealand Army land. Permission required.
- By walking upstream from the Taihape–Napier road.
- By helicopter from Taupo, Turangi or Taihape. However choppers are not permitted to land anglers upstream of the Otamateanui confluence.

Middle reaches

- Walk downstream from the Taihape–Napier road.
- From Oturarei Road, which leaves the Taihape–Napier road north of Taihape and leads to Mangaohane (Matawhero) Bridge.
- Between Taihape and Mangaweka the following roads lead off SH 1 to the river: Kotukuraeroa, Tuhoe, Toetoe, Kauwhatau Valley and Mangawharariki.
- Otara and Vinegar Hill roads, running east off SH 1 between Mangaweka and Hunterville.

Lower reaches From roads running east off SH 1 between Hunterville and Bulls. These are Putorino, Onepuri, Reu Reu, Kakariki and SH 3, the last of which crosses the river just south of Bulls. Downstream from Bulls there are fishing accesses from Taylor, Campion and Rosina roads.

Season Above Mangaohane (Matawhero) Bridge, 1 October–30 April. Below Mangaohane Bridge the river is open for fishing all year.

Restrictions

- In the wilderness section upstream from the Otarere confluence, only one trout can be taken and this must be less than 55 cm in length.
- Between the Otarere confluence and Mangaohane Bridge, four fish can be taken but all must be less than 55 cm in length.
- Artificial fly or spinner only is permitted above Mangaohane Bridge.
- Below Mangaohane Bridge there is no bag limit or size limit and bait fishing is permitted.

The wilderness section of this river is a unique trophy fishery, hence the restrictions on size and number of fish that can be taken. If any trout taken are tagged, please return the tags to the Wellington Fish and Game Council with full details.

Over the past three years, the average length and weight of trout has fallen to the point where double-figure fish (over 10 lb or 4.54 kg) are now rare. The cause of this decline is at present unknown. The upper Rangitikei contains fish that are larger and older than those in any other river in New Zealand, the only other similar fishery being the upper Ruakituri River. Overseas anglers and guides frequently visit the upper reaches by helicopter and raft in search of a trophy.

This valley is very exposed to the south and extremely cold in winter. The river winds through the heavily bush-clad mountains of Kaimanawa Forest Park. There are sheltered camp sites in the valley, with Ecology Stream and the Mangamaire River confluence being popular. Fish numbers thin out somewhat around 2 km upstream from Ecology Stream.

This is a medium-sized river in the wilderness section and, although there are some large, deep pools, the river can be forded at selected sites in low-water conditions. Some crossings may be deep, however, and the rock and stone riverbed can be slippery. The water is very clear and seldom discolours with rain. Trout can be sighted but are very wary as their vision is extremely good — especially in the deeper, slow-flowing pools. It is often difficult to reach fish from below as it is not unusual to find the majority lying in deep water two thirds of the way down a pool but still out of casting distance from the tail. Occasionally on a bright, calm, sunny day when the fishing pressure is minimal, trout feed along the edges of runs. Once disturbed, however, it may be a day or two before they resume feeding.

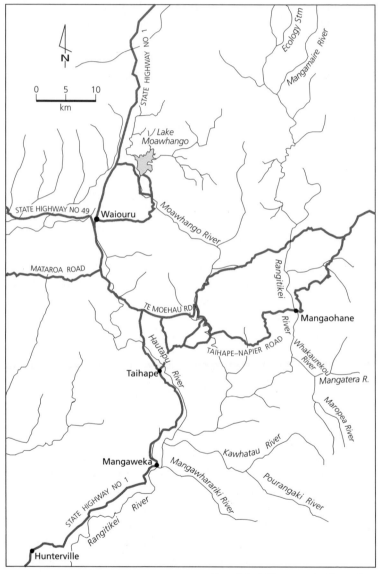

Rangitikei River and tributaries

Fish can be taken on well-sunk nymphs, lures, dry flies and spinners. A sinking line fished from above with a long trace and two heavy nymphs may be needed to cover difficult fish. Most of the trout in these upper reaches are rainbows. The brown trout population has increased gradually over recent years and there are a few very large browns. Be prepared to hike off downstream when you hook a good fish as it is likely to fight with tenacity.

In the middle reaches, access can be difficult on some stretches because of gorges. However, there is still plenty of fishing water as the river becomes quite large below Mangaweka. There is good water at the Mangawharariki confluence and trout often lie in the bouldery runs. Rainbows are more prolific than browns and, although fish up to 3 kg can be taken, the average weight is around 1.4 kg. The river has a shingle, rock and papa bed with long glides, pools and riffles overhung by cliffs. Crossings can still be made at the tail of some pools but one should be careful. Some areas are willow-lined but generally there are no casting obstructions. Mature fish tend to move upstream toward the headwaters in the autumn but an excellent stock of 1–2-year-old rainbows remains. These respond to well-weighted nymphs, well-sunk lures, spinners and live bait, especially late in the season.

Downstream from Bulls the water quality deteriorates but at times some of the locals enjoy interesting winter fishing.

Mangamaire River

Location and access This medium-sized river lies in a very inaccessible part of Kaimanawa Forest Park. Most anglers fish the lower reaches by walking upstream from the Rangitikei confluence. For trampers, the river can be reached after a long day's tramp from Boyd Hut. Others simply helicopter in to the middle reaches.
Season 1 October–30 April.

This clear, rock and stone river, winding across tussock flats and through patches of scrub and bush, offers 15 km of wilderness sight fishing. There are some deep, stable pools and, although the river can flood dramatically at times, it is usually well confined. There are plenty of sheltered camp sites in the valley and fish stocks are good, with an occasional rainbow weighing up to 4 kg. The lower bush-clad section has been more heavily fished and trout numbers have fallen over recent years. The middle section in the more isolated tussock country holds a better stock.

Moawhango River

Location Drains the Kaimanawa Mountains east of the Desert Road, flows south east of Waiouru and joins the Rangitikei at Taoroa.
Access From the Taihape–Napier road, and Oturarei and Kotukuraeroa roads east of Taihape.
Season Open all year.

Unfortunately, this river has been de-watered at the headwaters for hydro-electric power generation. It is now a relatively small river but, although it discolours readily in a fresh, it still holds a moderate stock of browns and rainbows. The gorgy section near the Taihape–Napier road is not easy to get to but access improves further downstream. In low-water summer conditions, weed growth becomes a problem as the water warms.

Hautapu River

Location Drains Ngamatea Swamp and the southern Kaimanawa range south-east of Waiouru. Flows in a southerly direction through Taihape to join the Rangitikei south of Utiku.
Access *Upper reaches* SH 1 follows the river and crosses north of Taihape.
Middle reaches Turn off SH 1 5 km north of Taihape to Mataroa. Further upstream there is access beneath a railway viaduct, through a DoC reserve and across private farmland.
Lower reaches From SH 1 both north and south of Taihape.
Season 1 October–30 April.
Restrictions Above the SH 1 bridge by the Taihape Golf Club is fly fishing only. Bag limit is two trout.

This small stream, flowing through hilly pastoral land, holds a good stock of relatively large brown trout. The average weight is around

1.4 kg but fish up to 2.5 kg are not unusual. Although the stream easily becomes silt-laden in a fresh and takes a few days to clear, fish can be spotted and stalked in normal conditions. Pools are well defined, the countryside is attractive, with patches of native bush and kowhai trees growing along grassy banks, and the stream can be waded and crossed without difficulty.

The heavily bushed section of river at the DoC reserve near Mataroa holds some large trout but the river is overgrown and very difficult to fish.

The Hautapu River holds challenging brown trout for the dry fly angler

In low-water summer conditions, trout become very wary and need careful stalking. An accurate and delicate first cast with a fine tippet is important as they spook easily.

In optimal conditions, this stream is a delight for the skilled fly angler keen on sight fishing. It pays to carry a landing net.

Whakaurekou, Maropea, Mangatera, Kawhatau and Mangawharariki rivers

Location and access These five tributaries of the Rangitikei River all drain the Ruahine Range east of Mangaweka. Access is generally through private farmland although the headwaters of the Maropea, Mangatera and Kawhatau lie in Ruahine Forest Park. The Kawhatau is accessed from Toe Toe and Kawhatau Valley roads, while the Rangitikei needs to be forded in low-water conditions upstream from Taoroa Junction to reach the Whakaurekou and its tributary, the Mangatera River.
Season The Whakaurekou River is open all year while the others open on 1 October and close on 30 April.

At times, especially early and late in the season, these tributaries hold fish. However, they are all unstable with moving shingle riverbeds, are prone to flooding and do not provide a good trout habitat. The Mangawharariki holds a few good browns while the headwaters of the Maropea, Mangatera and Kawhatau contain a few resident rainbows in the more stable pools. Sight fishing is often difficult because of silt, and when these rivers are low and clear in summer, most fish have dropped back downstream to the main river. While they may be interesting to explore, their fish stocks are not great and some are difficult to access.

Manawatu River and tributaries

Manawatu River

Location This large river drains southern Hawke's Bay, the southern Ruahine Range and the northern Tararua Range. The main river follows a southerly course to Dannevirke, where it turns west to enter the Manawatu Gorge 8 km west of Woodville. It emerges from the gorge at Ashhurst, meanders across farmland to Palmerston North and finally reaches the sea at Foxton Beach.

Access Many roads follow and cross this large river throughout its course. The following is a list of some of the suggested accesses to explore.

Upper reaches above Woodville
- SH 2 crosses north of Norsewood.
- Kopua Road, which leaves SH 2 between Takapau and Norsewood.
- Garfield Road, which leaves SH 2 19 km north of Dannevirke, to Makotuku, then take Donghi or Rakaitai roads.
- Cowper and Weber roads from Dannevirke.
- Oringi Road leaves SH 2 10 km south of Dannevirke.

Middle reaches from Woodville to Palmerston North
- SH 2 crosses the river south of Woodville while SH 3 follows through the Manawatu Gorge.
- Raukawa Road leaves SH 3 south of Ashhurst.
- From roads in Palmerston North city.

Lower reaches
- South of Palmerston North there are many access points from SH 3 including Shirriffs, Walkers, Karere and Poplar roads.
- SH 1 crosses south of Foxton.

Season Above the Mangatewainui Stream confluence near Ormondville, 1 October–30 April. Below this confluence the river is open to fishing all year.

The Manawatu River offers over 150 km of river to fish, but for the fly angler the most interesting water lies in the upper reaches north-east of Dannevirke. Here the river is manageable, being relatively small and easily crossed in most places. The good water quality in these upper reaches allows sight fishing to a reasonable stock of brown trout. There are pools and runs as the river winds its way across farmland, but casting can be difficult in some willow-choked stretches. Fish respond to dry flies and nymphs, with soft hackle wets being useful in the evenings for the caddis rise.

Between Oringi and Dannevirke the river becomes larger with long glides, deep pools and wide shingly riffles. Trout become difficult to spot on the shingle and mud bed but the high fish population is sufficient to allow good quality blind fly fishing, with an evening caddis rise likely on warm summer evenings. Fish can become selective during the evening rise and a small seine net or nylon stocking can be very useful in determining the hatch during difficult evenings. When all else fails, a small soft hackle wet may restore your ego. Captain G.D. Hamilton successfully fished this river one hundred years ago with soft hackle wet flies. Crossings are still possible at the tail of some pools but cliffs can make access tricky.

Downstream from Woodville, the water quality deteriorates and the river becomes much larger. Although fly fishing is possible, the water is better suited to spinning. A few rainbows are now present

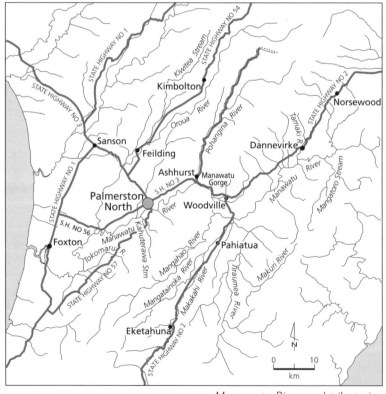

Manawatu River and tributaries

in the middle reaches. The gorge does not hold many fish as there are few places for them to hide when the river floods.

At Ashhurst, the river is heavily fished because of its proximity to the city of Palmerston North. Wet fly, live bait, spinning and nymphing with two heavy nymphs and an indicator are all popular. The mouth of Kahuterawa Stream and the water near Linton Army Camp are hot spots during April and May, when the spawning run begins. The Kahuterawa Stream itself is worth a look either early or late in the season. Note it opens on 1 October and closes on 30 April.

The water quality deteriorates even further at Opiki and the lower 20 km are tidal.

Makuri River

Location Drains the Waewaepa and Puketoi ranges east of Pahiatua. Initially the river flows south-west, but a few kilometres south of Makuri village it turns north to enter the Tiraumea River at Ngaturi.
Access East of Pahiatua on the Ngaturi–Makuri road. Makuri Domain offers basic camping, an even more basic 9-hole golf course and easy access to the river.
Season 1 October–30 April.
Restrictions Fly fishing only above the Makuri township bridge.

This small tributary of the Tiraumea River is highly rated by fly anglers and heavily fished in the region of the Makuri settlement. Here, the willow-lined stream has good water quality enabling sight fishing for browns averaging 1.2 kg. It is best early in the season before angling pressure has alerted the fish — they become very spooky. Success usually only comes from using small flies on a long fine tippet, a very careful approach and an accurate first cast. Pools and riffles are stable although in my experience farming operations have dirtied the river on more than one occasion.

Downstream the river enters a limestone gorge with bush overhanging the river. Access is very difficult but there are some good fish lying in the sink holes for scrub-bashing 'mountain-goat' anglers. Below the gorge the river is channelled and soon enters the Tiraumea.

Makuri River

Because of poor water quality and sediment, neither the Tiraumea nor the Mangaone rivers east of Pahiatua are recommended. The Tiraumea is slow, sluggish and channelled. Near Kohinui there is a section of river where cruising trout can be spotted but access is not easy.

Location Drains the Puketoi and Waewaepa ranges, flows north through Waitahora and enters the Manawatu River south-east of Dannevirke.
Access Take Waitahora Road from Dannevirke and turn left onto McGibbon Road.
Season 1 October–30 April.
Restrictions Fly fishing only.

This small, clear stream winds through hilly farmland and offers 8 km of sight fishing for a few good-sized browns. There are some gorgy sections but access is generally good and the stream is easy to cross. Trout will rise to attractor pattern dry flies in summer.

Mangatoro Stream

Mangatainoka River

Location Flows north parallel to and between SH 2 to the east and the Mangahao River to the west. Enters the Manawatu River south of Woodville near Ngawapurua.

Access There are many access roads, and 13 bridges cross this river. Take roads west off SH 2 at successive turn-offs to Mangamutu, Konini and Mangamaire and to Hukanui from Hamua. Mangatainoka Valley Road can be reached west of Eketahuna. SH 2 crosses the river at Mangatainoka close to the DB Brewery.

Season Above the Makakahi River confluence, 1 October–30 April. Below this confluence the river is open all year.

This medium-sized river, which is protected by a water conservation order, is highly rated by anglers and consequently heavily fished. There is 45 km of fishable water. Early in the season the upper reaches near Putara offer good sight fishing with well-formed pools and bouldery runs. However, when the river warms and the flow lessens, fish drop back downstream to more highly oxygenated waters. The upper reaches tend to be unstable during floods.

Mangatainoka River

The middle and lower reaches, where there are deep pools, long glides and shallow shingly runs, provide good all-season fishing. Fish are not easy to spot in these reaches but stocks are sufficiently high for satisfying 'blind' fly and spin fishing. Low, willow-lined banks and gravel beaches generally permit unobstructed fly casting from at least one side of the river. River crossings are not difficult but in summer the stones become slippery from algal growth. There is often a good evening rise. Dry flies, nymphs and soft hackle wets all take fish.

Brown trout in the 0.75–2 kg range can be expected from this popular river.

Makakahi River

Location and access This tributary of the Mangatainoka River follows SH 2 from Eketahuna to Pahiatua. SH 2 crosses the river twice. Permission must be obtained to cross private farmland.
Season Above the main road bridge at Eketahuna, 1 October–30 April. Open season below this bridge.

This is not an easy river to fish as it is willow-infested in parts and slow flowing. Fish tend to cruise the slower reaches but often the water quality deteriorates in summer making sight fishing difficult. Crossings can be made in this small river but the stones are very slippery from algal growth in summer. Best early in the season for bow and arrow casters and before weed growth causes frustration.

Mangahao River

Location Rises in the Tararua Range and flows north-east to enter the Manawatu River at the eastern end of the gorge, south of Woodville. Flows parallel to but west of the Mangatainoka River.
Access *Headwaters* These flow through Tararua Conservation Park above the hydro dams. There is a dam access road south-east of Shannon via Mangaore.
Middle reaches Turn off SH 2 south of Pahiatua to Mangahao, Nikau and Marima.
Lower reaches and mouth From SH 3 and Gorge Road.
Season Above the Marima Reserve bridge, 1 October–30 April. Below this bridge the river is open all year.

The hydro dams are de-silted every March and over the years this action has caused considerable deterioration in this fishery. Silt covers the clean, stony nymph habitat, thereby depleting trout food. There are a few large fish in the headwaters well above the dams but most fishing is done with spinners down towards the mouth. Not highly recommended.

Pohangina River

Location Rises in the Ruahine Range east of Kimbolton, flows south-west through the foothills of the eastern side of the main range and enters the Manawatu River near Ashhurst.
Access Turn north at Ashhurst, where roads follow up both banks.
Season Open all year.

Although the water quality in this small river is generally good, fish numbers are low as the river is very unstable and not well contained and often alters course during a flood. Holds browns averaging 0.75 kg. It is willow-lined with wide shingle beaches and few stable pools.

The headwaters offer tramper/anglers some wilderness sight fishing but, again, trout numbers are low. Combining fishing with a family picnic or camping at Totara Reserve is a pleasant way to spend time — this valley is very scenic.

Oroua River

Location Rises in the Whanahuia Range and flows south-west parallel to but east of the Kiwitea Stream to join the Manawatu River at Opiki.
Access From side roads running east off SH 54 between Feilding, Kimbolton and Apiti. There are numerous marked anglers' accesses from Almadale, Barrow, Millers, Geanges and Clarks roads.
Season Open all year.

This is a popular, small to medium-sized river with the middle reaches between Kimbolton and Apiti being favoured. The water quality deteriorates below Feilding and the Kiwitea confluence.

Like its neighbour the Pohangina, the Oroua has an unstable, poorly contained shingle bed that moves during a fresh.

The upper reaches have patches of native bush along the banks and provide reasonable sight fishing early in the season for the fit angler prepared to walk. Best fished early or late in the season.

Kiwitea Stream

Location and access Flows west of Kimbolton and Cheltenham, in a south-westerly direction, to join the Oroua River near Feilding.
Season 1 October–30 April.

A small tributary that flows across farmland and holds a moderate stock of small brown trout. It has a shingle bed but weed growth and reduced flow in summer cause problems. Best early in the season but is not heavily fished.

Tokomaru River

Location and access Rises in the Tararua Range, flows east and is crossed by SH 57 just south of Tokomaru. Access to the upper reaches extends from Tokomaru Road to Horseshoe Bend Recreation Reserve, but permission is required as this is private property.
Season 1 October–30 April.

The mountainous headwaters of this small stream are rough going for tramper/anglers seeking a few good fish. In the middle reaches above the railway line, where the stream crosses farmland, fish tend to be smaller but more numerous. Below the railway line the river becomes slow, sluggish and eel infested, more so during long, hot summers.

 Ruamahanga River and tributaries

Ruamahanga River

Location Rises in the Tararua Range north-east of Masterton, flows south across farmland east of Masterton and discharges into Lake Onoke at Palliser Bay.

Access *Upper reaches*
- Tramp up the true right bank from the SH 2 bridge at Mt Bruce. Permission is required from the landowner.
- From Putara and the headwaters of the Mangatainoka River.

Middle reaches
- From the Masterton–Gladstone road.
- From Papawai and Morrisons Bush, south-east of Greytown.
- From Martinborough.

Lower reaches From the Martinborough–Lake Ferry road.

Season Open all year for fishing.

This large river offers over 100 km of fishable water, beginning in the headwaters as a pristine, bubbly mountain stream and ending at Lake Onoke as a wide, deep, willow-lined, sluggish river. There is good sight fishing in Tararua Forest Park for anglers keen on tramping. Although fish are not plentiful, there are enough medium to large browns to sustain the interest. It is quality fishing in quality water upstream from Mt Bruce.

Between Mt Bruce and Masterton the fishing is unreliable as the river is unstable and subject to shingle extraction.

From Masterton to Martinborough the river is large but manageable with deep pools, long glides and shallow riffles. Crossings can be made at selected fords and the shingle riverbed is safe to wade. Willows line the banks. Fish stocks are good with browns averaging 1 kg, although the odd rainbow is now present having escaped from Henley Lake in Masterton. There is often a good evening rise in summer but fish can be very selective during this time. It pays to identify what insect is hatching and also whether fish are taking duns on the surface or emergers in the surface film. When all else fails try a small soft hackle wet fly fished across and down. A splashy rise usually indicates caddis escaping from the surface film. There are some interesting backwaters to look into where fish can be carefully ambushed with a small nymph or willow grub imitation. Popular access spots include Wardells Bridge, the cliffs just south of Masterton, Te Whiti Bridge and Ponatahi Bridge.

Spin anglers also have success although low-water summer conditions make spinning difficult.

Below Tuhitarata, the river becomes slow flowing and very deep. In winter some large sea-run browns can be caught legally by trolling from a boat.

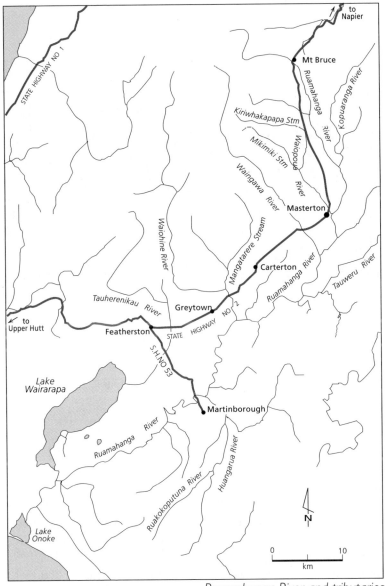

Ruamahanga River and tributaries

Below Masterton there are also some good-sized perch and these will take a fly.

Ruamahanga River

Kopuaranga River

Location Rises just south of Eketahuna, flows south following the railway line and joins the Ruamahanga at Opaki, 5 km north of Masterton.

Access Turn off SH 2 just north of Opaki on the road to Kopuaranga and Mauriceville. There is easy access from side roads off this road.

Season 1 October–30 April.

Restrictions Fly fishing only in this river.

This spring-fed, willow-lined stream meanders across swampy farmland and is highly regarded by local fly anglers. Above Mauriceville, willows choke the river making casting extremely frustrating. The lower and middle reaches are recommended, sight fishing being possible on bright days. Browns in the 0.5–1.5 kg range are present but they become very spooky as the season progresses. Trout food consists of mayflies, caddis and willow grub. As the water warms in summer, weed can be a nuisance.

Waiopoua River

Location Rises near Mt Bruce, flows south-east parallel to and west of SH 2 and joins the Ruamahanga River just east of Masterton.
Access From Mikimiki and Paerau roads, which leave SH 2 north of Masterton near Upper Opaki.
Season 1 October–30 April.

This small, fast-flowing stream is a spawning tributary of the Ruamahanga River. It fishes best early or late in the season but does hold a few resident browns. Blind nymph fishing is the most productive way to tackle this stream.

Two small tributaries of the Waiopoua, the Mikimiki and the Kiriwhakapapa, also offer the same type of early season fishing for small browns but fish stocks are not high. They are willow-lined in parts, have a shingle bed and can become weedy in summer. Watch the slippery riverbed!

Waingawa River

Location Rises in the Tararua Range north-west of Masterton and flows south-east to join the Ruamahanga River 9 km south of that town.
Access *Upper reaches* Take Renall Street west from Masterton to Kaituna and Tararua Forest Park.
Middle and lower reaches Via SH 2, which crosses just south of Masterton. Alternatively, Norfolk Road follows up the true right bank.
Season This river is open all year.

Below Kaituna, this small to medium-sized river is unstable and flood prone. There are a few browns in the more stable pools but these are few and far between.

The upper reaches above Kaituna and in Tararua Forest Park

offer good sight fishing for anglers prepared to tramp and ford the river frequently. Fish numbers are low but the quality of angling more than compensates for that. Best in mid-summer, when water levels are manageable for river crossings.

Tauweru River

Location and access Flows in a southerly direction east of Masterton to join the Ruamahanga River at Gladstone just upstream from Ruamahanga Bridge on the Gladstone– Carterton road.
Season 1 October–30 April.

Only the slow-flowing lower 3 km of this small river are worth exploring early in the season as the middle and upper reaches are willow-infested. Sight fishing is possible when the light is adequate but the river is not highly rated. Willow grub imitations work well in summer on cruising fish.

Waiohine River

Location Drains the Tararua Range west of Carterton, flows east a little south of this town and joins the Ruamahanga River east of Greytown.
Access *Upper reaches* Take the road to Walls Whare and the Waiohine Gorge from SH 2 south of Carterton. This leads to Josephs Road west of Matarawa and Tararua Forest Park.
Middle and lower reaches SH 2 crosses the river just north of Greytown. Swamp Road on the true left bank and roads running west from Greytown provide easy access.
Season Open all year round.

This medium-sized tributary holds brown and rainbow trout. The upper reaches above Woodside, and especially between Walls Whare and Totara Flat, offer wilderness sight fishing for good-sized trout. As there are two bush-covered gorges with deep holes and bluffs, the upper reaches are best for tramper/anglers in low-water, conditions in summer, when the river can be safely forded. Fish stocks are not high but the quality of the angling, the impressive scenery and the chance of landing a trophy fish more than compensate. Trampers can be a disruption in summer.

The middle reaches below Woodside are shingly, braided, flood-prone and unstable. Catchment activity has contributed to the poor fish habitat.

The lower reaches near the Ruamahanga confluence offer larger river fishing for spin and bait anglers.

Mangatarere Stream

Location and access This small spawning tributary of the Waiohine is accessed from Carrington, north of Carterton.
Season 1 October–30 April.

There is 10 km of easily accessible water. Best early in the season before weed and algal growth choke the stream. Sight fishing can be difficult but good blind nymph fishing may be enjoyed early in the season.

Tauherenikau River

Location Rises in the southern Tararua Range, flows generally south and is crossed by SH 2 between Greytown and Featherston. Empties into Lake Wairarapa.
Access *Upper reaches* From Kaitoke on SH 2 there is a tramping track through scrub and native bush. The river is reached in two hours.
Middle reaches Take Underhill or Bucks roads north of Featherston. SH 2 and SH 53 both cross the river.
Lower reaches Take Murphys Line from Featherston and Lake Wairarapa.
Season Open all year.

The upper reaches in Tararua Forest Park hold a few good brown trout in clear pools. However, a lot of walking is required between trout.

The middle reaches are unstable and hold few fish.

The lower reaches near Lake Wairarapa offer slow, deep water for bait and spin anglers. Fish stocks are reasonable with anglers just as likely to catch perch as they are brown trout.

Huangarua River

Location Flows north to join the Ruamahanga River at Martinborough.
Access From Ponotahi and Hinakura roads.
Season 1 October–30 April.

A small, shingly, willow-lined stream that dries in summer but can hold fish early in the season in the lower reaches.

Ruakokoputuna River

Location and access Drains Haurangi Forest Park, flows north-east and enters the Huangarua River south of Martinborough. Access south of Martinborough on Ruakokoputuna Road for the lower reaches and Haurangi Road for the upper reaches. Permission should be obtained before crossing private farmland.
Season 1 October–30 April.

This small stream has a mudstone bed and easily becomes silt-laden after rain. The water is never very clear except after a dry spell in early summer, when some sight fishing is possible. As the stream dries during a long hot summer it is best fished early in the season, when a few browns can be spotted in some of the more stable pools. The lower reaches are willow-lined whereas the upper reaches are enhanced by patches of native bush. Not heavily fished.

Henley Lake

Location and access Lies on the eastern outskirts of Masterton. There is easy, safe access.
Season Open all year.
This small, artificial lake covering 12 ha has been stocked for junior anglers. Holds some good-sized rainbow trout and perch.

Location and access Lies east of Gladstone on Te Wharau Road.
Season Open all year.

This lake covers 11 ha and contains stocked rainbow trout and
perch. Wadeable areas are limited but there is some shoreline fishing available. Most fish are caught from small boats. In summer the
lake becomes weedy and after rain it can become discoloured.
Some large rainbows have been caught, usually on a black night
lure or Woolly Bugger.

Lake Wairarapa holds both brown trout and perch but is generally
heavily silt-laden and better suited to spinning or live bait fishing.
Stream mouths are the most profitable locations.

The Otakura Stream, accessed from Diversion Road via
Lake Ferry Road, holds a few large browns but the water
quality is poor.

Pahaoa and Wainuioru rivers south-east of Martinborough also
hold a few trout but are not recommended as the water quality is
often poor and the rivers can dry in summer.

 Horowhenua rivers

Ohau River

Location Flows west from the Tararua Range to enter the sea south
of Levin.
Access *Middle reaches* From Parikawau Road off SH 1 just north of
the Main Road bridge. This leads to a riverside rest area beneath
the bridge.
Lower reaches From Waikawa Beach Road and Soldiers Road from
Kuku Road.
Season Open all year.

Generally, fishing is best in the lower reaches of this medium-sized
shingly river, downstream from SH 1. Willows line the banks where
there are well-developed pools and shallow, ripply runs. Most of the

browns average around 1 kg but a few larger estuarine or sea-run fish enter the lower reaches. Wading is safe and the river is easy to cross. Blind nymph fishing and spinning account for most fish taken. Unfortunately, flooding, gravel extraction and toxic discharges have all taken their toll on the fishing.

The middle reaches are unstable and only a few fish inhabit the upper reaches.

Two small feeder streams can hold fish early in the season. These are the Makaretu and the Makahika. Both can be accessed from Gladstone, east of Levin.

Otaki River

Location Drains the eastern Tararua Range, flows west and enters the sea near Otaki.

Access *Headwaters and upper reaches* Otaki Gorge Road follows the true left bank upstream to Otaki Forks. This road has recently been in bad repair and a 4WD vehicle may be required to reach The Forks. The headwaters can only be reached on foot by tramping upstream from The Forks into Tararua Forest Park.

There are good access roads downstream from SH 1.

Season Open all year.

The headwaters of this medium-sized river offer wilderness sight fishing for fit tramper/anglers. Stocks are not high but there are a few good brown trout.

The middle reaches around The Forks have some very deep holding pools but, again, fish numbers are low. Spinning accounts for most fish landed in these reaches.

Trout chase whitebait in the lower reaches so use a spinner or smelt fly. The river is shingly and willow-lined here. Unfortunately, this river has also been affected from time to time by floods and gravel extraction.

Waikanae River

Location Flows west from the Tararua Range to enter the sea at Waikanae.

Access *Upper reaches* From the Upper Hutt–Waikanae road through the Akatarawa Gorge.
Middle reaches From Otaihanga.
Lower reaches Reikorangi Road from Waikanae.
Season Open all year.

The upper reaches of this small river meander through patches of rewarewa and tawa. There are stable pools against rocky bluffs but the trout population is low. Early in the season, the most productive water lies above the railway bridge and below Reikorangi. In the warm summer months with low water flows fish drop back downstream to the stretch between Otaihanga and the water treatment weir. Here there are willow-lined pools, glides and runs. This is a pleasant, easy river to fish but because of floods, fish stocks can vary from year to year.

Other small streams in the Horowhenua district holding small brown trout are the Waikawa Stream north of Manakau and at Waikawa Beach, the Mangaone Stream near Te Horo and the Waitohi Stream near Otaki. All fish best early in the season before the water warms and weed growth chokes them.

 *Hutt River and tributaries*

Hutt River

Location Drains the southern Tararua Range and flows south down the Hutt Valley to enter Wellington Harbour near Petone.
Access There are many roads, access tracks and parks along most of its length. River Road between Upper Hutt and Silverstream offers especially good access.
Season Open for fishing all year.
Restrictions The headwaters are closed for domestic water supply.

Because it flows through an area of high population density, the medium-sized Hutt River has in the past been subjected to a wide range of pollution. Although sight fishing is difficult in the main river, the water quality has improved considerably over recent

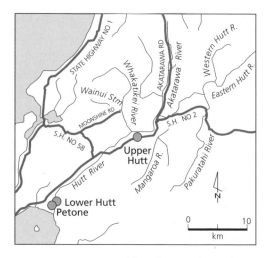

Hutt River and tributaries

years. Drift divers have counted a good population of brown trout, especially between the Akatarawa River confluence and the Silverstream bridge. However, fish tend to move both up- and downstream depending on the time of year, the food supply, the water temperature and the spawning urge. The average weight of fish landed is around 1 kg but sea-run browns up to 4 kg have been

A broad reach on the Hutt River at Moonshine Park

caught. Recently, a very large quinnat salmon was taken from the mouth, but this is most unusual.

There are well-established pools, long glides and shallow, shingly riffles. Willows line some stretches of the river but crossings are possible at the tail of most pools and wading is safe, although the stones can be slippery.

All methods of fishing, including well-weighted nymphs, dry flies, soft hackle wet flies, lures, spinners and live bait, can bring results. Considering the Hutt River flows through a heavily populated area, it is an excellent fishery with many kilometres of river waiting to be enjoyed.

Pakuratahi River

Location Drains the hills north of Wainuiomata, flows north and joins the Hutt River near Kaitoki.
Access From Waterworks Road, Kaitoki, and from the Rimutaka Incline Walkway.
Season 1 October–30 April.

This small, clear-water tributary runs through a narrow, confined,

Pakuratahi River near the forks

bush-covered valley. The pools are deep and stable but access is difficult in parts because of bouldery runs and rocky bluffs. Fish numbers are low but sight fishing is easy on a bright day. The lower reaches at Kaitoki are more open and hold the most fish.

Mangaroa River

Location and access From Wallaceville Road between Trentham and Lower Hutt. Or from Mangaroa Hill Road off SH 2 at Maoribank, then Flux and Mangaroa Valley roads.
Season 1 October–30 April.

This small tributary of the Hutt River is a spawning stream, but although fish move back downstream when the water warms in summer, there is still a population of resident fish, particularly in the deeper holes. Sight fishing is impossible north of the Wallaceville Road as the water becomes peat stained from Te

Cows in the middle reaches of the Mangaroa River.
Stream degradation such as this is becoming more common

274

Pango swamp. Weed and algal growth interferes with fishing after Christmas but this stream is known for rising fish.

Akatarawa River

Location Flows generally south down the Akatarawa Valley to join the Hutt River near Upper Hutt.
Access From the Upper Hutt–Waikanae road, which follows up the true left bank.
Season 1 October–30 April.

This small to medium-sized tributary of the Hutt River flows through gorges, native bush, pine plantations and farmland. The brown trout population is greatest away from the gorges where the valley opens out at Karapoti and Cloustonville. Access is difficult in parts but in sunny conditions fish can be spotted and stalked as the water quality is good. Although trout numbers are relatively low, fish are larger than those in the Hutt River. Fishes best early in the season before the water warms.

Whakatikei River

Location Flows roughly parallel to and south of the Akatarawa River and joins the Hutt River in Upper Hutt.
Access *Lower reaches* Cross the Hutt River at Whakatikei Street and walk upstream until a gorge makes access difficult.
Middle and upper reaches Turn off SH 58 onto Moonshine Road, then Bull Run Road. Then walk down the Wainui Stream for 300 m to reach the Whakatikei.
Season 1 October–30 April.

This small, relatively inaccessible mountain stream offers wilderness type sight fishing remarkably close to Wellington. Brown trout numbers are low but fish can be spotted and stalked providing you don't mind walking, scrambling and crossing the stream frequently. If anyone is fishing ahead of you it is best to find another river. Considering this stream is so close to Wellington, catch and release would seem a wise restriction.

Scrambling upstream on the Whakatikei River

Location Rises in the Rimutaka Range east of Lower Hutt, flows south through Wainuiomata township and enters Cook Strait near Baring Head.

Access Coast Road follows down the true left bank from Wainuiomata to the mouth. Permission may be required to cross private farmland.

Season 1 October–30 April.

Restrictions Fly fishing only below the main township bridge. The headwaters are closed owing to draw-off for the domestic water supply. Bag limit is two trout or salmon.

The most productive stretch of river begins 8 km south of Wainuiomata. There is 20 km of slow-flowing, deep, weedy, fishable water, and trout can be spotted in these middle reaches. There is a good stock of browns averaging 1 kg. The water quality deteriorates in the lower reaches and sight fishing becomes difficult if not impossible.

The river meanders its way across farmland and through patches of gorse. High banks and a silt riverbed make fish spotting easy between the weed banks but trout soon see you on the skyline and disappear. Stalking on hands and knees is often necessary and the help of a mate can be very useful. Delicate fine fishing with a long tippet and small nymphs or dry flies is required. Fish can be fussy so it pays to examine the insect life.

A light southerly is good for this valley but a strong northerly kills the fishing. Fishes best early and late in the season, when eutrophication is suppressed.

Other fishing spots worth mentioning in the Wellington district include small, stocked lakes at Porirua and Whitby. These are for junior anglers. The Makara Stream at Makara Beach, the Pauatahanui Stream flowing into Porirua Harbour and the Korokoro Stream near Petone all hold a few small browns early in the season for anglers keen on small-stream fishing.

Index